He u ♡ P9-DLZ-234

She hadn't expected that . . .

Not that such a trivial thing mattered. Nora forced herself to study him not as a woman, but as Robert often studied a rival's art: with a detached sense of curiosity.

Even from afar, she understood why the actresses loved Hatcher. This was a man designed to gain attention, with his rumpled, wheat-streaked hair and strong, chiseled features. As he drew closer, she noted the high, prominent cheekbones and sharp nose. Broad shoulders atop a lean build. But it was more than that. As the Americans said, he had *dash*—a certain panache that lent him an air of superiority. Perhaps it was the money, but Nora did not think so. New York was dripping with rich men and none of them looked like Julius Hatcher.

In a word, he was perfect.

By Joanna Shupe

The Four Hundred series
A DARING ARRANGEMENT

The Knickerbocker Club series
MAGNATE
BARON
MOGUL
TYCOON

JOANNA SHUPE

A DARING ARRANGEMENT

THE FOUR HUNDRED SERIES

AVONBOOKS

An Imprint of HarperCollinsPublishers

A DARING ARRANGEMENT. Copyright © 2017 by Joanna Shupe. All rights reserved. Printed in the United States of America. No part of this book may be used or reproduced in any manner whatsoever without written permission except in the case of brief quotations embodied in critical articles and reviews. For information, address HarperCollins Publishers, 195 Broadway, New York, NY 10007.

First Avon Books mass market printing: November 2017

Print Edition ISBN: 978-0-06-267889-8
Digital Edition ISBN: 978-0-06-267890-4

Cover illustration by FictionArtist.com.

Avon, Avon & logo, and Avon Books & logo are registered trademarks of HarperCollins Publishers in the United States of America and other countries.

HarperCollins is a registered trademark of HarperCollins Publishers in the United States of America and other countries.

FIRST EDITION

17 18 19 20 21   QGM   10 9 8 7 6 5 4 3 2 1

To those who persist and never give up . . .
even when it's super hard.

A Daring
Arrangement

Chapter One

*Thirty-Seventh Street
and Fifth Avenue
New York City*

February 1890

The pressed tin ceiling was about to cave in on their heads.

Lady Honora Parker glanced upward once again, fascinated by what was taking place on the second floor of Sherry's, one of New York's most exclusive restaurants. Each raucous thump and horrific crash from above shook the huge gold and crystal chandelier in the main dining room and caused the black-coated waiters to wince. It sounded as if a herd of elephants were up there.

From what Nora had seen and heard of the reckless Americans in the last month, she would not be surprised if it *were* elephants. Nothing seemed off-limits here, no idea too big or too wild. Giant houses, like English country estates, lined Fifth Avenue. Imported marble, bright limestone, and shiny gilding blinded from every street corner. Tall buildings stretched high up into the sky. There was a sense of urgency in New York to buy more, build more, *do* more. It made her long for the dirty, crowded, yet civilized streets of London.

"Nora, dear," her aunt's gentle voice interrupted her thoughts. "Mr. Van Rensselaer asked you a question."

She turned to the older, heavyset man on her right. Her uncle had arranged the dinner, one of many meetings designed for her to find a "suitable" man. But the idea of marriage to a man old enough to be her father made Nora's skin crawl. Even her aunt disapproved of Van Rensselaer, saying he was, "a set of heavy eyebrows with a stick up his behind."

It must be said that Nora adored her aunt.

More importantly, Nora did not desire a suitable American man, not when a perfectly suitable artist awaited her back in London. Her father hadn't approved of said artist, unfortunately, which is how she now found herself in America, being trotted around New York like a prized thoroughbred up for auction. *That's the earl's daughter,* they whispered behind her back. *Here to find a husband.*

No, she absolutely would not. Nora had no intention of marrying anyone here. "I apologize," she replied to the eyebrows. "You were saying?"

"Perfectly understandable." Mr. Van Rensselaer smiled tolerantly at her, as if Nora were some flighty nitwit incapable of following a conversation. Commence additional skin crawling. "I asked if your ladyship missed London."

Yes, I miss Robert terribly. Her heart squeezed in a tight grip, an ache settling in her throat. A young painter, Robert Landon had no money or title to speak of, but she didn't care. He'd been the first person to see Nora for who she truly was, not just her father's daughter. He was sweet and romantic and all she desired in this world. After they married, they planned to travel across Europe so Robert could hone his craft. She would keep him company and continue to serve as his "muse," as he often called her.

Her father, the Earl of Stratton, hadn't approved. He'd been horrified when Robert and Nora were caught together—a scene orchestrated for the earl's benefit at a dinner party—and from there, things had taken a disastrous turn. Instead of forcing the young lovers to marry, as she'd hoped, her furious father rushed Nora off to his sister in New York. *"No one there will have heard of the scandal yet,"* he had said. *"Your aunt will help you find a proper husband in America. Do not return without one. Now, do not disappoint me, Nora."*

Was that not what she'd been doing her entire life, disappointing him? He'd wanted a boy; she'd been born a girl. She had studied, practiced, and tried to be the perfect daughter, and he'd only ignored her. She'd smiled through her debut, eager to make him proud, and he hadn't bothered to attend any of the balls or dances.

Attempts at playing the good daughter, the proper society young woman, had gotten her nothing. Worse, they'd resulted in a trip to a strange city to be dangled in front of every fortune hunter and insufferable snob twice her age.

So that proper society young woman was no more. A new Nora had emerged on the cross-

Atlantic voyage four weeks ago, one who had decided to take matters into her own hands by concocting an infallible way back to London.

The plan was simple. If her father wanted her to find a husband, she'd find the most outrageous man in New York, a fiancé noteworthy and unsuitable enough to land in the papers. An actor? A politician? She hadn't quite settled on how to achieve it yet . . . but she would. She had to. The news must become public enough to reach the earl's ear across the Atlantic, horrifying him into summoning her home.

To Robert.

Three sets of eyes were staring, so she returned her attention to the conversation at hand. "I do miss it. Certainly not the weather, however."

Aunt Beatrice, Uncle James, and Mr. Van Rensselaer laughed, and conversation droned on until another loud thump sounded from above. Her uncle's mouth flattened. "I cannot comprehend why that hullabaloo is permitted to continue."

Mr. Van Rensselaer wiped his mouth with the linen serviette. "From what I understand, Mr. Hatcher is up in the ballroom. Some sort of exclusive dinner. This is why your country is superior to ours, Lady Nora, because the undesirables here have no idea how to conduct themselves properly."

By *undesirables*, it was clear he meant men who had earned their wealth, not inherited it as he had. Had he any idea how pompous that made him sound? Though Robert had no money, he was a kind, decent, and loving man with brilliant wit and unshakable morals. That was the perfect man, not one like Mr. Van Rensselaer, who'd visibly sneered at the modest blue silk gown she wore tonight. While it might be conservative compared to the fancier American gowns throughout the dining room, she believed the color showed off her dark chestnut hair and golden-brown eyes.

"Mr. Julius Hatcher?" Aunt Bea asked. "The financier?"

"Indeed. The man's a scourge on everything decent and upstanding in this city." Van Rensselaer cut into his asparagus spears. "Do not worry, though. He doesn't exactly run in the best circles. In fact, he's tried numerous times to buy his way into polite society over the years, but they won't have him."

Though she'd only been in New York a month, Nora had heard of Julius Hatcher. A handsome, brash swell with more money than sense, he threw elaborate parties and associated with a string of high-profile actresses, at least according to the gossip pages. He'd even built a replica of a sixteenth-century French castle on Upper Fifth Avenue—complete with a moat.

Though the newspapers touted his exploits with glee, society thought him outrageous and improper. A society he'd apparently tried to buy his way into—and failed. And here her father had disapproved of Robert when there were scoundrels like Julius Hatcher running amok. However was that possibly fair? It would serve the earl right if she brought Hatcher home for—

Her brain froze for an instant, stuck on the delicious idea. Oh, indeed, it would serve the earl right. Her father would never approve of Hatcher as a husband, a scoundrel who would bring shame to the venerable Parker name. Surely that would force her father to see Robert in a more favorable light. It would certainly prove that a hardworking, decent man like Robert was good enough to marry the earl's only daughter.

Moreover, the second her father caught wind of her connection to Hatcher and the depravity of his reputation, he would undoubtedly bring her home posthaste.

Mr. Hatcher sounded like the answer to her prayers.

Another thud sounded from above. *This is my chance.* She had to find Hatcher and try to convince him to help her. Right now. Immediately. Before she lost this opportunity. She started to push her chair back and a waiter rushed over to assist her. "If you will excuse me, I am feeling a bit overheated."

"Shall I come with you?" her aunt asked as the two gentlemen politely rose as well.

"No, please," she rushed out a little desperately, then tempered her tone. "Enjoy your meal. I'll put a cool cloth to my neck and return in moments."

NORA SOON LOCATED the main stairs and hurried up, holding her skirts with both hands to keep from tripping. A waiter appeared just as she reached the top step. "Ma'am, are you lost?"

Even here in America, women were not supposed to dine upstairs, alone. No doubt he thought her a hussy, strutting about without a male escort. She gave him a blinding smile and spoke rapidly.

"Oh, I am ever so sorry, sir. We just finished dining and I believe I left something in one of the upper dining rooms. Would you mind terribly if I quickly searched for it? I promise I shan't take long."

The tips of the waiter's ears turned red and he moved aside to let her pass. "Of course, ma'am. Go right ahead. I didn't realize you was a proper British lady. We get a lotta questionable characters on the upper floors. Would you like me to come help?"

"No, thank you. Undoubtedly, you are quite busy. I'll be but a moment." Relieved, she glided past him toward the private dining rooms.

After he departed, she began searching for the source of the noise. The ruckus grew louder as she approached a pair of large wooden doors on the right. Pressing her ear to one of the panels, she heard more thumps and booming male laughter emanating from within.

Here.

She thought of Robert and their future together. Traveling Europe and spending lazy mornings surrounded by him and his paints. A man who wanted *her*, not the heirs she might expel from her womb or the status associated with her father's title. Taking a breath for courage, she turned the knob and slid into the ballroom. Then she came to an abrupt halt.

Good heavens. There were . . . horses everywhere.

Horses. Inside. The. Ballroom.

With men in the saddles.

All twenty or so male guests were dressed in black evening suits, silk hats, and eating off trays secured to saddles. Waiters, outfitted as grooms, scurried back and forth. The room smelled like a barn drenched in cigar smoke.

Dinner on *horseback*? Had these Americans lost their minds?

She could not wait to tell Robert about it.

One man broke off from the group and maneuvered his horse to where she stood. He tipped his hat, an affable grin on his handsome face. "Good evening, miss. May we help you?"

"You have horses. In a restaurant. On the second floor."

He chuckled and lifted one shoulder. "It's my friend's birthday, and he never does anything in half measures. Believe it or not, the horses were fairly easy to get up the freight elevator."

She couldn't imagine how much this all cost, though she would never ask. Better to stick with her purpose. "I am looking for Mr. Hatcher."

"Of course you are. All the pretty ones do." He pointed to a hatless man waving a champagne bottle and weaving in the saddle. "He's over there, the blond one with the bubbly. Shall I fetch him for you?"

The ballroom floor had been covered in hay and dirt—and that was before one considered the horses. In hopes of preserving her shoes, she nodded. "Yes, if you would be so kind."

He wheeled his horse around and walked to where Hatcher was holding court. Hatcher appeared to be telling a story, gesturing wildly with his hands, which he moved to his chest as if cupping a pair of large breasts. Nora felt her skin heat as she turned to the wall. His obnoxious behavior only solidified this plan in her mind. *I'll see you soon, Robert.*

A few seconds later, the earth shook under her slippers. Glancing up, she found Mr. Hatcher trotting toward her. He was handsome. She hadn't expected that—not that such a trivial thing mattered. She forced herself to study him not as a woman, but as Robert often studied a rival's art: with a detached sense of curiosity.

This was a man designed to gain attention, with his rumpled, wheat-streaked hair and strong, chiseled features. As he drew closer, she noted the high, prominent cheekbones and sharp nose. Broad shoulders atop a lean build. But it was more than that. As the Americans said, he had *dash*—a certain panache that lent him an air of superiority. Perhaps it was the money, but Nora didn't think so. New York was dripping with rich men and none of them looked like Julius Hatcher.

In a word, he was perfect.

He brought his horse to a stop and peered down at her. His blue eyes were glassy and rimmed red. Full lips slid into a confident, impish grin, and some sort of bizarre reaction occurred in Nora's stomach. "McDaniel's outdone hisself this year."

She blinked. Though his speech was slightly slurred, she had heard every word. "McDaniel?"

"The man who paid you, sweetheart." He leaned forward in the saddle and let his eyes linger over the length of her body. Extra attention was paid to her bosom, which she knew was nothing more than average. Still, he must have liked what he saw because he said, "Damn, but whatever you charged him wasn't enough."

"Charged him?" she repeated. "I am—"

"You're the best birthday present I've ever received. Give me an hour or so to sober up and then I'll take you somewhere nice. We'll get a suite at the Fifth Avenue Hotel."

Though he pronounced it "shweet," she well knew what he meant. God above, he believed her a loose woman. For his birthday. And he had a friend who gifted him with such each year? Hatcher was even more odious than she'd been led to believe.

"Sir, I am not your birthday present. I am dining downstairs."

"You're English."

"Yes, I am. My name is Lady Nora Parker. I am staying with my aunt, Mrs. Cortland."

The horse shifted, shaking its large head in impatience. Hatcher absently stroked the animal's neck. "Know her husband, Jim. Big in oil stocks. And you're a lady, you say?"

"Indeed, I am. My father is the eighth Earl of Stratton and a bunch of lesser titles not worth repeating at the moment. May I speak with you?"

He glanced over both shoulders dramatically. "Are we not speaking now?"

"I meant . . . Forget it." Staring up at him pained her neck. If he were a true gentleman, he would've dismounted and addressed her properly.

Sighing, she searched the room and noticed a chair resting near the wall. She strode over, grasped the chair back, and dragged the piece closer to Hatcher. Before she'd even placed her slipper on the seat, a waiter rushed over to assist her up. In seconds, she stood nearly eye to eye with her quarry. "I have something I wish to discuss with you."

The sly smile returned. "Anythin' you want, sweetheart."

She took a deep breath and ignored the insinuation. The man had filth on the brain. "For reasons that are irrelevant to this conversation, I should like to return to England as quickly as possible. However, my father wishes me to find an American man to marry. I need an outrageous fiancé—are you *asleep*?"

Hatcher jerked, his eyes stretching wide. "No," he lied, as if she hadn't seen him clearly dozing off. "I'm awake. But p'haps you could get to the point."

She did need to hurry. No doubt her aunt was growing concerned in the dining room. "I'd like for you to pose as my fiancé, just long enough to anger my father and get me summoned home."

"Fiancé? Me?" His voice had turned shrill, startling his horse. With a competent press of his knees, he steadied the beast and then stroked its neck with a gentle hand. He shook his head. "I am never marryin' anyone, not even a woman as gorgeous as you."

"We would not marry. I merely need my father to think we will."

"Why?"

"Reasons. Meanwhile, I'll gain you entrance into all the society events. When my father learns of our association, he'll summon me home and then you'll be released from our agreement."

He swayed, his brow lowered in concentration.

She had no idea if he were attempting to stay in the saddle or contemplating her offer. His hooded gaze stared at her mouth. "Would I be allowed to kiss you?"

A strangely exhilarating wave of heat rolled through her. The idea of kissing him should *not* tantalize her under any circumstances. She pushed those thoughts aside, permanently. "Absolutely not."

The lines on his forehead deepened. "Hardly seems fair."

Life was not fair, she wanted to tell him. Falling in love with a decent man her father refused to accept was unfair. Being a woman and not having the right to decide her own fate was unfair.

She could go on.

"Nonetheless, that is my offer. Do you accept?"

"You and me, showin' up those Knickerbockers?"

It took her a minute to decipher the words. "Yes, precisely. Showing up those Knickerbockers. Will you do it?"

"Hell, yes! Where do I sign?"

God save her from inebriated men. She just prayed he remembered this conversation come morning. "No papers, Mr. Hatcher. Merely your word."

"I like papers," he murmured. "But for you, I can make an 'ception." He thumped his chest with his fist. Hard. "My word, then. You and me, sweetheart."

Relief flooded her. "Thank you. I knew you were just the man to see. I am so grateful I was in the dining room when you—"

Hatcher's lids fluttered and he slumped forward,

his body becoming lax. Before she could do anything, his horse sidestepped and Hatcher slid out of the saddle. He fell onto the floor with a thunk.

Horrified, Nora covered her mouth. Was he *dead*? She stepped off the chair and rushed closer, ready to assist in whatever way necessary . . . and then he groaned.

"We've got him, miss," one of the grooms said as he hurried over.

Certain her new fiancé hadn't expired, Nora slipped out of the ballroom and briskly walked back to the dining room. Her heart pounded with newfound hope.

Based on what she just witnessed, she'd be back in England—and Robert's arms—before the month was out.

Chapter Two

Julius Hatcher never missed the start of a trading day.

Even this morning, with a throbbing head and queasy stomach, he was in his office chair when the exchange opened and the ticker started humming. The opening stock prices were like fortunes, their numbers predicting the rest of the day. What was in demand first thing in the morning? Any wild speculation or takeovers? Did he need to travel to the exchange to oversee his interests personally?

On a normal day, he would check the numbers, see all was normal, and then move on to other business matters. Today, he very well might go back to bed instead.

Last night had been wild, even by his standards. Wasn't often a man turned thirty, so he'd spared no expense for the event. He just wished he remembered more of the evening. Last thing he recalled was Alfie's suggestion to order that one-hundred-and-fifty-year-old bottle of brandy. It had come from

Louis Sherry's private stock and had cost over four thousand dollars. The first glass had been heaven. The rest, a blur.

His stomach roiled and he rang for a footman. When one appeared, he said softly, "Breakfast. As bland as Mrs. Bell can make it."

"Of course, sir."

Julius winced. "Quietly, Michael."

The footman nodded, though he probably hadn't been all that loud. Nevertheless, Julius's head throbbed like a damned drumbeat.

He checked the ticker tape. The numbers flew by, each one registering in his brain. No surprises thus far. Excellent. He didn't like surprises much, at least not when it came to finances. A memory nagged, something from the night before. Had there been a surprise at the party? Try as he might, his brain could not fully grasp the wisps of the thought.

He let it go. It hurt too much to think.

Despite last evening's debauchery, he didn't often drink to inebriation. Yes, he liked excess in most things, though not when it came to ceding control. Weak men were ripe to be taken advantage of. Bought out. Swindled. *Buried*.

Like his father. Warren Hatcher had been the trusting sort, quick to accept a man's word instead of an ironclad contract. Once, Julius had asked his father about this eagerness to believe, his blind faith in humanity. *"You cannot live your life doubting everyone and everything around you,"* his father had answered.

Unfortunately, the rosy attitude had led to the

family's destruction in the Panic of '73. The month before the bottom fell out of the economy, good ol' Warren had organized an investment deal with, "some honest, upstanding Knickerbocker men." When the banks collapsed, the bank called in the demand note from his father. The other investors—men who could easily afford the loss of a few thousand dollars—then backed out of the arrangement, which left Warren Hatcher responsible for the entire loss.

Creditors had swooped in. The Hatchers became destitute.

They hadn't been alone, of course. Hundreds of thousands were ruined thanks to railroad overexpansion. Investors started declaring bankruptcy, banks and factories went under, and workers were suddenly unemployed. Whole damn country slipped into a depression, with violent riots frequently breaking out in big cities. It had been a vicious, uncertain few years, a time Julius would never forget. Even today the thought of an unruly mob bent on destruction turned his blood cold.

Their family hadn't been the same after the creditors. His father had taken his own life shortly after, but not before ranting and raving for five drunken nights about the society men who had cheated him. He'd never mentioned any names, however, not even when asked. And when Julius found his father's lifeless body hanging from the stable rafters, he'd sworn revenge against those responsible. He didn't know their identities but he'd find—and ruin—them if it took his entire life.

The office door opened and his proper British valet, Weaver, entered with a tray. Julius rubbed his temples. "I'll give you two hundred dollars if there is coffee on that tray."

Weaver set the silver filigreed tray on the edge of the desk. He began arranging Julius's breakfast. "There is indeed coffee, sir, yet it would be most improper for you to compensate me for that fact."

"You have no sense of humor, Weaver. You're in America now. You're allowed to laugh."

"I apologize, sir. I hadn't realized you'd made a joke."

Julius sighed. He'd hired Weaver away from a duke's household two years ago because everyone knew British valets were the best—and Julius made a point to surround himself with nothing but the best. Just like his butler, Brandywine, who'd been hired away from one of the smaller royal residences in London.

Weaver certainly hadn't disappointed. The valet was a dashed marvel, and the man well knew it. Efficient and knowledgeable, he was always ready with whatever Julius needed. For this, Julius tolerated Weaver's dry personality and thinly veiled insults. He also enjoyed needling the servant whenever possible.

"You know, I'm certain there's a doddering old marquess or vicar we could ship you back to."

"I believe you mean 'viscount,' sir, as no vicar would be capable of hiring a valet of my stature."

Julius ignored the rebuke and nearly lunged for the china coffee cup Weaver offered. He took a sip, letting the fragrant liquid slide down his throat and warm his stomach. He leaned his head back and closed his eyes.

"Do you feel well enough for buttered toast?"

Bile rose in Julius's throat. "Perhaps in a moment." He checked the tape once more, cataloging and sorting the stock prices in his mind. He liked numbers, always had. Numbers made sense. One could take them at face value and not worry about being lied to. He'd shown an aptitude for math and calculations since boyhood, one his father had encouraged.

Weaver set the toast aside. "Very good, sir. Incidentally, a young woman is here to see you. Brandywine has placed her in the rose salon."

A young woman? Julius gulped more coffee. He felt more human with each passing second. "Why is she here?"

"I could not say, sir. Will you be attending to your appearance before receiving guests?"

Julius glanced at his respectable, perfectly pressed brown tweed suit. There were no discernible stains or loose threads. Before descending the stairs, he'd bathed, shaved his face, and cleaned his teeth—all without Weaver's help. "No, why?"

Weaver pursed his lips. "No reason, sir. Perhaps the unkempt look is appreciated by the fairer sex nowadays."

Julius dragged a hand through his half-combed hair and then straightened his necktie. "It's as presentable as I get the morning after my birthday, Weaver. Besides, she's uninvited. Turn her away."

"I do not think that is wise, sir. She is Lady Nora Parker, the daughter of the Earl of Stratton. She has her maid with her."

Another memory, stronger now, tugged at Julius. That name was familiar. He drank the rest of the coffee and then held out the cup to Weaver. "Have I met her before?"

His valet took the china cup and set it in the saucer. He poured more coffee and added sugar, the way Julius preferred. When the cup had been returned to Julius's hands, Weaver said, "I would say the answer to that question is an unequivocal yes, sir."

Julius tried to picture her. A hair color or general body shape. A hint of anything that might remind him. The daughter of an earl, Weaver had said. Julius hadn't met any British ladies recently. "How are you so certain I know this woman?"

"Because the lady says you are her fiancé."

HE NEARLY RAN into the room.

From her perch on the sofa, Nora watched as Julius Hatcher skidded to a stop on the Italian marble floor. With his adorably mussed blond hair, rumpled clothing, and the dark circles under his blue eyes, he had obviously just been roused from bed. His coloring hinted at a Nordic ancestry. A Viking warlord's younger scapegrace brother, perhaps.

His brows dipped as he looked her over. Flat, dispassionate eyes reflected none of the teasing warmth from the night before. His mouth held no flirtatious smile, no hint of mirth. Hard to believe this was the same man atop the horse at Sherry's.

But there was no mistaking those roguish features, even when heavily frowning. "Are you some sort of charlatan? Or confidence man?"

Disappointment pierced her chest. He didn't recognize her, which meant he'd no doubt forgotten their agreement. "I am neither. And if you are asking, that means you do not recall our conversation last evening."

He dropped into the chair on the left and massaged his forehead. "Listen, you're not the first woman to try and trick me into marriage. I don't know who you are or what you're about, but we are *not* engaged."

"You gave me your word we were, sir."

A strangled sort of embarrassed amusement escaped his mouth. "I was three sheets to the wind. I would have promised anything to anyone."

He could not back out, not now. Not after Nora had spent the night planning and hoping. Dreaming of Robert. No, her plan needed to progress. She needed to return to England where she could marry Robert. Elope to Scotland, if necessary.

And Julius Hatcher was a perfectly horrible choice for a husband. Even this house was outrageous. A French limestone fantasy, the massive castle had turrets, balconies, gables . . . even gargoyles on the corners. Ducks had been swimming in the moat as she'd climbed the wide flight of steps leading to the giant stone portico. And inside, impressive stained-glass windows lit the light yellow Caen stone walls.

Her father would book her passage on the first ship home the moment he heard the news.

She drew in a breath and decided to start over. "Sir, my name is Lady Nora Parker. You and I struck a mutually beneficial bargain last evening. If you will permit me to explain?"

He waved his hand as if to hurry her along. "Permission granted. Get to the point, milady."

She ignored the sarcasm lacing his words. "My father has sent me here to find a suitable American husband. I wish to return to London, unmarried, instead. I need my father to hear of an unsuitable fiancé, which will result in his ordering me home."

Hatcher squinted and pointed at his chest. "And I'm the unsuitable?"

"Yes." No need to lie. This could not be news to a man with Hatcher's reputation.

She had no idea what to expect, but Hatcher surprised her by throwing back his head and laughing. Not just a chuckle or a titter. A full-out belly laugh. She thought his eyes might be watering, too.

When he stopped, he wheezed, "As a flimflam, I must tell you, this is the best I've ever heard. Brava, madam." Placing his hands on the armrests, he pushed up out of the chair. "Feel free to have Brandywine call for my carriage to see you home. Good day."

"Wait." She shot to her feet. "You cannot leave."

Heaving a sigh, he turned around. Exhaustion lined his face. "Why not?"

"Because I have not told you the rest of it."

"And what is the rest of it?"

"Rumor has it you are eager to ingratiate yourself into New York society. I am able to assist with that."

He crossed his arms over his chest, appearing

more imposing by the minute. She began to see why he was so successful in business. "And just how do you propose to assist me in that endeavor?"

"I'm the daughter of an earl. As well, I am staying with my aunt, who is the sister to an earl. We are received everywhere here."

"Define everywhere."

She listed the most recent invites. "The Fishes, the Astors, the Van Rensselaers, the Cooper Hewitts, the Posts. Oh, and the Roosevelts. I'm certain there have been more, but that was just this week."

"This week? It's only Wednesday." When she nodded, he said, "I don't believe you. No daughter of an earl would show up at my house—me, a bachelor with a wild reputation—by herself first thing in the morning. Even your carriage waiting outside would cause a stir."

She cleared her throat. "Well . . . as to that. I might have let it slip to certain parties that we are engaged."

"You _what_?" He stalked forward, his shoulders tight with anger and recrimination. He pointed a finger in her face. "You had no right to do that."

She shoved his finger away. "You agreed last night! You gave me your word." It hadn't escaped her that he might not remember agreeing to her scheme, so telling others of the betrothal had seemed a clever way to ensure Julius's cooperation.

He stopped, closed his eyes, and took a few deep breaths. "Weaver!" he suddenly shouted, the sound reverberating off the papered walls of the cavernous room.

Seconds later, a tall, well-dressed servant appeared. Not a footman or the butler, so she guessed a valet. "You *rang*, sir?"

She nearly laughed at the sly insult over Hatcher's bellowing. Hatcher did not seem to catch it, however. "Weaver, thank God. Come in and shut the door."

"Of course, sir." He entered and clasped his hands behind his back. "How may I be of assistance?"

Julius indicated Nora. "She claims to be the daughter of an earl. Lady Nora something or other. I need you to tell me if she's speaking the truth."

"The lady is indeed Lady Honora Parker, the daughter of the eighth Earl of Stratton. I have seen her portrait at the home of the dowager countess, her ladyship's grandmother. The Parkers have held the earldom since King James the First bequeathed the title on her ancestor, Rowland Parker."

Nora hadn't heard that. "Is that true? Rowland?"

"Oh yes, my lady. His lordship, the first earl, had been a Scottish childhood friend to the king. It is believed he appropriated the name Parker to sound more English."

"Fascinating," she said, awed by Weaver's knowledge of her family. "What was his surname prior to Parker?"

"I have heard Munro but there is no solid evidence to confirm it."

"You are a marvel. Have you memorized all of Debrett's?"

He beamed with pride. "Of course, my lady. One never knows when such information will become useful."

"What about—"

"*Thank you, Weaver.*" Irritation laced Hatcher's voice. "That will be all."

Weaver's lips twitched and Nora had the impression he was fighting a smile. "Very good, sir." He withdrew, closing the door softly behind him.

She lifted one eyebrow, not even attempting to conceal the smugness.

"Fine. You are the daughter of an earl." Hatcher shifted his weight and thrust his hands in his trouser pockets. "Who have you told about this engagement?"

"My aunt and uncle. Your staff. And I wrote to Mrs. Billings to let her know you would be escorting me to the ball on Saturday evening."

"A ball?" When Nora nodded, Hatcher's gaze narrowed. "What if I have plans? What if I refuse?"

"If you are interested in gaining society's acceptance, this is an excellent place to start. Nearly everyone of importance in New York will be there. Why on Earth would you refuse?"

"Perhaps because I do not appreciate being ordered about by a woman I've never met? Or maybe I have changed my mind about entering society."

"Have you?"

She could tell by his expression he hadn't. Though they were nothing more than strangers, determination lurked under his skin. She would bet once he set his mind to a task or goal, there was no talking him out of it.

"So why not take me up on my offer?" she asked. "You have nothing to lose and everything to gain."

He rubbed his jaw as he studied her. "Tell me

the reason for your desperate wish to return to England."

She considered telling him about Robert, admitting her love for another man. Likely it would set Hatcher's mind at ease to know he'd have nothing to fear in regards to an unwanted emotional attachment from her.

But the admission felt too private. Hatcher was nearly a stranger after all. He might not understand why the daughter of an earl yearned to be with a simple artist, one who loved her for herself and not her title. Or he might conclude affection was not a reasonable motivation for lying to everyone in New York.

The decision on whether or not he could be trusted hadn't yet been made. And until she knew, Robert would remain a secret.

She countered with, "Tell me the reason for your desperate wish to join society."

"Doesn't everyone long to join society?"

Something in the flippant statement rang false, and she knew he had a reason. One he was not sharing.

It turned out they both had secrets.

Fine. She needed neither his trust nor his friendship. What she needed was for him to be as outrageous as possible. Word would reach her father quicker that way.

She closed the distance between them. His tall frame towered over her, yet she faced him squarely and ignored the tingling along the back of her neck. Without liquor's influence, his eyes were really the most startling shade of blue. Clear and bright, with a hint of gray in them, and framed by long blond lashes. Drunk, she'd believed him attractive in a roguish way.

Sober, Hatcher was downright devastating.

Robert had a softer, more boyish form of good looks. Thick black hair and dark eyes that showed his sensitive, sweet soul. He also didn't loom over her. Moreover, he never argued or disagreed with her. They had a deep, serious connection, one she'd never shared with another person. One she missed terribly.

Resolved, she boldly struck out a hand. "Never mind. Whatever your reason, I am willing to help you as long as you do the same. Do we have a deal?"

WEREN'T ENGLISH GIRLS renowned for being timid?

Obviously, no one had informed this English girl of that fact. Lady Nora hadn't a timid bone in her body, from what Julius had seen. He glanced down at her outthrust hand, the moment stretching into years, as he debated whether or not to accept. Her idea seemed insane. Outrageous. Potentially scandalous.

Which perhaps explained why he liked it so damn much.

On the other hand, posing as a fiancé meant spending a lot of time with this particular woman. This wouldn't be a hardship if she were his usual type: experienced, bold, and well endowed. But Lady Nora possessed only one of those qualities, the one on which he placed the least amount of importance.

Julius had no patience for virginal debutantes.

Especially beautiful ones with dark curls, full lips, and gypsy eyes that changed color depending on the light.

A memory surfaced. He pictured her up on a chair and staring him down. "Last night, you stood on a chair."

Her hand dropped to her side and she stared at him in surprise. "You remember."

"Not all of it." He grimaced. "I don't usually drink that much. It was my birthday."

"So your other parties, the ones I've read about, those were anomalies as well? Like when you rented out the ballroom at the Hotel Astor and held a ten-pin bowling tournament for your friends. Or the time you constructed an enormous fountain where the waiters had to ride in canoes just to ladle the rum punch."

"The canoes were tiny," he muttered, frowning down at her. Was he supposed to feel guilty about spending his money the way he wanted? "And that's enough about me. How old are you exactly?"

"Twenty. How old are you?"

Christ. Nearly a baby. Just his presence in the same room would corrupt her. "Thirty. Which is why you should turn around, go home, and tell everyone you were mistaken."

"You'll never work your way into society if I do." She lifted a brow, almost daring him not to agree to this insane plan.

And God help him, he was considering it. "What would my responsibilities be in this arrangement?"

"Very little," she said quickly, almost eagerly. As if asking for more would scare him off. "Merely a few evenings together each week. I thought we would begin at the opera Friday night. Then a ball on Saturday."

"And all I need to do is escort you?"

"That and mingle. I'll take care of the rest."

He scratched his jaw. She made it sound easy . . . but the carrot she dangled was tempting. The names of his father's investors had eluded Julius for thirteen years. Rubbing elbows with the fancy set would give him a better opportunity to figure out who had ruined his father's life, which was why he'd tried to buy his way into society over the years.

A man lives and dies by his word.

How often had his father repeated that phrase in the last days of his life? Probably a thousand times. No matter how long it took, Julius would find those three men—men who had left his father on the hook for everything—and destroy every single one of them.

She lifted her hand, regaining his attention. "Also, I should have an engagement ring of some sort. Is that a problem? I wouldn't normally ask, but my aunt will wonder if I am not wearing one after a few days."

A sensible request. "I can provide an appropriate ring. My mother has a dozen or so she left behind." Refused, actually.

He'd been foolish enough to repeatedly buy his mother impressive jewelry after he made his initial fortune. Each piece had been returned without explanation. Like a fool he'd continued to spend more on bigger stones and elaborate settings, thinking to win her over. The opposite had occurred. Now his mother barely tolerated him.

"Is she . . . ?"

"My mother is very much alive. She's also long since ceased keeping an eye on me, your ladyship. She left the city to move in with my oldest sister when I turned eighteen."

In fact, he only saw her twice a year, once on Christmas and again in April for her birthday. He'd come to dread these excruciatingly awkward interactions.

When he'd started earning money on the exchange, he purchased a large house for her in Albany. However, other than him covering the upkeep and expenses on the property, she'd asked him for nothing over the years. Nor would she accept gifts from him. Trips were refused. Paintings returned. Clothes donated to the poor. If he didn't know better, he'd think she had turned Quaker on him.

She disapproved of his money and the way he chose to spend it. This left them at an impasse, because he had no intention of giving up either his money or his lifestyle.

Speaking of lifestyle, he'd have to speak with Poppy as soon as possible. The popular actress had been Julius's mistress for three months now, but their relationship needed to cool until after the engagement ended.

"Mr. Hatcher—"

"Julius," he corrected. "If we're engaged, you might as well use my first name in private."

"Please, you may call me Nora. Do we have an agreement?"

"What happens if this fails?" he had to ask. If her father refused to summon her home, what then? Julius had zero interest in this arrangement becoming permanent. "Perhaps we should agree to a certain length of time for the engagement."

"I suppose that makes sense." She tapped two fingers against her lips. "Would three months be acceptable?"

Three months of the Metropolitan Opera House instead of Tenderloin dance halls? Twelve weeks of tepid champagne, chastity, and idle society chit-chat? He'd lose his mind.

How quickly could he find his father's investors? Perhaps not long if he made good use of his time at Nora's side. Sink his hooks in with society so deep that calling off the engagement wouldn't get him blackballed. Then he could continue to search, if necessary, even after she returned to London. "Two months."

"Ten weeks," she countered like a seasoned negotiator. "My father is busy with Lords and may not spare me a thought until the session wraps up for Lent."

"Lent begins in five weeks."

"Yes, but he may need time to catch up with the goings-on in New York."

He didn't like it. Ten weeks seemed forever but he could force her to reevaluate if he found his father's business partners before then. "Fine, ten weeks."

She beamed at his capitulation, and he couldn't

help but return it with a smile of his own. She appeared so inordinately pleased, almost as if she'd doubled her money on a shorted stock—

Of course. Why hadn't he realized it sooner? A *man*. There was a man back in England to whom she wished to return. Things began to fall into place. He wondered briefly who she'd fallen for. A footman? A groom? Had to be someone completely unsuitable for her father to ship her off to America.

The woman had secret depths. He liked that. Perhaps this would not be so terrible after all.

He put out his hand, which she readily accepted. His palm pressed to her smooth, soft skin as they shook. "You have yourself a fake fiancé, Lady Nora."

Chapter Three

During the New York social season, the Metropolitan Opera House buzzed with activity on Friday evenings. Much like the opera at Covent Garden, anyone worth knowing attended, sitting in one of the tiered boxes to best be seen.

The inside of the new building was far grander than anything they had in London. Paintings adorned most every surface of the light and airy space, and the furnishings were sumptuous. Rich reds and golds, with ornate carvings every which way one turned. Thousands of gas lamps created a warm atmosphere, the light reflecting off the heavy decorative gilding. Americans had no sense of subtlety, Nora thought as they wound through the corridors toward their box.

Her fake fiancé also lacked subtlety, apparently, judging by the three-carat pink diamond betrothal ring delivered earlier today. She'd been forced to buy a special glove just to fit over the enormous thing.

They entered the salon attached to the Cortland box. A man unfolded from the sofa to greet them.

Julius Hatcher had already arrived.

One could not help but admire him. His hair had been slicked back, which highlighted the sharp planes of his roguish face, and he wore a fitted black swallowtail coat and white waistcoat, shirt, and tie. He had a barely leashed elegance, sort of like a wild animal one brought indoors in hopes of civilizing it. "Mr. Hatcher." She moved forward and held out her hand. Julius bowed over it, a small smile playing on his lips.

"My lovely Lady Nora," he murmured in a voice too low to be heard by the others. An involuntary shiver worked its way along Nora's spine.

Before she could wonder on that, he straightened and faced her aunt and uncle, who were staring at the pair with avid curiosity. She threaded her arm through Julius's and pressed tight to his side. Goodness, his frame was as solid as a block of marble. "Uncle James, Aunt Beatrice, allow me to present Mr. Julius Hatcher, my fiancé."

Her aunt and uncle came closer and Hatcher greeted them both respectfully. This surprised her. He'd clearly been hiding proper manners under that ne'er-do-well exterior.

"This has come about suddenly." The ostrich feathers in her aunt's hair bobbed as she gestured between Nora and Julius. "I wasn't aware you two were acquainted. Nora tells me you met in the park?"

She had already crafted a plausible story regarding their initial meeting, one she'd used when breaking the news of the engagement to her aunt days ago. Undoubtedly, her family now wished to hear Julius's side, so instead of speaking, Nora tilted her face toward her fake fiancé and waited.

"I saw her on a walk in Central Park. Intrigued, I struck up a conversation. Soon, I was bewitched. I began meeting her each morning." He stared at her with such genuine tenderness and devotion that even Nora was nearly fooled. "I haven't been able to stay away since."

Her aunt and uncle knew she walked in the park each morning, so the story was entirely believable. That is, if one believed Hatcher roused himself out of bed before noon. Scoundrels were predictable, after all, no matter the country in which they reside.

"Then allow me to offer our most heartfelt congratulations." Her uncle slapped Julius on the back. "Welcome to the family, Hatcher."

"Thank you, Cortland."

"Shall we enjoy a cigar before the performance starts?"

"I'd like that." Julius lifted Nora's gloved hand and pressed it to his lips, and Nora's heart started galloping. Goodness, the man was potent.

Julius followed her uncle and disappeared into the corridor, leaving Nora alone with her aunt. She exhaled, grateful for the reprieve to gather her thoughts. Did finding her fiancé attractive make the deception easier to carry out?

"He is very handsome," Aunt Bea said as she studied Nora's expression. "I can see you are fond of him."

She swallowed the urge to deny it. While she disliked lying to her aunt and uncle, who'd been nothing but kind and welcoming to their unknown niece, she had to remember her purpose. Returning to Robert, the sensitive artist who owned a piece of her soul. "Yes, I am quite fortunate. Mr. Hatcher is a fine man."

"He does have a bit of a wild reputation, however. Women, raucous parties. Gambling. I'm not certain your father will approve."

Goodness, I hope not. "Please give him a chance, Aunt Bea. I think you and Uncle James will come to like him. You shall see he is quite different than how he's portrayed in the press."

In fact, he is much worse.

Her aunt patted Nora's hand. "You know I merely want for you to be happy. And if you claim Mr. Hatcher is a good man, then I will believe you."

"Thank you," she gushed to her aunt. "That means so much to me. You and Uncle James have been so kind these past few weeks." Not a lie. She had honestly enjoyed getting to know her father's sister and her American husband. The couple hadn't visited London since the countess's funeral when Nora was seven.

In fact, Aunt Bea was almost *too* kind. Nora had originally hoped to use her aunt as an unwitting ally in escaping New York City. She'd thought the instant she showed interest in the wrong type of man her aunt would cable her father and a one-way steamer ticket would be purchased. Instead her aunt had surprised her. *"Marry for love, Nora, as I did. Take your time and find the right man, no matter his status. I'll not send your father reports, so stay here in America as long as it takes to let your heart guide you."*

An impossible feat, considering Nora's heart wanted to guide her back to England. Still, it had been hard to resent a woman as lively and considerate as Aunt Bea.

"Oh, my dear." The older woman's round face softened. "It is you who have brightened our doorstep. As you know, we've no children of our own and it's been a true joy to spend time with you."

Experiencing an unexpected rush of guilt at her pack of lies, Nora moved to the waiting ice bucket and poured two glasses of champagne. She handed one to her aunt and retained the other. "Have you ever regretted not moving back to England?"

"Goodness, no," her aunt said. "I hated it there. So rigid and constricting. I felt as if I could hardly breathe with all the expectation."

Nora knew exactly what her aunt meant. "How did you meet Uncle James?"

"He came to London for business. The Cortlands are descended from the Duke of Huntington, you know."

"No, I hadn't known."

"It's not something your uncle crows about, but yes. His great-great-grandfather, I believe. Anyway, he asked me to dance at some such ball the year I debuted. Swept me off my feet. We were married that year and moved to New York. I never considered living anywhere other than by his side."

"Did you not miss your friends and family back in England?"

"No, not really. All I had was your father, and he and I were never close."

That was news to Nora. "You weren't? I assumed because he sent me to you . . ."

Aunt Bea chuckled. "I can assure you, I was as surprised as you. Not that I am ungrateful. Whatever his reasons, I owe Bertrand a great debt for allowing you to come stay with me. You've been a breath of fresh air."

Despite the affectionate words, a dark thought suddenly occurred. Had her father another reason for sending her to a different country, one nothing to do with her scandal? "Is he . . . ?" She cleared her throat. "Did he send me here to be rid of me? For good, I mean?"

Her aunt's face crumpled, her kind brown gaze brimming with compassion. "No, my dear. Heavens, no. I cannot imagine your father wants to be rid of you. I'm certain he wishes for you to return to England once you and Julius settle down."

But not to live, a voice whispered in her head. Her father had ordered her to find an American husband, one who would undoubtedly prefer to reside in America. She recalled his anger upon discovering her with Robert, the only time in memory when she'd received a dressing-down from her father.

"All of London will soon hear you've ruined yourself with this fortune-seeker, Nora. No decent man will ever want you after this."

She had tried explaining that Robert had no interest in her name or her fortune, but the earl would not be swayed. He'd ordered her to New York, booking passage for her on the next trans-Atlantic steamship. Her room had been guarded, trapping her in the Mayfair townhouse, until the ship sailed. The only way to send a good-bye letter to Robert had been with the help of her good friend, Eva, who'd also been kind enough to keep Nora updated on all the happenings back in London.

Had her father sent her away for good? Was he too angry, too embarrassed about what she'd done? That would explain why he shipped her off to another country to find a suitable husband instead of allowing her to choose a man in England. He never wanted her to return to London.

Fortunately, she had another idea in mind.

THE SMOKING ROOM in the Metropolitan Opera House overflowed with men eager to escape their wives and mistresses. Julius had visited the cramped space once or twice before but never lingered since he did not smoke.

Tonight, he trailed Cortland into the hazy room. The smell of tobacco and cigar nearly choked him, smoke burning his eyes. Christ, the ventilation was terrible in here. He'd tagged along so as to not offend Nora's uncle. That, and he suspected James Cortland wished to have a private word.

Of course, circulating with the Knickerbocker men before the performance would serve his purpose nicely—not that he expected someone to walk up, shake his hand, and admit to ruining his father. But he hadn't risen to the top of New York finance by not learning how to read people. He would watch facial expressions and mannerisms to discern patterns and spot abnormalities. All he needed were a few clues as to who might remember his father.

Cortland stopped and reached inside his jacket pocket, clearing his throat. "I would have preferred you asked for her hand properly, Hatcher, but I cannot quibble over silly rules. As long as you and she are happy, then Beatrice and I gladly give our blessings."

"Thank you, sir. I appreciate that. The proposal was very impetuous of me. Thankfully, Nora did not seem to mind."

Cortland withdrew two cigars and offered one to Julius, who shook his head. Cortland's brow shot up in surprise. "Don't smoke?"

"No, not since I was a teen." He'd tried for a while after his father's death but never developed a taste for it. He lifted a shoulder. "One vice I never acquired, I suppose."

Nora's uncle began the process of clipping and lighting his cigar. Shorter than Julius, Cortland wore bushy white sideburns that matched his hair. He came from one of the most respected families in New York, the kind who had settled along the Battery when the rest of the island was wilderness. Before tonight, the two men had never been more than passing acquaintances.

Cortland took several puffs then said, "About those vices. I suppose you'll speak to Miss Desmond now that you're engaged."

"I've already done so, in fact." He'd met with Poppy last evening to break things off. The popular actress had not been thrilled to learn of Julius's engagement, which he'd allowed her to believe was real. She'd cursed a blue streak, calling him every name she could think of, before ordering him out of her apartments.

"Good. I'm glad to hear of it. I expect you to have a care with my niece's reputation."

"I shall, sir."

"Because I'll be greatly displeased if she's hurt. The girl is under my protection until after the wedding."

Message received. Little risk in ruining her, however, as she was in love with another man. At least, he assumed that was her reason for concocting this plan in the first place. Why else would a gorgeous, vivacious, and intelligent woman such as Nora be so desperate to return to boring old London?

"I understand. I would not see her harmed."

"Good evening, Cortland." A man joined them, one Julius recognized from about town. Mr. William Pendleton, one of the Knickerbocker elite and the current president of the exclusive Gotham Club.

"Evening, Pendleton. Do you know Mr. Julius Hatcher?"

"Of course." Pendleton struck out his hand. "Congratulations are in order, I hear, Hatcher."

Julius shook the older man's hand. "Thank you. I am a lucky man, indeed."

"Now that you're in the family, perhaps James will sponsor you for membership at the Gotham. We're always looking for fresh blood."

Julius nearly laughed outright. The Gotham Club had turned down his membership application back in '87, as had all the other fancy society clubs uptown. Instead, he'd joined Edwin Booth's artistically inclined Players Club down in Gramercy Park, which he happened to quite enjoy.

But circulating inside the blue-blooded clubs could provide him with additional opportunities to ferret out the men who'd ruined his father. So he forced a smile. "Thank you, Pendleton. I appreciate the offer."

"I'd be happy to," Cortland said. "Hadn't realized you weren't already a member, Hatcher."

Julius doubted that very much but said nothing.

"Incidentally, Hatcher," Pendleton said after taking a sip of what looked like whiskey. "You've certainly got the golden touch on Wall Street. Which stocks grab your fancy these days?"

The question set Julius's teeth on edge. So here was Pendleton's price for the club membership. Several men nearby quieted, conversation waning as they unabashedly listened for Julius's answer. He threw back the rest of his champagne. "Both Great Lakes Railroad and Pratt's have shown strong growth this quarter."

"Excellent." Pendleton's eyes glittered with anticipation. "Appreciate the tip. Hope to see you both soon. Will you be at the Billings event tomorrow?"

"Yes," Nora's uncle said. "We plan to be there. My niece is anxious to share a dance or two with her new fiancé."

Dance? Julius nearly cringed at the thought. He hated dancing.

Pendleton departed and Cortland soon finished his cigar. The two men started back to the family's box and the women. His fiancée. Strange to think of Nora that way. *Strange to think of any woman that way.*

He'd sworn never to marry. Having a wife and family put considerable burdens on a man. Weighted you down with responsibilities that resulted in rash, desperate decisions, oftentimes with disastrous results. With only himself to look after, Julius could focus on what truly mattered: himself.

Temporary, the engagement was merely temporary. Nora would soon be shipped back to England, the men to blame for cheating his father would be ruined, and Julius could return to life as a bachelor.

"Hatcher!"

Julius's head shot up to find his good friend and attorney, Frank Tripp, coming toward him in the corridor. They had known each other for years, both having the same thirst for parties, gambling, and ladies. Often all at once.

"Evening, Tripp." He quickly introduced Nora's uncle.

"I thought that was you." Tripp slapped Julius on the back. "Say, I heard the funniest joke yesterday. Someone's going around claiming you're engaged. I told them there was no chance because just the other night you—"

"If you'll excuse us, Cortland," Julius said to Nora's uncle. "I'd like to have a private word with my friend."

Cortland looked considerably uncomfortable and latched on to the escape. "Of course. See you at the box, Hatcher." With a nod in Frank's direction, Cortland hurried away.

"You idiot," Julius snapped. "That is my fiancée's uncle."

Frank's face fell, his eyes searching Julius's face. "Jesus, you're serious. You have a fiancée? What about Poppy?"

"Cast adrift, I'm afraid. And I do have a fiancée. Her name is Lady Nora Parker."

"A lady? I cannot believe this. But you swore . . ."

Never to marry.

He could not trust Tripp with the truth, that the engagement was a sham. The fewer people who knew, the better chance they had at maintaining the ruse, even amongst friends. "People change. And she's a wonderful woman. I'm fortunate to have her."

"I don't understand."

"You don't have to understand. Just accept it and be happy for me."

Tripp held up both hands, palms out. "I beg your pardon. I'm merely having a hard time wrapping my head around all this. How long have you known her?"

"Not long. We met in the park, took to walking together every morning." He didn't see the need to deviate from the agreed-upon story.

"Walking in the park? In the morning? *You?*" Tripp threw his head back and laughed. "Now I know you're pulling my leg."

Julius grabbed Frank's arm and tugged him closer to the wall. He leaned in. "Do not make me hit you. Stop questioning me and just believe it for now."

Frank drew back. "For now? What does—oh, I see." Understanding dawned in his eyes. He gave

Julius an exaggerated wink. "Say no more, Hatcher. Engaged it is."

"No, wait. You misunderstood."

Tripp patted Julius's shoulder. "No, I don't believe I have—and stop worrying. Your secret is safe with me. Listen, some of the boys are down in the Patterson box. We're throwing dice for some of his silver mine stock. You in?"

Julius grimaced. He should say no. The Cortlands and Nora would wonder where he'd wandered off to if he did not return promptly. But Patterson's stock was an almost irresistible lure . . .

"Come on. I know you want to," Tripp encouraged. "Ten minutes, that's all. Your fancy fiancée won't even miss you. No doubt you've been eyeing that stock."

Of course he'd been eyeing that stock. It had tripled in value in two years, and throwing dice was all probability. His mathematical skill at calculating the odds made him nearly unbeatable.

Damn it.

Julius darted a glance on both sides of the nearly empty corridor. The performance had started again. Could he sneak away? For all Nora knew, Julius might still be in the smoking room. What was ten minutes? "All right. Ten minutes, that's all. I need to hurry back. After winning, of course."

ONE QUARTER OF an hour later—and five hundred shares of Patterson mining stock richer—Julius returned to the Cortland box. An empty salon greeted him, the rest of the group already in the seats. He continued into the main theater box and dropped into the empty chair between the wall and Nora.

She sniffed and then leaned over to whisper, "You smell like a tobacco factory."

"A result of visiting the smoking room, I'm afraid." He noticed her face was pale, her golden-brown eyes flat. Had something upset her? "Is everything all right?"

"It's nothing."

An obvious lie, but he had no way of tearing the truth out of her. "Would you care for some air?"

She darted a quick glance at the boxes around them, filled with New York's elite. Was she worried about attracting attention? Ridiculous. No one stayed in a seat for the entire performance. Besides, hadn't this entire scheme been about attracting attention?

He stood and held out a hand. "Come."

After a few soft words to her aunt across the narrow aisle, Nora rose and led the way to the salon. When she was settled on the tiny velvet sofa, he poured her some champagne and himself a whiskey.

Strains of the German opera floated through the heavy curtains as he handed her a crystal glass. He lowered himself next to her, maintaining a respectable distance. *Remember the agreement and stop admiring the long graceful curve of her neck.*

When he'd first seen her tonight, the breath had left his chest. She was all regal elegance and voluptuous beauty in a cream opera gown with gold and brown beading on the skirt. White gloves came up past her elbows and tasteful, expensive jewelry adorned her throat and wrists. Her brown hair was pinned into a simple hairstyle that had him longing to rumple the glossy strands with his bare hands. She was an absolute vision.

And off-limits.

Lowering his voice so as to not be heard by the others, he asked, "Did your aunt or uncle say something to upset you?"

"No, not really. Merely a realization on my part. I'd really rather not discuss it."

"Do you want to call this off?"

Her eyes cut to his. "Whatever would cause you to think that?"

"I assumed you were having second thoughts."

"No second thoughts. None whatsoever." She took a healthy swallow of champagne. "Did you know my aunt and uncle hardly ever travel to England? Prior to four weeks ago, I hadn't seen them since my mother's funeral."

"My condolences. How many years ago did she pass away?"

"I was seven."

"It's difficult to lose a parent so young."

She stared at him intently, the gaslight playing across her face as she waited for him to elaborate. When he didn't, she remained silent and he found himself strangely disappointed. "You may ask me, you know."

"It's impolite to pry. I assumed you'd offer up whatever information you wished to share."

"I'd rather you merely ask me whatever it is you're curious about."

She avoided his gaze and smoothed her skirts with her free hand. "I shouldn't like to offend you."

"Nora," he said through a chuckle. "I'm American. You prim and proper Brits cannot offend us Yankees."

He liked the wide smile that overtook her face. "Is that so? Now I shall truly attempt to try."

The moment stretched, the two of them grinning at each other, until she broke away to inspect the wall. He took a long swallow of his drink. "You are an interesting puzzle, Lady Nora."

"How so?"

"A woman who seeks me out at Sherry's, arranges for a fake engagement, and then is worried about overstepping her boundaries? That is most definitely a puzzle."

She lifted a shoulder, let it drop. "I suppose you are right. Some days, I feel as if I am caught between two worlds. Never doing what is expected of me."

Ah, he was beginning to understand. He'd often experienced similar thoughts. "Life would be quite boring if we always did what was expected of us."

"True, but I find that usually results in disappointing everyone."

"Except ourselves." He toasted her with his cut-glass tumbler. "We have but one life, Nora. Best to live it the way we'd like, eh?"

"Is that what you do? Live only for yourself?"

"Yes, I do. Simpler that way."

"Lonelier, too."

Lonely? No, definitely not. He had friends, lovers. Companions whenever he desired, solitude at other times. He would not trade his life for another, not in a hundred years.

But the rules were vastly different for men and women. Had Nora been lonely in England? That could explain how she'd ended up in love with a man ill suited for her.

"They say you are some sort of financial genius," she said. "Is it true?"

"Not sure about genius, but I do like numbers. Always have. Just have a head for figures, I suppose."

"What is six hundred and twenty-two thousand multiplied by eight hundred and thirty-seven thousand?"

The numbers aligned in his mind without much effort. "Five hundred twenty billion, six hundred and fourteen million."

"I'm impressed. So how does that translate into acquiring a fortune?"

"If one is able to remember patterns of numbers and use them to predict trends, like which companies are growing and which are contracting. I can discern the inflated stocks and the ones undervalued. It's a constant puzzle with no end."

She nodded, as if this information unlocked some hidden meaning into his personality. "Another puzzle."

"Yes, but one not nearly as interesting as you."

The line escaped his mouth before he could stop it. He hadn't meant to flirt with her. They were partners, not lovers, but he hadn't been able to control himself. Which was unusual, to say the least.

Dangerous. This woman is dangerous.

She laughed, thank goodness. "There is no need to flatter me, Julius. We are allies, nothing more." She rose and placed her empty glass on a side table, sparing him the need to offer up a response. He stood and finished his drink as well, happy to give his runaway mouth something else to do.

"We should probably return to our seats," she said. "The purpose in coming tonight was to be seen together, and thus far we have failed in that endeavor."

"Not completely. I'd wager every person in our tier noticed us leaving. And news of the engagement has already spread like fire in a match factory."

"Excellent. Then things are progressing quite nicely, I'd say." She took his elbow. "Incidentally, what did my uncle say to you in the smoking room?"

Keeping his voice low, he said, "He was disappointed I didn't properly ask for your hand. Warned me to have a care with your reputation."

She snorted, a sound he found endearing. Were proper British ladies supposed to snort? No wonder Nora's father had shipped her to America. She must have scandalized society in London over and over again.

"You think he's wrong to worry?" he asked.

"Things are hardly ever what they seem, Mr. Hatcher," she said cryptically. "Come along. Let's return to our seats."

Chapter Four

On the surface, society events in New York were not very different from those in London. They each had a large ballroom for dancing, with a nearby room set up with food and tables for conversation. Card room for the gents and retiring room for the ladies.

What set the American parties apart, Nora had noticed, was the grand scale of it all. The houses were bigger, the decorations more lavish. The Billingses' dining table had a large ice sculpture of Poseidon in the middle, surrounded by freshly shelled oysters and clams. A champagne fountain flowed. Vegetables had been painstakingly carved into flowers. The wine had been shipped in from France, and wooden trellises covered with lush pink and white roses adorned the walls. And, of course, Delmonico's, the most popular restaurant in the city, had provided the extensive buffet.

And not even *that* was enough. It was common practice here to depart the party with a favor or two. At a ball last week, the host had gifted solid gold pencil cases and porcelain figurines to her guests. Whatever Mrs. Billings planned for this evening, no doubt it would be comparable.

Nora had weightier issues on her mind, namely getting herself back to London. She examined the sea of dancers on the floor. The ball was in full swing, but Julius had disappeared on her. Again. If she did not know better, she'd think the man was trying to avoid her.

Which made no sense. They needed to circulate together to attract attention. News of the engagement had spread but no one seemed overly shocked or scandalized. For his part, Julius had acted perfectly respectable thus far, merely a doting fiancé smitten with his choice of bride, before wandering off into the throng of male guests.

She caught a flash of brownish-blond hair and found him in deep discussion with two men across the room, one shoulder propped against the wall, a glass of champagne in his hand. He seemed right at home, comfortable in his own handsome skin, even surrounded by the blue bloods of society who'd reportedly rejected him over the years. How did he accomplish it, to fit in wherever he went? She had struggled for years with a father who didn't want her, a society that curtailed her individuality, and a world that viewed women as second-class citizens.

She pushed her way through the crowd, closer, until she stood in his line of sight. Catching his eye, she motioned to the dance floor.

Raising a brow, he mouthed, *Later.* Then he straightened and led the two men farther into the bowels of the mansion. Farther away from her.

Nora tried not to gape as her blood simmered. The nerve of that man. Had he forgotten their purpose? This was unacceptable. He could not ignore her. He hadn't even asked her to dance.

She clenched her fists. As far as outrageous fiancés went, Julius Hatcher left much to be desired.

Whirling away from the dance floor, she took a step toward the card room—and two young women suddenly blocked her path. Nora drew up short and tried to place their names. Both had brown hair, were about her same age, and dressed in the latest Worth gowns.

"You are she. You are Lady Nora," one of them said, her eyes wide.

The other woman took Nora's elbow and began leading her toward the edge of the room, where the crowd had thinned. "We have been dying to meet you. I am Kathleen Appleton."

"And I am Anne Elliot. You're the one who snagged Mr. Hatcher."

Nora dipped her chin and tried to look pleased. "Nice to meet you both. I suppose I have snagged him." *For the time being.*

"There is no need for modesty, my lady." Anne leaned in. "Julius Hatcher is the most delicious man in New York."

"And the most unattainable." Kathleen's brows rose. "I would be bragging up and down Ladies' Mile for months if I'd landed him."

"Except your mother would kill you first," Anne told her, then turned back to Nora. "Amongst the mothers, Mr. Hatcher was always off-limits. Definitely in the 'look but do not touch' category whenever we saw him in public."

"But, oh . . . to touch," Kathleen said on a dreamy sigh, her hand over her heart. "The mere thought has me perspiring."

Nora couldn't help but laugh. These two were amusing . . . and refreshingly honest. "He is quite handsome. And intelligent."

Anne waved her hand. "No one cares if a man that pretty can hold a conversation."

Kathleen lowered her voice. "Indeed. I hear his skills reside in other important areas."

All three broke out in laughter, though Nora's face felt as if it were on fire. "Are all New York debutantes so bold?"

"No, the rest are bores," Kathleen said. "We are the fun ones. Our fathers say it's because our mothers were raised by wolves."

"They weren't really," Anne explained. "But they are first cousins."

"So you two are second cousins?"

"Yes, and thick as Five Point thieves," Kathleen confirmed. "So tell us. How did you manage it?"

"Manage what?"

"You and Mr. Hatcher," Kathleen said. "He's never circulated in polite society and my mother would die if I approached him."

"He spends most of his time with his mistress, Poppy Desmond." Anne put a hand to her mouth. "Unless you didn't know?"

"I had heard the two were acquainted, yes," Nora confirmed. Everyone in Manhattan knew

Miss Desmond and Julius had been lovers. So was he still seeing her? A strange heaviness expanded behind Nora's ribs, one that she ignored.

"I cannot imagine she fancied the idea of him marrying someone else." Kathleen shared a look with Anne. "She bragged quite openly about how they'd marry one day."

"Really?" Nora wondered over that. Had Julius promised the woman a future together? Not that it mattered. Once Nora had her ten weeks and a summons home, Miss Desmond was welcome to him.

Anne nodded. "Yes. No one believed her, though, even if she is one of the most beautiful actresses in the city."

"Women like that aren't for marrying," Kathleen said. "Besides, she's not nearly as beautiful as your ladyship."

"Thank you. And I'm just Nora among friends."

Kathleen beamed and clapped her hands. "Annie, you hear that? She called us friends. You know what that means? Bridesmaids!"

Anne grabbed her cousin's arm. "Good heavens, it'll be the event of the season. I can hardly wait." She turned to Nora. "Have you set a date yet? You simply must go to Paris and let Mr. Worth design your gown."

"Well, about that." Nora cleared her throat. "We haven't discussed the details. I'm still awaiting word from my father regarding his schedule."

"Isn't he an earl?" Kathleen asked. "How exciting. You are the luckiest woman in New York."

"The woman who tamed Julius Hatcher!" Anne beamed. "The two of you will be on every guest list."

Nora's brain tumbled over the first statement. "Wait, tamed? What does that mean?"

Kathleen's brows flattened, her mouth turning into a pretty frown. "Oh, everyone is talking about it. Haven't you heard?"

"Heard what?"

"That you're the one who has brought Julius to heel. Everyone is starting to wonder if they were wrong about him."

To heel? She hadn't wanted him *tamed*. She needed him scandalizing New York society. Creating a ruckus. Outraging her father. Not winning everyone over. She ground her teeth together.

He'd wanted to find his way into New York society. And he has now accomplished it.

No. She refused to believe Julius no longer needed her. They had a deal. He'd given his word. Shaken her hand.

She forced the lingering doubt away and bid farewell to her new friends. As much as she missed the companionship of girls her own age, she had a more important agenda tonight. This new, stronger Nora was tired of waiting. It was time for Julius to live up to his end of the bargain, for the two of them to set tongues wagging.

And if he wouldn't do it, then she certainly would.

JULIUS HAD ONE furious fiancée.

Even as he congratulated himself for smoothly suggesting the gentlemen follow him to a quieter place for conversation, he knew—deep down, he just *knew*—Nora would not take this delay kindly. She struck him as the sort of woman with little to no patience. She'd accosted him during a scandalous party at Sherry's, for God's sake.

Still, he couldn't worry on that at the moment. While mingling, he'd encountered two men near his father's age. They were discussing poor investments from the last few years. Stocks that had crashed. Businesses that had failed. Promises made and broken. Hopeful, he'd pressed the two for more stories. What else did they remember?

"What about you, Hatcher?" one of the men asked as they moved into the portrait gallery. "Where did you lose money in the last few years?"

Julius shrugged. "I haven't."

The other man, Mr. William Young, narrowed his eyes. "Come now, no one gets it right every single time. There must have been one or two investments you've regretted."

"Not a one. Not since I started investing at age seventeen."

"I don't believe you," Young said, his voice crisp. "The hiccup with the Allegheny Railway in '86? Everyone I knew nearly lost his shirt."

Julius remembered it well. The price-to-earning ratio on Allegheny had been shit. He'd cleaned up in the aftermath on the exchange. "I pulled out two weeks before. Thought the stock was overvalued. Turns out, it was."

Both of the men gaped at him. "What system do you use to evaluate them?" This was from Mr. Van Allen, the other member of their trio.

"Ah," Julius said with a sly smile. "That is a secret of the trade."

Young's gaze turned speculative, as if he were

seeing Julius in a new light. "They said you were some kind of wizard on the exchange. I hadn't believed it until now."

Julius sipped his whiskey and fought the urge to lob a sarcastic remark. How did these men think he'd acquired his wealth? A gift from the gods? Investing took guts, intelligence, and foresight. Most of these Knickerbocker men couldn't lay claim to any of the three.

"What is your family's background, Hatcher?" Van Allen asked. "Am I familiar with your father?"

"He died some years back." He purposely kept the answer evasive. If someone offered more in-depth information, that could be telling.

Young snapped his fingers. "Wait, I seem to recall—"

"Mr. Hatcher! There you are."

Julius's stomach sank at the interruption. What had Young been about to say? Something about Warren Hatcher? Damn it.

Clenching his jaw, he turned to find Lady Nora descending upon his trio. His fake fiancée's sense of timing left much to be desired. "My lady," he greeted and bowed over her hand. "Perhaps you could allow us a few more moments to conclude our conversation?"

She ignored him. "Good evening, Mr. Young. Mr. Van Allen."

"My lady," they each said and bowed over her hand as well. Julius ground down his back molars and waited for her to come to the point.

"I do apologize for interrupting," she started. "But I wonder if I might steal Mr. Hatcher for a dance?"

"About that," Julius said. "Why don't I meet you in the ballroom after I'm done here?"

"Nonsense," Mr. Van Allen said. "If a pretty lady wants you to dance, Hatcher, you hop to it."

Young lifted his glass toward Nora. "Yes—and an earl's daughter, no less. You cannot leave your fiancée wanting for your time. We shall see both of you later on." He sauntered away, heading toward the card room for gentlemen.

"Indeed. Enjoy your dance. Perhaps later you'll recommend a few stocks, Hatcher." Van Allen inclined his chin and hurried after Young, who was already halfway along the gallery.

Julius watched them go, his muscles tight with annoyance. He slapped his glass down on a side table. "Are you out of your mind? A *dance*, Nora? That couldn't wait ten minutes?"

The flecks of gold in her irises sparked in the dull electric light. "I've been waiting for over an hour. You've been ignoring me most of the evening. How long was I supposed to stand around and wait for you to notice me?"

Notice her? He'd done hardly anything all night *but* notice her. Having her in the vicinity distracted him. Her expressions, her laugh . . . the exquisite bow shape of her upper lip. His obsession with watching her had been part of the reason he'd asked Young and Van Allen to the portrait gallery. And such an obsession irritated him. He needed to remain focused on his purpose, which had nothing to do with wasting time on the dance floor with the loveliest woman in the room.

Sarcasm laced his words. "I know you are English, where the women are timid and meek, but in America, we prefer our women with a little more independence. Ten more minutes without me would not have killed you."

Her lips flattened into an angry line. "And I know you are American, where manners were apparently hurled into Boston Harbor with all that tea, but English gentlemen do not abandon their fiancées."

"A pity you were unable to locate a fake English fiancé, then."

"You are odious and insufferable, Julius Hatcher."

"Two qualities I believe you referred to favorably when selecting me as your partner in this venture—or am I wrong?"

Her shoulders drooped slightly and she studied the landscape painting on the wall. "I need you to be odious and insufferable to everyone else *but* me. If we are truly partners, then you cannot dismiss me the instant we arrive."

Fair enough. She had a point. He felt himself relax, his own anger dissipating. "I apologize. I was involved in an important discussion and did not wish to cut it short."

"An important discussion about what?"

"Nothing," he lied.

"You're lying. Why don't you want to tell me?"

Because it's private. Because I've never told anyone. "We were talking about investments."

"Oh. Were you asking their advice?"

Julius couldn't help it: he snorted. "Hardly. I

don't take anyone's advice but my own, and if I did it wouldn't be from those two. They're still convinced telephones are a passing fancy."

"That must be why Mr. Van Allen asked you to make recommendations. I suppose you get quite a bit of that, considering your reputation."

Nearly everywhere he went. Men were desperate to acquire an advantage when it came to the exchange, where fortunes could be won or lost in a single day. But Julius did not play well with others. Likely a lingering effect of his father's failures and subsequent death, but he didn't trust easily—especially when it came to business. He preferred keeping his thoughts and ideas to himself, listening to his intuition on how to best proceed, never relying on anyone else.

"I do. I rarely answer, however." Ready to put an end to the probing conversation, he held out his arm. "Will you honor me with a dance, Lady Nora?"

"I thought you'd never ask." She placed her hand on his sleeve. "Literally, I believed you would never ask."

He started them toward the ballroom, the silk skirts of her gown rustling in the cavernous silence. "I would have asked eventually. I know my duties, Mrs. Hatcher."

"Ha. I bet it feels strange to call a woman by that name."

"*Strange* is indeed the precise word. Marriage is not on my list of items to accomplish before I die."

"You might wish to inform Miss Desmond of that fact, then."

He stopped short. "What did you say?"

"Miss Desmond. Your . . ." She waved her hand, her creamy skin turning a fetching shade of rose.

"Mistress?" he supplied, merely to cause her more embarrassment. She did not disappoint, blushing deeper. Even the modest area above her neckline changed color. How far had the blush spread over her body?

He shook away those thoughts. Nora was not the type of woman with whom one dallied.

"Yes, her. I hear she believes the two of you shall one day marry."

Poppy . . . his *wife*? Had they ever discussed it? He couldn't recall the topic even being raised. If it had, he would've let her know his feelings on the subject.

He took Nora's elbow and began walking once more. "That will never happen."

"Because she is an actress?"

"No. A woman's profession makes no difference to me. If I loved her enough, she could be a shop girl, a debutante, or a prostitute. But I'll not marry anyone."

"Now, or ever?"

"Ever." He glanced down to see Nora's brows furrowed. "Does that surprise you?"

"Yes, it rather does. I thought every wealthy man wanted to see his legacy passed down."

"Not this one."

"Live only for yourself?"

So she remembered their conversation in the salon last night. He nodded once. "Exactly."

They reached the doorway. Nora put a hand on

his shoulder, stopping him. "Wait, we forgot to discuss what we shall do out there."

"I thought we were planning to dance."

"Yes, dance. But what else?" He must've stared at her blankly, because she said, "How do you plan to cause a scene?"

And get himself thrown out? Barred from further events? He'd barely delved a toe into these upper-crust waters and now she wanted him to raise a ruckus? "I'm not planning to cause any sort of scene, Nora."

She shifted to face him, leaning in so as to not be overheard. "My dear man, the entire purpose of engaging an outrageous fiancé was for you to be outrageous. Otherwise, how will we scandalize them?"

"I have no intention of scandalizing them, my dear lady."

"But you agreed!"

"I did no such thing. I agreed to squire you about New York for ten weeks, acting as your fiancé. I never promised to ruin your reputation—or mine, for that matter."

"You have no reputation to ruin. Everyone already knows you're—" She cut herself off, closing her mouth abruptly.

Julius stiffened. He could fill in the rest of that sentence with a dozen different words, all of them unflattering.

And everything just became clear.

"I see. You chose me because you thought I wouldn't fit in here. That they would never accept me, so I'd willingly thumb my nose at them."

"No, that's not entirely true." Her voice was weak, not at all her usual decisive tone.

"Just mostly." He heaved out a breath and took a moment to analyze the situation. In the end, he cared little for what this English rebel thought of him. What mattered was staying in society long enough to discover the connection to his father—and actually staying in society was paramount to the cause. Acting the obnoxious buffoon would not accomplish that.

Nora, he'd come to realize, was not a patient woman. Unfortunately, she was impetuous and quite stubborn when she set her mind to a task. If she decided to forge ahead with this scandal idea on her own, both of them might suffer social recriminations.

He had to stall her. Pretend to help while guiding her toward respectability. Keep her on the straight and narrow. Because no matter what, he would not allow her to get him thrown out of society two minutes after he'd found his way in.

He gave her a charming smile. "Let us dance, then, and discuss how we may best proceed."

"Do you know most everyone here?"

Nora tilted her face up at Julius's question. They were on the dance floor, twirling to the strains of Strauss, and she'd been lost in thought, marveling over Robert's short poem that had arrived in yesterday's post. Twelve sweet lines that had tugged at her heartstrings and caused her to miss him terribly. Yes, he'd rhymed *mine* with *spine*—a shame, really, when one considered *thine, wine,* and *fine*—but she'd never had a man write her poetry before.

"Not everyone," she answered. "I've met many of the older ladies and gentlemen, as they are the same age as my aunt and uncle. But the younger ones are mostly a mystery. What about you?"

"The men are somewhat familiar, at least those active in business. The ladies are a blur of petticoats, though. My path hadn't exactly crossed with debutantes before tonight."

Precisely why she'd asked him to pose as her fake fiancé. Mothers hid their daughters from men like Julius—unless the men were titled, of course. A title meant a man could act as idiotic or terrible as he liked and mothers still shoved daughters into his path. "Yet you were anxious to join society. Any idea when you'll tell me why?"

A muscle flexed beneath the rough skin of his jaw. "I think I'll wait a little longer, if it's all the same to you."

She did not press. A woman with secrets of her own had no right to pry. "So how shall we cause a stir?"

He shrugged slightly. "You know the rules far better than I. Perhaps you should offer up some suggestions?"

"Fair enough. What if we perform an exaggerated twirl and my skirts raise to mid-calf?"

The edges of his mouth turned down as he gave a small shake of his head. "Let's refrain from dancing the cancan until all other options have been exhausted. What else?"

"You could hold me inappropriately. You know, wandering hands . . ."

"And risk your uncle tearing my limbs off? No, thank you."

She thought for a moment. They needed to set tongues wagging, enough that someone either cabled her father or the gossip pages printed it. This whole thing started because she and Robert had been caught kissing during one of her father's dinner parties. "We could sneak off together."

"Would that be scandalous for an engaged couple?"

"Yes, in London, at least. I am assuming the same applies in New York." Was a secret rendezvous scandalous enough? "Or we could kiss right here on the dance floor."

"Absolutely not," he snapped, his body jerking. "Sneak off together it is. When and where?"

"Half an hour and we'll meet in the gardens. The key is to be noticed as we each leave the ballroom."

"That shouldn't prove difficult. Who leaves first?"

"I suppose it should be you. Then I'll venture outside, stroll about for fifteen minutes, and return to the ballroom."

"No." His hand tightened on her waist. "I do not like the idea of you wandering the gardens by yourself. I'll leave first and wait for you just beyond the circle of torchlight."

"I am certain it's perfectly safe out there."

"Spoken like a woman raised in the English countryside. This is New York, Nora. Do not argue—and do not go off by yourself, even at a fancy society party."

She huffed and waited for a nearby couple to dance out of earshot before she murmured, "I've spent a considerable amount of time in London. We have a fair number of criminals there, too. And you are surprisingly bossy for a fake fiancé."

He leaned in, his mouth close to her ear. "While we are engaged, fake as it may be, you are my responsibility, one I take quite seriously."

A shiver worked its way along her nerve endings, though she couldn't say why. The sensation resembled attraction, which was insane considering the circumstances. Attraction . . . for *Julius*? Utterly laughable. Yes, he was handsome and intelligent. Reasonably charming when he wanted to be. But the two of them were partners, nothing more. Nora's only goal was to return to Robert.

She stepped back and put distance between them. "I appreciate your concern, but I am shockingly self-sufficient."

"And young." His bright blue gaze narrowed on her. "Do you argue with everyone, or is it just with me you insist on disagreeing?"

She couldn't remember any argument with Robert since they'd become acquainted, but she wasn't about to let Julius believe himself special in some way. "A pity you find me so objectionable. Which is indeed interesting coming from a man I saw drunkenly fall off a horse a few days ago."

He deftly guided her toward the far end of the room, his steps sure and quick on the dance floor. "A neat way of avoiding the question. Besides, I already told you that was my birthday celebration."

"I see," she said, though she really did not. Did every wealthy American man throw a bacchanal on his birthday? More horrifyingly, there was a hint of defensiveness in his tone, as if he only acted so outrageously one day a year. *That would be a disaster*, she thought. One day a year would not shock her father. She needed Julius hosting parties on horseback every week.

At that moment, the song ended and Julius led her to the edge of the parquet dance floor. He kissed her gloved hand but did not relinquish his hold after he straightened. Instead, his lips curved into a devious half smile. "Twenty-five minutes, my lady."

A strange warmth seeped into her belly, so she snatched her hand back. When they met outside she would need to tell him no more flirting. No more whispering in her ear or holding her hand too long. And absolutely no roguish smiles, either. She did not want to *like* him, for heaven's sake.

They were temporary partners to accomplish a common goal. That was all it ever would be.

After managing a brisk nod, she spun and hurried away. There was no reason to run, but she had a sudden desire to *flee*. To get away from this house, this city. To put as much distance between herself and Julius Hatcher as possible.

Chapter Five

"I cannot make up my mind."

Julius spun to find Beatrice Cortland directly behind him in the dining room. He'd been circulating through the crowds, trying to patiently wait out the twenty-five minutes before venturing outside. Nora's aunt frowned up at him, though he had no idea what he'd done to displease her. "Ma'am?"

"About you. I cannot decide if you are exactly who people say you are, or if you are the complete opposite."

His reputation had been greatly exaggerated in the press, but he wasn't about to tell her that. "Perhaps it's a bit of both?"

"I certainly hope not." She plucked two glasses of champagne off the dining table and handed one to him. "For Nora's sake, I hope you are far more serious than the newspapers make you out to be."

"Why?" he had to ask.

"Because my niece has unfortunately inherited my rebellious streak and the young man waiting for her back in England no doubt encourages it.

Some fortune hunter, I'd wager. What she needs is a levelheaded man to keep her grounded." She took a sip from the crystal glass, her eyes never leaving Julius's face. "And it would be nice if said man were American."

"Oh." His mouth dried up as questions flooded his brain. Did Mrs. Cortland suspect the engagement to be a lie? How had she learned of Nora's young man back in England, something Julius had merely suspected? Was she seriously hoping Julius and Nora developed a fondness for one another?

"You're white as a sheet." Nora's aunt chuckled. "You young people, thinking we're stupid merely because we're older. Do not worry, I shan't say anything to Nora about this."

"How did you learn of the man back in England?"

"The letters. He writes her one nearly every day. Same masculine hand and cheap paper. I haven't read any, if that is what you're thinking. I would never invade her privacy in such a disrespectful manner."

"I didn't assume you had. Is this man why her father sent her off to America, then?"

Mrs. Cortland took a long sip of champagne and studied him over the rim. "The honest answer is that I don't know. However, even if I did, I'm not certain you have her best interests at heart. Until I feel you are trustworthy, you'll get nothing out of me."

"I do not wish her harm, if that's your concern."

"Yes, but you have your own reasons for agreeing to this scheme, one I suspect was her idea. Interesting that she disappeared for so long during our dinner at Sherry's, where you happened to be hosting a raucous party. You see, I looked for her after a few minutes, just to check on her, but she was not to be found."

Obviously, Nora could not fool her aunt. Part of him wanted to warn his fiancée; the other part wanted to enlist her aunt's help in curtailing Nora's outrageousness. He decided to go with honesty. "Yes, that is where she first approached me. Do you plan on revealing us?"

"No. As I said, I have purely selfish motives for encouraging the two of you. And, based on what I have observed, I am quite hopeful."

He blinked a few times. "Hopeful? I don't understand."

She stepped in closer, lowering her voice. "I've seen the way you look at her. She is unlike any woman you'll find here in America, Mr. Hatcher. Girls here are raised as if they are made of sugar, treated like precious objects. Coddled. Nora is steel and spice, with centuries of British female resourcefulness in her genes."

Yes, that summed up what he knew of Nora thus far.

But he had to ensure this woman harbored no false hope. "I have no intention of actually marrying her, Mrs. Cortland. Or any woman, for that matter. Just so we are clear on where matters stand."

Her lips twisted into a sly smile, mirth dancing in eyes that closely resembled her niece's brown gaze. "Powerful men like to cling to their bachelorhood as long as possible, Mr. Hatcher. But you all fall eventually. All it takes is the right woman." On that, she swirled away in a cloud of silk skirts, leaving him rooted in place.

Julius watched as drops slid down the large ice sculpture, Poseidon's crown now more like a tiny tiara. For the first time since agreeing to Nora's scheme, he wondered if he might be in over his head.

No, he would remain firm. This was a business arrangement. Yes, he was attracted to Nora. What red-blooded American man wouldn't be? She was challenging, intelligent, and fearless—not to mention distractingly beautiful with full pouty lips and a healthy bosom.

But this was only a short-term solution to a problem that had long plagued him: finding the men responsible for his father's demise.

That was all.

Lifting the champagne glass to his mouth, he threw back the contents and swallowed. He wished for something stronger but had no time to seek that out now. He needed to make his way outside to meet Nora.

It was not easy. Most of the doors were in full view of the crowd, and Julius had no intention of being seen departing for an illicit rendezvous. He'd been serious when he told Nora he would not cause a scene. Getting himself thrown out of society so soon served absolutely no purpose. The men who cheated his father would never be found then.

He located a window in one of the empty sitting rooms that would lead to the edge of the terrace. Throwing up the sash, he climbed over the sill. The night was unusually warm for February in New York. Surprising, then, to find the terrace empty.

He'd thought more guests would long to escape the heat of the ballroom.

Taking the stairs at the edge, he soon ended up on the ground near the gardens. He leaned against the stone wall and checked his pocket watch by the torchlight above. Exactly twenty-eight minutes. Had she beaten him outside?

After another few moments he pushed away from the wall and started into the gardens. Perhaps she'd wandered down the path to find him. The tall hedges would come up over her head, which meant he couldn't easily spot her. "Nora," he called in a stage whisper.

Another turn on the stone path led him deeper into the foliage with only the light of the moon to guide his way. He hadn't seen a garden quite like this outside of Central Park. Trees and bushes lined the walk, with trellised archways on the corners. Julius needed to have a serious discussion with his gardeners.

He wound around a corner and still did not see her. "Nora," he said louder. "Are you here?"

She popped out from the side of the bushes directly ahead, nearly scaring him. "Julius!"

He blew out a breath and stopped by a large oak tree. "Thank God. I worried I'd have to send a search party after you."

"I came out and didn't see you," she said, drawing closer. "So I assumed you'd already walked into the gardens."

Never mind that he'd expressly said he would wait for her, that she shouldn't wander the gardens alone. He got the sense Nora did not take orders well. He thrust his hands in his pockets. "Well, what do we do now?"

She came to stand in front of him and lifted one shoulder. "Wait a few moments and then go back inside."

"Separately or together?"

"We wait here together and then enter the ballroom separately. Have you never carried out an illicit rendezvous before?"

"I've never had a reason to be secretive before." He flashed her a grin and waggled his brows. "All of my illicitness is quite public."

"This coming from the man who did not want to hold me improperly on the dance floor."

His grin faded. "Is that truly what you'd like, a man to defile you in front of a room full of matrons and gentlemen?"

She sniffed and rubbed her upper arms with gloved hands. "I never said defile. Grope, yes. Defile, no."

"It's the same thing in their eyes, and you know it. You must have given your father fits."

"Why do you say so?" Her gaze narrowed on him.

"I can only imagine him as a very proper aristocrat who continually tried to stop his daughter from calamity."

"You would be wrong. I'll have you know I was a model daughter and young woman of society. There were no calamities—well, except for one."

"Oh, this I must hear."

"Absolutely not. Forget I mentioned it."

He opened his mouth to push her on it but a crunch of gravel nearby caught him off guard. He locked eyes with Nora, who seemed to be holding her breath.

"Say, who's there?" a voice called from behind them, the footsteps coming closer.

His only thought was to protect Nora. No one could discover her here, alone with him.

Without blinking, he grabbed her waist and lifted her, putting her back to the tree trunk and covering her with his body. The only thing left to do was to keep her quiet.

He quickly angled his head and started kissing her.

JULIUS'S LIPS PRESSED to hers and Nora froze, her mind trying to understand what was happening. One minute she'd been standing in the path talking to Julius, and the next moment he had her pressed against a tree, kissing the daylights out of her.

Kissing her. Julius was *kissing* her. On the mouth.

Confusion became quickly overshadowed by the pull and drag of his lips as they molded to hers, confident and sure, as if they had done this a thousand times. Warmth spread through her veins, a slow rush of unexpected heat. Bark dug into her back but she hardly felt it, not with Julius's fingers digging into her hips as he teased a response from her, coaxing, guiding her toward wickedness. She knew this was wrong, knew she should put a stop to it . . . but found herself kissing him back instead.

His large body jolted and he growled in the back of his throat. "Yes," he breathed before tilting his head and deepening the kiss, attacking her mouth with a determination that weakened her knees. Her lids fluttered closed and she relaxed, melted, and acquiesced into a sea of sensation, her pulse an erratic rhythm in her chest. She forgot about the cold, the strange surroundings, that most of New York society was just steps away. It took all her concentration just to hold on to him and keep breathing.

Large hands traveled up her rib cage while his tongue teased the seam of her lips. She opened her mouth to allow him inside and he took immediate advantage, his tongue sliding past her lips to twine with hers. Slick and rough, his tongue tasted her with slow, deliberate thoroughness, as if savoring the experience. Exploring. Learning. He surrounded her, inside and out, a safe haven where she could be this new bold, carefree woman enjoying an illicit kiss with a near stranger. No plotting and scheming, no worrying about her future. There was only now. Only Julius.

"Say, who's there?" the strange voice said again.

Julius's mouth broke off from hers and he pressed her face directly into the warm skin of his neck. She heard him snap, "Leave us."

"Oh, Hatcher. Apologies. Thought you were someone else."

Panting, she tried to clear her mind. Julius had kissed her. Outside. In the gardens. Of the Billingses' ball. Her nose was buried in his throat and she took a deep inhale. He smelled heavenly, like dark woods and spice. Why were they here? Right, she'd asked him to meet her to start a scandal. And someone else had just caught them. Therefore, she should be calling attention to her presence. Why was she so dashed light-headed? Heavens, that kiss had scrambled her brain.

Drawing in a deep breath, she lifted her head and opened her mouth. "Wait, sir," she rasped.

Hands abruptly left her waist. Julius stepped away, dragging fingers through his rumpled hair. "Don't bother. He's gone."

She put her palms on the trunk behind her to steady herself. "Gone? But he was right here a second ago."

"A little longer than that, princess. Regardless, he cannot hear you any longer."

Shame and anger began coiling in her chest, a hot ball of regret to replace the tingles from moments earlier. Dear heavens, she'd just kissed a man who wasn't Robert. Sweet Robert, who pined for her back in London. This was *not* how the evening was supposed to turn out.

She latched on to the outrage, a much safer feeling that required no examination or explanation of any kind. There would be time enough for recriminations later, once she had reflected on all that had happened. "How dare you kiss me! The only reason I came out here was to be discovered—and you just prevented that!"

His head snapped toward her, blue eyes narrowed. "No, you wanted to be seen leaving the ballroom. Not cavorting alone with a man in the gardens."

"I was hardly cavorting—and nothing untoward would've even occurred if you hadn't kissed me."

"It was the only thing I could think to do to save your reputation."

"Oh, save my reputation by kissing me? Really, Julius." She rolled her eyes. "That is the most ludicrous thing I've ever heard."

"Nevertheless, it's true. I knew whoever caught us would recognize me, assume the worst, and leave. Which is precisely what happened. And you are welcome." He straightened his waistcoat and then his tie, which had become askew. Had she done that? Knowing she'd pawed at him caused her fury to grow hotter.

"I am not thanking you!" she said. "You are the most aggravating man. Your plan to save me from ruin is to ruin me yourself?"

"Kissing is hardly ruining you, Nora. Unless you are truly that innocent?"

"I know what it means to be ruined—and you are missing the point. I *want* to be ruined!"

"No, you don't. Trust me. Scandal is one thing. Ruin is another matter entirely."

She put her hands on her hips. "I had no idea you were such an expert on society's rules, seeing how this is your first foray into society. Anything else you should care to explain?"

He exhaled harshly. "I'll not allow your reputation to be dragged through the mud. I'm certainly no expert, but I do know that society frowns on this sort of thing between unmarried couples."

"You should not be kissing me."

"Why not? You wanted me to grope you on the dance floor." His voice crept up in volume, a flush creeping over the edge of his collar. "Why is kissing worse?"

"Because we were alone. The groping was for the benefit of the ballroom."

"And that kiss was for the benefit of the man who almost discovered you out here." When she just glared at him, too furious to speak, his expression cleared. "I understand what is happening here. You enjoyed our kiss. That's why you're so upset."

"I did not *enjoy* that kiss. You caught me by surprise and took advantage."

His eyes went huge and a sound of disbelief erupted from his throat. "I took advantage? So that wasn't your tongue in my mouth? The small whimpers you gave or the way your fingers—"

"That is enough." She marched forward and stuck a finger into his chest. "We will not speak of this after tonight. Keep your hands to yourself—and you're never, ever to kiss me again. Are we clear?"

"As crystal. And no need to panic—I have no intention of repeating what happened, not when you are so ungrateful."

"What did you expect? I am the daughter of an earl. Do you think I would jump at the chance to kiss an American nobody?" She hated the cruel words, hated the way they sounded, like the snobbish, high-born society women who could slice deep with one syllable. But the rash reaction was tangled up with all the emotions roiling in her chest. She had kissed this man . . . and enjoyed every minute. He knew it, the cad. What sort of woman did that make her? Why hadn't she pushed him away? Why hadn't she thought of Robert once?

Hurt flashed across his face before the edge of his lip curled into the semblance of a sneer. "No, I suspect not. I won't make the mistake again." Turning on his heel, he strode down the path and disappeared around a corner.

As soon as he was out of sight, she wilted, all

her bravado and anger evaporating and leaving her spent. How could she have let that kiss happen? More importantly, why hadn't she stopped it once she realized what was happening?

She rubbed her eyes with the tips of her gloved fingers. Her lips were still swollen from Julius's mouth, her back raw from the rough trunk. For now, she had to return to the ballroom and forget the kiss. Otherwise, guilt would eat her alive. She couldn't tell anyone of this. What happened here in the gardens would not happen again and Robert would never find out. *Julius didn't kiss you because he wanted to. He kissed you to protect you.*

And if not for that triumphant, "*Yes*," he'd whispered against her lips she would almost believe it.

ANGRY AND FRUSTRATED, Julius stomped through his front door. "Evening, Brandywine." He handed over his cane and top hat. Removing his gloves, he asked, "Anything I need to know before I drink myself into a stupor and fall into bed?"

"Good evening, sir. Mr. Tripp is waiting for you in the billiards room."

Drinking all the good whiskey, no doubt. Was Frank Tripp here about work, or to ask questions regarding the engagement? His friend had been caught off guard by the news last night. Julius should probably smooth over any ruffled feathers on that front. "I'll see what he needs before I head up."

Exhaustion set aside for the moment, Julius hurried through the house until he reached the billiards room. His friend was playing a solo game on the massive table, the long cue smacking the colored balls over the green baize. The two of them had met while Tripp was finishing law school, with Julius still making a name for himself on the exchange. Tripp preferred words while Julius preferred numbers, but they both came from modest families with a dark history, and they both had held a deep appreciation for the city's vices during their youth.

"Hello, Tripp."

Tripp's brown-haired head snapped up and he straightened to his full height. "Thank God. The boredom had me nearly betting against myself in this game. Come, give me a challenge."

"Let's make it a quick one," Julius said as he selected a polished stick off the rack. "I cannot stay awake all night."

"All your fancy society parties and dinners wearing you out?"

"Something like that."

Tripp began collecting the balls into the wooden triangle so one of them could break. "Or perhaps it's your beautiful fiancée wearing you out?"

That came up sooner than anticipated. "Any chance we can avoid a discussion of said fiancée?"

"Not a chance," Tripp said through a grin as Julius removed his coat. "I'm dying to hear the details of this so-called engagement. It's the reason I am wasting my Saturday evening here instead of a gentleman's house of leisure in the Tenderloin."

"It is not a 'so-called' engagement. It's real."

"Please. You say that as if I haven't been your closest friend for the last decade. I'll give you the break, then." He removed the wooden triangle, leaving the balls in a perfect pattern, and stepped aside.

Julius went to the edge of the table, lined up, and let his stick fly. The cue ball smacked into the group of balls at the opposite end, scattering them toward the rails. Three dropped in.

"So why are you pretending to want to marry this Englishwoman?"

Instead of answering, Julius took another shot. The ball missed the pocket and he conceded the table, walking to the sideboard and pouring a glass of whiskey. "You're not known for keeping a secret, Tripp."

"True, but I've kept many of yours over the years." He let loose with an impressive shot where the ball banked off two rails and dropped into the pocket. "Consider it covered under client's privilege. As your attorney, I'm bound not to disclose whatever you confess."

Julius sighed. Perhaps having his friend's support would come in handy at some point. He quickly told Tripp of meeting Nora that night at Sherry's and the arrangement they'd agreed upon. "Her father sent her here to find a suitable husband but she wants to return to England as soon as possible—without a husband. She's settled on me as the fellow to most upset the earl, the one that'll get her called back home."

"Christ, now I wish I hadn't been out of town for your birthday party." Tripp frowned as he bent over the table. "So why would you upset her father the most? Half the young women in New York are angling to marry you."

Julius swallowed a mouthful of whiskey. He grimaced as the burn spread down his throat and throughout his belly. "She has a beau back in London and the father doesn't approve. Man's probably not of their class. Regardless, she's desperate for a scandal that'll cause her father to bring her home."

"Ah, the plot thickens." Another ball dropped in. "Wait, you haven't said why you agreed to this scheme in the first place."

Julius didn't immediately answer. Though he had client's privilege with his attorney, he didn't particularly feel like dredging up the black story of his father's demise. He went with a half-truth. "She got a yes out of me while I was flat-faced drunk at the party."

Tripp laughed so hard that he missed his next shot. He chuckled all the way to the side table where he'd placed his drink. "Serves you right, then. What is she suggesting for this scandal? *In flagrante delicto?*"

"In a manner of speaking. Tonight, she wanted it to appear as if we'd left the ball to engage in a tryst outside."

When Julius missed his next shot, Tripp rested the stick on the floor, and leaned against it. "Did you do it?"

"Yes, unfortunately."

Tripp waited for him to continue. When he didn't, his friend smirked. "Allow me to guess. You tried to seduce her."

The kiss in the gardens replayed itself in Julius's head, every lusty, delicious second. He craved her even now, after her verbal set-down. She'd kissed him with determination and gusto, no hesitation whatsoever. With an implicit trust, like she'd been thinking of kissing him for days—just as he'd been thinking of kissing her.

Yet he couldn't admit any of this to Tripp. "Don't be ridiculous. One cannot seduce an earl's daughter in the gardens during a ball."

"Really? I once saw you seduce the governor's daughter during intermission at the Met. You took her to an alcove—"

"That's enough—and she was more than willing, by the way."

Tripp reached for his drink. "My, we are touchy this evening. I think I like this earl's daughter."

"If you want any more of my whiskey, I'd advise you to remember whose side you are on." He cursed under his breath after missing his next shot. "And I don't want a scandal."

"Why not? You've never shied away from one before."

"This is different. The reputation of an earl's daughter is at stake."

"Ah, you're worried you'll get saddled with a wife if things go sour."

Not quite, because Julius wouldn't allow himself to be forced into a marriage no matter what . . . but Tripp didn't need to know the exact reason Julius needed to stay in society's good graces. "Precisely. And if I ruin her, there will be hell to pay from society on both sides of the herring pond."

"Hmm. So you need a way to keep your fiancée from creating a scandal when she's hell-bound and determined to do it."

"Yes." Now that he thought about it, perhaps he should confide in Tripp more often. His friend's quick intelligence had never failed Julius before, his lawyer's brain able to twist hypotheticals where Julius could only see straight facts.

"Can the regard for her London beau be shaken somehow, I wonder?" Tripp's arm jerked forward, the stick careening into the cue ball. Another ball dropped into a pocket. "That way she wants to remain in New York."

"Another man, you mean?"

"Yes, but it would be difficult to bring another man into the situation while she's betrothed to you. That means *you* must be the other man."

"Wait a minute—"

Tripp straightened and grinned, his free hand gesturing at Julius. "I like this. Yes, this is exactly what you should do. Flirt with her, charm her, until she begins to doubt her feelings for the boy across the ocean. Because if she develops feelings for you she won't be as eager to get kicked out and sent home."

"That feels dishonest. And calculating."

"Of course it is, which is why it's my idea and not yours. It'll work, I promise. And what's the harm? You've already kissed her, haven't you?"

Julius thought of the trusting way she'd melted into him and kissed him back tonight. "It's wrong to deceive her."

Tripp glanced heavenward. "Please. I've seen you charm a serving girl for an extra pint of ale. Remember that time told a dancer you were shipping out with the Navy the next day and needed one last free dance? Come now, my friend. One or two small lies seems perfectly reasonable to me."

As far as buying himself some time to investigate, the idea was a solid one. The longer he kept Nora on the straight and narrow, the longer he could circulate through society and find his father's investors. But Tripp's plan had one major flaw. "I don't want a wife, Frank. You're risking the very thing I'm trying to avoid. It makes no sense."

Tripp started pacing as he often did when reasoning out legal problems. "Would you marry her if you ruined her?"

"No."

"There you go, then. In public, you're proper and polite. No one will know how you treat her in private. In a few weeks she either returns to her beau in London or discovers she didn't truly want him after all. Either way, you fulfill your obligation and move on. Everyone wins."

He made it sound so simple. Yet Julius knew the best-laid plans could go awry. "I'll think on it."

"Good. A little harmless flirting is all you need. If she truly loves this man in England, perhaps she'll be able to resist you."

That made sense, actually. If her feelings for the young man were unshakable, then the two of them would end up together, no matter what Julius did. Was there such a thing as harmless flirting, however?

"Hardly seems as if the idea is a stretch, if your face is anything to judge by," Tripp said. "Let me know how things progress. I might lay odds on the outcome."

"I haven't agreed yet—and no betting. You're terrible at calculating odds."

Tripp finished his drink and set the tumbler down on the table. "That is what I have you for. And in case you missed it, I just beat you. Shall we play again? Loser has to wear a satyr costume at your annual masquerade."

Shit, Julius had forgotten about his yearly pre-Lenten bacchanal. Based on the Mardi Gras and Carnival celebrations, the party required everyone to wear masks and colorful costumes. The city's actors and dancers always came out in droves, reveling in the debauchery. The timing could not be worse, however. "I'm not certain it's wise to host a masquerade this year."

Tripp's jaw fell open, his face gone slack. "What do you mean? You always host a masquerade."

"I'm betrothed. No scandals, remember?"

Tripp gawked like Julius had lost his mind. "This isn't an event for wives and fiancées, Hatcher. I don't think you need to worry about her reputation while we're dancing with half-naked girls at the Gilsey House."

Julius sighed. Society may've been willing to overlook these things before his engagement but now he wasn't so sure. Was one night of hedonism worth the risk? And yet he did love that masquerade . . . "I'll think on it." He snatched the chalk and smoothed it over the tip of his stick. "In the meantime, let's play again. Loser has to cover the winner's tab at Sherry's for a full year."

"You're on."

Chapter Six

The morning after the ball, Nora descended the hack and quickly paid the driver. Her
aunt and uncle were attending church services and
she had very little time before they returned home.
To escape their watch, she'd pled a headache, then
set off for Julius's obnoxious castle the second she
was alone.

She hurried up the walk, determination in her
stride as she crossed over the moat, the morning
papers cradled in her arms. She rapped on the
front door and waited. Within a minute, the ornate wooden panel swung inward to reveal Julius's
proper English butler. "Good morning, my lady."

"Good morning." She stepped inside without
giving him a chance to refuse her. "I must see him.
You'll have to wake him, I'm afraid."

"Oh, Mr. Hatcher has already started his day, my
lady. He has been in his office since eight."

She froze in the process of removing her gloves.
In his office? Since eight? On a Sunday? "Is that . . .
unusual?"

"No, my lady. Not a bit."

"But . . ." She let her voice drift off. It sounded silly to admit aloud that she'd assumed him to sleep most of the day away. After all, that was what the scoundrels in London did, waking up and stumbling to their clubs in time for supper.

You mean the scoundrels who inherited their money?

Yes, she could see how a man who'd made his own fortune might behave differently. Julius obviously prioritized his work, considering the staggering amount of wealth he'd amassed in a short period of time. So she shouldn't have found it surprising . . . yet she did.

And when would Julius stop surprising her?

"If your ladyship will follow me," the servant said and opened the door to the same rose-colored receiving room she'd been shown to earlier in the week. "Shall I bring refreshments?"

"No. I shan't be staying long."

"Very good. I'll let Mr. Hatcher know your ladyship is here."

He withdrew, shutting the door behind him, and Nora perched on the sofa and removed her bonnet. She had to give credit to Julius's decorator. The space was elegant compared to the rest of the ostentatious house. Crown molding wrapped the room and accented the rose walls, and gilded French furnishings were positioned just so. A large Persian rug covered the parquet wooden floor and silk draperies adorned the huge rounded windows overlooking Fifth Avenue. The highlight was an octagonal-shaped inset carved into the ceiling, the interior of which had been painted to resemble the sky and clouds.

It was a room designed to subtly emphasize the owner's wealth. Having redecorated her father's various houses over the years, Nora had an idea what this must have cost and she was suitably impressed.

Based on these surroundings, she could well believe him a financial genius. Julius had been humble about the title, but no man rose from nothing and lived like this without remarkable intelligence. Another reason to feel duped by her choice in fiancé, not that she could back out now. Unfortunately, they had to last the rest of the season together.

Heaven knew a broken engagement would not shock her father. He'd merely believe she had her eye on someone better. No, she had to work this out with Julius, make him understand this only succeeded if her father objected to the match and summoned her home.

Most importantly, they must refrain from kissing again.

The door opened and she turned. Julius appeared, his dark blond hair slicked back to show off slashing cheekbones and startling blue eyes. Those eyes were too pretty by half, boring into her from across the room, so she focused on the rest of him. His gray wool suit pulled across wide, sturdy shoulders, and a waistcoat of dark navy silk accentuated a trim torso and narrow waist. She swallowed, her mouth gone dry at the memory of clinging to his frame, the feel of the hard ridges and firm muscles under her fingertips.

You are my responsibility, one I take quite seriously.

Why on earth did that sentence cause her heart to flutter?

"My lady," he said, leaving the door slightly ajar. "You are out early today." He slipped his hands in his trouser pockets and cocked his head. "Is something wrong?"

"You left the ball. After . . ." She couldn't bring herself to say it, so she continued on. "By the time I returned inside you'd snuck away like a thief in the night."

His shoulders relaxed and his lips twisted into a small smile. "Nora, you make it sound as if I were trying to avoid you. Which would be ridiculous, considering the circumstances. An urgent matter required my attention. That's all."

"And what matter was that?"

He slid into a chair opposite the sofa and brushed his trousers. "A boring business matter. I'm certain you'd rather not hear the details."

A business matter at *midnight* on a Saturday? Poppycock, as the Americans said. She lifted her chin. "You would be wrong. I adore details."

"Fine. I promised my assistant to review a contract yesterday and forgot. I needed to have it completed before this morning."

A contract—not the kiss—had caused him to flee the ball? She could tell by the tensing of his jaw that Julius was prepared to fall on the sword of his lie. Arguing would get her nowhere. She gestured toward the morning papers she'd placed on the low table. "Have you seen these?"

"Yes."

"I don't understand. You are always in the papers. In the brief time I've been in New York, you've been mentioned no less than four dozen times."

"In the business pages, perhaps—"

"And the gossip pages. Where you went for dinner, who you were with. You and Miss Desmond are practically regular features. Yet since our engagement, nothing. Not even a single mention. What are we doing wrong?"

Julius shifted in his chair and smoothed the fabric of his trousers. "We're not doing anything wrong. It's unfair to compare the two situations. Miss Desmond is very popular here. She's one of the most popular singers and performers in America."

"And your mistress."

"No longer, but yes, she was that, too."

So he'd ended his association with Miss Desmond. This was news. Part of her felt relieved . . . and the other part of her was horrified at said relief. Why should he not have a mistress? He and Nora were business partners, nothing more. Which did not explain why the idea of him with another woman turned her stomach.

Her gaze flicked to his mouth, those full lips that had ravaged hers the night before. *You liked kissing him. Admit it.*

No. She would admit nothing of the sort and the entire episode needed to be erased from her mind. Enough time had been spent ruminating on that kiss last evening.

"And the places I took Miss Desmond were designed to attract attention," Julius continued. "Notoriety is what performers crave."

Places designed to attract attention. Nora paused, her brain absorbing. Yes, that was definitely the difference. She wasn't thinking broad enough in her plan. Society events were predictable and hardly worth noting in the papers. A whole city existed out there, with seedy and immoral destinations perfect for a scandalous outing. "What were these places?"

"Well, there's the Haymarket. Delmonico's and Sherry's, of course. Bare-knuckle prizefights. Bicycle races. Horse races at Sheepshead Bay. She liked the German beer gardens as well."

The Haymarket was an outrageous dance hall in the Tenderloin district. An earl's daughter would never, ever visit there . . . but the new Nora Parker would go in a flash. "Those all sound terribly exciting."

His handsome face grew wary. "I don't care for that look. What are you plotting?"

"I think it's obvious, isn't it? You and I will visit these places, too. Then the papers will begin mentioning us and word will reach my father's ears."

"Now, wait a moment," he said, rising. "Most of those places are in dangerous neighborhoods hardly suitable for an English lady. Forget scandal— you could be seriously hurt."

"That's why you are coming with me. To offer your protection."

"No, absolutely not." He put his hands on his hips, his shoulders stiff and unforgiving beneath the fine tailoring. "Even if I could protect you, things occur in those places that no gently bred woman should ever witness."

"Let me worry about my delicate sensibilities. Do you not see? This is an absolutely perfect plan."

"You're asking me to treat you like a mistress, Nora. It's impossible." His hand swept the air to indicate the length of her body. "And inappropriate. Look at you."

"Why?" She glanced down at her perfectly pressed yellow day dress. It molded to her curves without revealing too much and complemented her skin tone. "What is wrong with the way I appear?"

"Nothing, for an earl's daughter. You're perfectly put together. A mistress dresses entirely differently."

"How, exactly?"

His hand flopped ineffectually at his side. "I don't know. They dress to entice."

Her feminine pride wilted a bit. *He doesn't find you enticing.* Hadn't he said as much after their kiss last night? *"Don't worry—I have no intention of repeating what happened."*

Well, neither did she. They were partners in this sham engagement. Time to act like it. "Fine. I can do that. What else does a mistress do?"

JULIUS COULDN'T HELP it. One of his brows shot up as if to say, *Really?*

A delicate flush swept over her neck, meaning he wouldn't have to spell it out for her. Again he wondered if she were innocent. He suspected the boy back in England had taken liberties, which was why she was determined to return to him. Women, especially those of Nora's class, were taught to hold on to their virginity until marriage. Doubtful she'd have given it away without serious emotions involved. Regardless, her past was none of his business.

Still, he couldn't help but wonder if she kissed the English lad the same way she'd kissed him last night?

"I meant other than *that*, of course," she said.

He exhaled and pinched the bridge of his nose between two fingers. The day had hardly begun and already he longed for a stiff drink. "This is a ridiculous conversation—"

She clasped her hands together, pleading with him. "Come now, Julius. I need your help. You know these places. Take me to one or two of them so we may cause some gossip."

"What you're asking will result in getting me thrown out of society ten seconds after I've barely been let in."

"No, it won't. Society is very forgiving of men and their escapades—and they've already accepted you. I saw you cozying up to the gentlemen last night. They all couldn't wait to bend your ear."

"For stock tips, Nora. They aren't exactly inviting me to dinner." He closed the distance between them so he could better see her eyes. "Tell me why returning to England is so important. Tell me about the young man waiting for you."

Her mouth formed a tiny O and he heard her swift intake of breath. Did she think him dense? Though he'd clearly shocked her, he said nothing. In business the most crucial advantage in a negotiation was silence. Relationships were no different in his experience.

"Why do you think there is a man?" she finally asked.

No need to tell her Beatrice Cortland had confirmed his suspicion last evening. For whatever reason, the older woman had kept the knowledge from her niece and Julius saw no reason to intervene. "Because I like puzzles and I'm fairly good at putting the pieces together." He tapped his temple with one finger. "Things have to add up in here or else I'm not satisfied. And it's obvious that's why you're so anxious to return home, not to mention horrified by what happened last evening."

Frowning, she shifted a few steps away, trailing her fingers along the wooden chair back. "Fine. There is a man. My father disapproves of him, which is why I've been sent here."

Knowing for certain that another man held her affections bothered Julius. He told himself it was because he liked Nora, found her courageous and entertaining. She deserved to be happy with a man deserving of her spirit, not some sniveling coward who allowed her father to keep them apart.

But he suspected his annoyance might stem from another reason altogether.

"Who is he?"

She avoided his gaze. "His name is Robert and he's an artist."

Julius bit his lip to keep from snorting with laughter. Of course her father disapproved. Julius could picture the lad: a brooding, dark-haired sensitive type who wrote sonnets to the curve of her ear while dreaming about her dowry. Jesus. Did she honestly believe a happily ever after awaited herself and this boy?

"Allow me to guess," he drawled. "A *struggling* artist."

Nora lifted her chin, her spine as straight as a tailor's pin, and Julius knew he'd struck a nerve. The woman was no fool; she had to know her family's fortune and status would attract all kinds of rogues and ne'er-do-wells. "Robert has been studying his craft. He's a painter and has been searching for an apprenticeship over the last year."

He didn't have the heart to tell her, *"searching for an apprenticeship"* was a polite way of saying *"searching for a wealthy patroness."* The sun had certainly smiled on dear old Robert the day he met Lady Nora. Was she really this naïve?

None of this was Julius's concern, per se, except the flagrant disregard she showed for her reputation. She had no desire to stay in society's good graces; her only motive was returning to London.

If she develops feelings for you she'll want to remain in New York . . .

His mind turned over this devious thought. At least then all this nonsense about visiting the Haymarket and the Tenderloin would be put to rest. Julius would remain in polite society to discover clues about his father's business partners, an agreeable Nora by his side. The nine remaining weeks would then expire and he'd be free from the engagement.

At which point Nora would either return to her artist or find a new husband, one she truly loved.

Engage in harmless flirting, he told himself. That was all. Just enough to hopefully spark an attraction that would have her questioning her attachment to the budding Michelangelo. Lord knew kissing her would certainly not be a hardship. "You want to visit those places, where I took Miss Desmond?"

"Yes, I do. Have you agreed to take me?"

He moved in closer. Shades of green and gold flickered in her brown eyes in the overhead light. "Not quite. I want to see if you can pull it off."

She cleared her throat but didn't move. Two spots of color appeared on her cheeks. "Pull what off?"

Lifting his hand, he traced the smooth edge of her jaw with a blunt fingertip. Damn, her skin was soft, as soft as her lips from last night. Warmth slid along his veins and through his groin. "If I agree to take you to those places, are you able to blend in with the other loose women? This isn't London, sweetheart. This is New York City and we can spot a fraud from a mile away."

She stared at him boldly, their gazes locked, and her lips parted as the rate of her breathing increased. The clock on the mantel kept a steady pace, though he could hardly hear the ticking over the pounding in his chest. *Thump, thump, thump.*

Then her eyes slid to his mouth and the tip of her tongue darted out to moisten her lips. The air in the room disappeared, his lungs filling with heat and longing instead. God, he wanted to kiss her right now, to feel their bodies pressed together. Was she thinking the same?

Suddenly, she pushed his hand away and stepped back. "I needn't prove a thing to you. If you refuse to take me, I'll merely go by myself. Or I'll find someone else to escort me."

A dark, unfamiliar pressure in his chest quickly replaced the lust. "No, absolutely not. You cannot gad about with another man. And furthermore, going there alone would put you in incredible danger."

She marched to the sofa and retrieved the bonnet she'd placed there earlier. "Julius, you are neither my husband nor my father. You are not even a true fiancé. I can hardly foresee any circumstance where I must follow your instructions."

His jaw clenched. Were all daughters of earls so willful and stubborn? So utterly unreasonable and maddening? She could not wade through the city's underbelly alone, nor did he want her traipsing about with some other escort in such a seedy, disreputable place. Damn and hell.

One outing will not hurt. You can prevent her from doing something outrageous. Flirt with her. Cause her to forget Robert the artist.

She'd almost reached the door when he'd finished arguing with himself. "Wait," he called, and she froze, her hand poised on the latch. "I'll take you. One time, to the Haymarket." He better knew the staff there and could minimize the risk more adeptly.

When she turned, the strength of her smile nearly knocked him off his feet. "Thank you, Julius. I knew you'd be reasonable."

Reason hardly factored into what he experienced at the moment. No, he was completely untethered, slipping down the side of an icy mountain while grasping at branches to try and save himself. He only hoped he didn't come to regret this decision. "You are welcome."

"I do have one request."

His mouth tightened. He was hardly feeling charitable. This conversation had already not gone according to plan—and now she had another demand? "Which is?"

She ticked off on her fingers. "No more kissing. No holding hands. No long, deep gazes. No flirting."

He smothered a strangled laugh and stared up at the ceiling. Had she read his mind? Because that had been precisely what he'd planned to do. Damn it. "You believe I have designs on seducing you?"

"I'm certain you don't but I prefer to be perfectly clear as to where things stand between us."

"And where is that?"

"As friends, of course. That's all. You know my affections are engaged elsewhere, and you have your . . . ladies. There is no reason for either of us to think otherwise."

"There isn't?"

"No, of course not. We're partners in a mutually beneficial agreement. I see no reason to ruin that with messy emotional entanglements."

Messy emotional entanglements? Was that what the British aristocrats called kissing? Still, he needed to put her at ease. It wouldn't do to have her constantly on guard. He forced an easy, friendly smile. "I concur. I'm not particularly fond of emotional entanglements myself." He stuck out his hand. "Friends."

She reached out and shook his hand. "Friends."

~~My dearest Robert,~~
~~Robert, my love,~~
~~Sweetest Robert,~~

NORA SCRATCHED OUT the salutation and then crumpled the piece of paper. She tossed it into the fire burning in the grate to join the others already discarded. Her letters to Robert were normally brimming with emotion, yet each draft since the Billingses' ball had been a meandering, boring mess of drivel. For some reason she could not seem to muster up the enthusiasm.

It was that damned kiss. The embrace had hung like a black cloud over her head for nearly five days. Part of her wanted to confess the betrayal to Robert, but she dismissed the idea. As Julius had explained, the kiss had been his way of protecting her from discovery. Nothing more. They had become carried away in the moment and both had promised the episode would not be repeated. He'd shaken her hand and everything.

They were friends. And while she found him attractive and interesting, she would retain a respectful distance.

A soft knock on her door was preceded by her aunt's voice. "My dear, are you busy?"

"No. Please, come in." She quickly shoved her writing papers under a bolster on the bed.

Her aunt opened the bedchamber door. "There are some letters in the morning post." She held out a stack of papers. "You must have quite a number of friends in London who miss you."

Nora merely smiled as she accepted the packets. Since the scandal broke in London, her only letters nowadays were from Robert and Eva. "Thank you." She set the stack on her bed.

"Incidentally, I heard from your father."

Nora's spine straightened as hope rose in her throat. Her father hadn't written to her since she'd come to New York. Doubtful he'd heard of the engagement this quickly, but perhaps he'd decided to bring her home regardless. "What did he say?"

"Nothing of importance, really. Just updates on Parliament and his schedule."

Updates on his schedule? Disappointment thickened Nora's tongue, yet she forced herself to ask, "Any message for me at all?"

"No," her aunt answered, sympathy brimming in her eyes. "But he isn't one for idle chitchat, my dear."

Yes, Nora knew that quite well. How many breakfasts had she tried to engage him in conversation while he pored over the morning papers? How many evenings had she read in his study merely to be in the same room with him, while he scoured paperwork at his desk? How many birthdays had he missed, sending a present with his secretary instead?

So why, then, was she surprised he'd ignored her now?

Because you're a fool, that's why.

The only thing that had attracted his attention was discovering his daughter kissing a man on the drawing room sofa during a dinner party. And Nora suspected he would have ignored even that if he hadn't been surrounded by a handful of his Parliamentary cronies.

She pushed aside the hurt and asked, "Was he always so closed off, even as a child?"

Her aunt lowered herself onto the edge of Nora's bed, shifting to get comfortable. "He was never gregarious, if that's what you mean. Being the earl . . .

well, you know the responsibility that goes along with the title. And he inherited quite young, after our father died. I fear poor Bertrand never had a chance of a normal childhood, whatever that was for English boys at the time."

"I wish I remembered more from when my mother was still alive."

"She was lovely, like you, and Bertrand loved her madly. I think it broke him when she died, from what I heard. He seemed to withdraw even more. I wish I had offered to bring you to New York then. Perhaps you wouldn't have been quite so lonely."

"I wasn't lonely," Nora said. "There were the servants. Neighbors. I made a few friends my own age. And I used to volunteer in the foundling hospital." Which was how she'd met Robert. He'd grown up at the hospital and often returned to teach the young boys to paint. Robert hadn't been afraid to talk to her, hadn't been intimidated by her title or her status. He had been interested in *her*.

Aunt Bea reached over to pat Nora's arm. "Well, then, I will stop berating myself for leaving you with your father. And you're here now, which is all that matters."

Nora smiled and tried not to feel guilty over her desperation to return to England. Her aunt had repeatedly expressed happiness at the chance to spend time with her, and here Nora was busy plotting and scheming to get away from New York. Including tonight's outing to the Haymarket with Julius, which would require sneaking out of the house once her aunt and uncle retired.

I'll not feel bad about wanting to choose my own husband. I'll not feel bad for loving Robert.

She picked at a loose thread on the bedding. "Do you believe my father will approve of Julius?"

"If you're happy, then I cannot imagine your father standing in the way of a match. It's not as if Mr. Hatcher is a fortune hunter, after all."

The words brought to mind Julius's sneer when she'd told him about Robert. *Allow me to guess. A struggling artist.* The tips of her ears grew hot. Robert was *not* a fortune hunter. In the first place, the subject of her family's money had never been raised between them. His love for her was genuine—not a scheme to ensnare an earl's daughter. Did Julius think her so silly as to not know the difference?

"There is indeed that," she murmured when she realized her aunt was staring at her. "Julius has more money than God, it would seem."

Her aunt chuckled. "Quite possibly. More importantly, because he lives an ocean away, your father won't have heard of Mr. Hatcher's wilder exploits."

Not if Nora could help it. She wanted her father to catch wind of every misdeed and outrageous moment of Julius's life. The more scandalous places they visited together, the higher the chance of it making the papers. Her father would be outraged and undoubtedly come to see what a terrible idea it had been to send her to New York.

"Do you feel up to paying afternoon calls today?" her aunt asked. "There are several we should return, including the Appletons. I thought you might want to visit with their daughter, Kathleen. I noticed the two of you speaking the other night at the ball."

"Oh, yes." Nora perked up at the idea. "I should like that very much."

"Very good." Aunt Bea glanced at the clock on the mantel. "We have an hour or so yet before we need to leave. I'll let you catch up on your correspondence."

"Thank you, Aunt Bea. For everything." She meant it. Her aunt had opened her home and her heart to this niece she'd barely known. Even after Nora returned to England, she would not forget this kindness.

"My pleasure. You'll see." Aunt Bea patted Nora's shoulder. "It'll all work out. We shall make a true New Yorker out of you yet."

When her aunt left, Nora dove for the letters and tore open the most recent from Robert first.

The poem at the top made her smile. He'd taken each letter of her name and written a line about her qualities. *O* was for her "Open and trusting manner, her Otherworldly beauty." Otherworldly seemed an odd description but she was not complaining. Certainly the thought counted in the art of wooing.

Halfway through the letter, her breath caught. *No, no, no. How . . . ?* She sat down heavily on the edge of the mattress and reread the words.

> *The earl paid a call yesterday. It was a civil meeting and I think he believed me when I said we had not been in contact. As always, I am counting the minutes until you are safely back in my arms . . .*

Papa had inquired whether she and Robert were corresponding. Why? More important, how had he learned where Robert lived? She checked the date of the letter and saw it had been written three weeks ago.

A cold unease slid over her skin.

She needed to return to England.

Soon.

Chapter Seven

Darkness cloaked the city as the carriage rolled downtown, away from the electrified mansions of Fifth Avenue and toward the seedy entertainment district known as the Tenderloin. Julius knew he'd well and truly lost his mind to participate in this scheme. Why couldn't he say no to this woman?

She looked dashed pleased with herself, too, nearly bouncing in the seat across from him in her excitement, her wide eyes tracking their progress through the streets, fascinated. He suddenly wanted to learn more about her. Know her secrets. He gathered she'd been fairly sheltered in London—until her father sent her away. "How did he discover you?"

She jerked at his abrupt question. "He, who?"

"Your father. You said he disapproves of Robert. How did he learn of the affair?"

"It isn't an affair," she snapped.

He had no desire to launch into an argument this soon in the evening, so he held up his hands.

"I mean no offense." There wasn't enough light in the carriage to see her expression so he plowed on. "How did your father learn of the *deep and loving relationship*?"

She cleared her throat. Twice. This caused Julius to inch a little closer on the seat, curiosity thrumming through him. She finally said, "I arranged for him and some of his Parliamentary peers to discover us together one evening."

Julius's jaw fell open as he tried to put this together. "You and Robert . . . found locked in an embrace . . . in front of a bunch of stuffy English lords?"

"That is about the right of it."

He ignored the edge in her answer and threw his head back, laughing. "Oh, God. He must have been humiliated."

"Who, Robert?"

"Your father. To have his daughter flaunt such disrespect under his nose . . . in front of his cronies? No wonder you were sent to America."

"I had to do it." Her skirts rustled as she straightened on the velvet seat. "If he'd been alone he may have just ignored it."

True, but no man wanted his daughter's intimacy thrown in his face. Julius never wanted kids of his own, but even he knew that. "What did you think would happen when they found you?"

She lifted a shoulder, her hands smoothing out her cloak. "What any father does when his daughter is caught with a man to whom she is not married."

"Well, that plan certainly failed," he said through a chuckle.

"Obviously. And I am so pleased to serve as a source of amusement for you."

He tried to rein in his mirth. This was clearly a sore spot, even though her scheme had been reckless at best. "I apologize. Are you close with your father?"

"Children of the British aristocracy are not known for being smothered by parental affection."

"So he ignored you?"

"No need to paint me a tragic figure. I had more advantages than most. And what of your parents? You said your mother lives upstate."

The swift change in topic was not lost on him. "Yes. She lives with my sister, Agatha. My father died when I was thirteen."

"Other siblings?"

"Clarissa but she moved to Chicago years ago. I go upstate once or twice a year."

"Do they ever come to New York?"

"No, never." His mother hadn't visited once since she left. He'd invited her countless times but she always made excuses. It had taken him a while to realize that his home, his wealth embarrassed her.

The carriage slowed as they arrived at Thirtieth Street. A large crowd had gathered on the corner in front of the legendary dance hall—a term used loosely considering the activity on the second floor—and he once more questioned his sanity in assisting in this endeavor.

"Stay with me," he told Nora. "Do not get lost in the crowd or separated—and absolutely do not go to the upper floors." He thought of the curtained alcoves designed for trysts. "Or the balcony."

Her wide gaze took in the brightly lit three-story building. Music and conversation drifted in, hints of the raucousness one could expect to find inside the walls.

"Is it always this lively?" she asked, not turning away from the window.

"Yes, whenever the doors are open." The area was one of the most popular entertainment destinations in the city, with saloons, opium dens, brothels, and restaurants all crowded on top of one another. Vice could be found at any time on any street corner. He and his friends had certainly proven that over the years.

The carriage door opened. Julius descended and then assisted Nora to the ground. "Perhaps you should put up the hood of your cloak," he suggested. "Just until we're inside." *And tucked into a corner somewhere, safely away from the crowd.*

"Why?"

He couldn't tell her the real reason: a desperate attempt at protecting her reputation. So he went with a lie. "It's not uncommon to see drinks thrown about. You wouldn't want to get drenched in whiskey."

"Oh." She drew the cloth over her head, which shrouded her hair and placed her features in shadow. Then she took his arm and they set off for the front door. A large band played a gay tune, a siren's song to the degenerates frequenting the wicked neighborhood, degenerates like himself. Hell, he'd been lured by similar tunes many times over the years.

Which was how he knew this was a terrible idea.

Cutting through the crowd, Julius worked toward the large, mustached man who guarded the entrance.

"Twenty-five for the gents. Ladies drink free," the man called out in a booming voice. The side of his mouth hitched when he saw Julius. "Mr. Hatcher! It has been a while. Good to see you again, sir."

Julius slid a dollar piece into the man's palm. "Hello, Jim."

They were quickly waved through the main door. Taking a deep breath, he led an earl's daughter into the very heart of New York City's debauchery.

THE HAYMARKET WAS billed as a dance hall, yet dancing seemed a distant secondary activity to the general merrymaking and mingling throughout the cavernous space. Nora gaped, lowering her hood for an unencumbered view as they entered, Julius staying close to her side.

Hedonism surrounded them from every angle. Serving girls moved briskly through the crowd. Ladies beneath plumed evening hats hung on the arms of well-dressed gentlemen, while women of a coarser nature strolled the wooden floors with working-class men. Each guest clutched a drink of some kind, whether champagne or ale, and the sound of laughter nearly drowned out the booming band. It was a wondrous mix of humanity—young and old, rich and poor—one she hadn't ever experienced in London.

On the stage were five dancing girls, their colorful skirts bouncing as they kicked their legs high. Men lingered close to the edge of the stage, leering, but the girls laughed and danced, ignoring the admirers.

Nora had a strong urge to dash up there and join the women on the stage. To bask in the freedom and conviviality of the hall.

"Let's find a table." Julius took her elbow and began navigating the crowds and small round tables. He passed scads of empty seats until they reached a dark corner, as far from the excitement as they could possibly get.

He held out a chair, but she shook her head. "I won't be able to see a thing from here."

"Yes, but it's quieter. We'll have a better opportunity to carry on a conversation."

Was he serious? "Is that why we're here? To converse with one another?"

He dragged a hand through his hair, and she immediately understood. This was an attempt to keep her away from the crowds and protect her reputation. Rolling her eyes heavenward, she spun on her heel and strode off toward the stage, not bothering to see if he followed.

Of course he'd follow. Instead of her conspirator, Julius was beginning to feel more and more like a chaperone. He'd ordered her to keep her hood up all night and not to talk to anyone. And not to leave his side. A long list of rules had been set down in the carriage, none of which she planned on following.

The small wooden tables near the stage were all occupied. Nora didn't let that stop her. Perhaps she could convince someone to share.

A large man with streaks of dirt on his face rose

at her approach, a shabby brown derby clutched between his hands. "Miss, would you like a seat?" He gestured to his table, where his friend was avidly staring at the women on stage.

"Are you certain?" she asked in her politest accent. "I would not care to disrupt your evening."

The man kicked his friend's chair. "No, we was just leavin'. You're more'n welcome to the table."

"Leaving?" his friend said without looking over. "I didn't say nothin' about leaving."

The first man kicked the chair once more, gaining his friend's attention. When he pointed at Nora, the second man shot to his feet. "I beg your pardon, miss . . . ma'am. Here, have our table."

Nora felt Julius behind her, but she ignored him. "Thank you ever so much," she told the two men. "I am visiting from London and this is my first time in the Haymarket."

"Then you should have the finest seat in the house." The man held out her chair.

She began to unfasten her cloak and the other man rushed to assist her with it.

"Do you mind?" she heard Julius snarl, now directly at her back. "I'm capable of helping my fiancée with her cloak."

Biting her lip in an attempt not to laugh, Nora threw off the heavy outer garment. Julius gave a quick intake of breath, and the two men who'd given up their table gaped.

He told me I should blend in.

The red silk dress, procured by her maid earlier today, was edged in black lace and clung to Nora's curves. The neckline was the lowest she'd ever worn in public, with so much of her bosom on display that she very well might catch cold. The tops of her breasts were thrust up, her waist cinched in tight, the dress designed to attract attention. To entice.

She lowered herself into the empty chair and sent a smug smile to Julius, who glared at her before reaching into his jacket pocket. He withdrew a billfold, peeled off a few bills, and handed them to the departing men. They traded handshakes, with Julius uttering a few words that had the men chuckling before they disappeared onto the dance floor.

"I hope you're happy," he grumbled over the ruckus as he sat. "Everyone in the place is staring at you right now."

Excellent. "Let them stare. That is why we are here, after all."

"You should not be dressed in something so . . ." He waved a hand in her vague direction. "Obscene."

"I was attempting to not appear as an earl's daughter. After all, isn't that what you wanted?"

His lips flattened as he motioned to a serving girl. "Why, Mr. Hatcher, hello." The girl's fingertips trailed boldly over the fine wool covering his shoulder. "What would you like this evening?"

"Just a bottle of champagne for now." He grinned and leaned back in his chair, closer to the girl, who stroked his jaw before turning and leaving.

The innuendo could not be thicker if it were molasses, Nora thought, her stomach clenching. If he were a real fiancé she would kick him right now. How dare he encourage that woman?

Even worse, why did she care what he did?

Nora forced the jealousy aside. *Friends. We are merely friends.* She studied him through her lashes. Such an interesting contradiction, this man. He appeared at home in the Haymarket, with his roguish features and elegant evening suit, yet he seemed equally comfortable in the throngs of polite New York society. How did he do it?

She angled closer. "How often do you visit this fine establishment?"

"Once or twice a month, I suppose."

Frequently, then. One of the dancers openly grinned at him, trying to catch his attention, though Julius wasn't watching her, his gaze trained on the surrounding tables instead. Was he concerned they might be set upon by roughs?

"But I usually don't sit up front," he continued.

"Why not?" Wouldn't he want the best seat in the house?

His gaze darted around the room, almost nervously. But that was ridiculous. What would he have to be nervous about? He lifted a shoulder and said, "I don't like crowds."

The champagne arrived then and was quickly poured. He slipped the serving girl a few bills, and she bent to whisper something in his ear before walking away. Nora hadn't been able to hear it but she could guess as to the nature of the remark. Probably something about services available upon request.

Julius handed over a glass and then retrieved the other for himself. He touched the crystal together in a toast. "To getting out unscathed."

She frowned. Now what in heaven's name had he meant by that?

The dance ended and applause broke out. Nora clapped, Julius adding in a few whistles. The dancers all bowed and fluffed their skirts, one even turning around and revealing her drawer-covered bottom to the crowd. Nora smothered a gasp, though the patrons roared their approval.

Julius leaned in. "If that scandalized you, we should leave right now. There's no telling what else you may see tonight."

"I am hardly scandalized, merely surprised—and we are not leaving."

He sipped the champagne, his full lips a sharp contrast to the delicate rim. Dangerous, devil lips. She thought of how they'd felt on hers, the heat rolling off his body as he'd kissed her, rough bark at her back . . .

No, stop. She must not entertain a physical attraction to this man. With a flick of her wrist she opened her black lace fan and cooled her face.

Setting down his champagne, he asked, "What do you hope to accomplish this evening? Are you hoping reporters are lurking in the crowd, pen in hand, waiting for a story? Or perhaps one of the gentlemen unable to stop staring at your bosom will come over and whisk you away from me."

Was that why he'd been studying the crowd?

"No one will try and whisk me away, Julius. Furthermore, you must stop complaining. The sooner we gain notice in New York, the sooner I'll be called back to London. Then you may return to your Miss Desmond, the Haymarket, and outrageous parties."

"I hope you realize you are threatening your position in society—as well as mine—with that dress and your presence here."

She waved her hand and swallowed more champagne. "I am not all that concerned with what society thinks. You'll soon learn to think the same."

He drummed his fingers on the table. "I need to circulate in society, Nora. I cannot be unconcerned with what they think, not just yet."

The way he said it, the choice of the word *need*, caught her attention. "Tell me, then. Why do you need to ingratiate yourself to them? It cannot be for the money or the status, because you have both."

He tossed the rest of the liquid in his glass into his mouth, swallowed. "My father—"

"Ladies and gentlemen!" A tall, mustached man had come out onto the small stage. "We have a treat for you this evening. One of New York's greatest actresses will perform a song from her new show. Please welcome Miss Poppy Desmond."

The crowd went wild. Nora immediately swung her head to gauge Julius's reaction. Her escort appeared slightly bewildered, shoulders stiff and his brows lowered. His stare remained fixed on the man on stage as if he couldn't believe what he was seeing. Nora hadn't ever considered that a woman of Miss Desmond's caliber would perform in a place like this.

She touched his arm. "Does she normally—?"

"No. Never."

He said no more, his mouth compressing into a tight line as a beautiful buxom woman glided to the front of the stage. Miss Desmond's wide smile did not falter as the patrons shouted and stomped their feet, though her gaze swept briefly over Julius. Had she known he was here?

An exquisite dress of shimmery light blue silk accented every nook and cranny of Miss Desmond's lush frame. The fabric shone in the light as she moved, drawing every eye in the room like a lighthouse in the dead of night. Her brown hair was piled in careful curls, a single red-and-black poppy tucked behind her ear, while jewelry sparkled at her ears and throat. She executed a slight curtsey and the applause rose in volume.

Patrons began moving toward the stage, men crowding the small tables at the front. Julius glanced over his shoulder and then cursed under his breath. "Come on, let's go."

Nora didn't want to leave. On the contrary, she was looking forward to this performance. Was Julius uncomfortable at the idea of watching his former paramour? If so, that was unfortunate. Nora couldn't wait to see if Miss Desmond's singing skills were as spectacular as rumored.

"No," she told him. "I want to stay."

A man jostled her chair as he rushed forward, and Julius grabbed her elbow. "This is not safe." He had to nearly shout in her ear to be heard. "You'll be hurt if we don't leave."

Before she could tell him to go to the devil, a voice started singing—a crisp, flawless soprano that instantly quieted the room. Everyone stared, entranced, as the notes rippled throughout the space. Lifting. Rising. Swelling with emotion and passion. Nora had never heard anything like it.

Factoring in Miss Desmond's looks, that this stunning woman sang so astoundingly seemed almost unfair.

Nora couldn't look away. The unfamiliar tune was about love and loss, about having one's heart broken by a careless man. Though the actress's gaze remained trained on the back of the room, Nora couldn't help but wonder if this was a message to Julius.

For his part, he watched the performance absently, his focus instead on the men crowding around the floor. He seemed concerned rather than annoyed or flattered. If he had any remaining feelings for his former mistress, he was doing a dashed fine job of hiding them.

Nora, on the other hand, remained fascinated. To command a room in such a bold, audacious manner, to hold and then revel in the attention . . . What must it feel like? She could well imagine the striking couple: Julius, with his cool Nordic handsomeness, and this dazzling firebrand. No wonder the city's newspapers had been so eager to follow their exploits.

The song built to its natural conclusion, the last note held for a full minute. When she finally stopped, Miss Desmond removed the poppy from behind her ear and tossed it into the crowd.

It landed on their table. Directly in front of Julius.

He scowled at the flower as if it were poisonous. Before Nora could ask him what was the matter, men lunged for their table. Nora gasped and flew to her feet as large sweaty bodies converged from all sides, sending the champagne bottle and glasses crashing to the floor. The flower was lost on the ground, and men fell to their knees, wrestling each other for it. Punches were thrown and Nora began to realize the seriousness of the situation.

The Haymarket had erupted into a full-out brawl.

Men pushed Julius aside in their quest for the flower, and he was soon lost from her view. Head swiveling madly, she tried to find him. An elbow jabbed her ribs. A shoulder bumped her back. Something kicked her leg. Spinning, she called, "Julius!"

Dear God in heaven, what if she couldn't get out of this mess?

She began pushing and shoving as best she could, attempting to extricate herself from the brewing insanity, edging toward the sides of the room . . . The group only thickened, however, and she found herself surrounded by drunk, eager men determined to retrieve the flower.

"Nora!"

Turning, she saw him a few feet away, his hair disheveled. He'd been cut above his eyebrow, red trickling along his temple. His face etched with determination, he began moving toward her, shouldering men out of his path.

He was nearly in arm's reach when one of the men jostled him. "You had the flower!" the man shouted in Julius's face. "Where is it?"

Oh no. If the crowd believed the flower to be on Julius's person, they'd rip him apart.

"I don't have it," Julius returned, but the man

did not appear convinced and tried to get inside Julius's inner coat pockets. Julius threw a punch but the man easily blocked it.

She had to do something. A bottle hit her shoe, so she reached down and grabbed the neck. When she straightened, Julius and the other man were engaged in a brutal shoving match.

The attacker had ripped the shoulder seam of Julius's frock coat in trying to wrestle it off. "He's got the flower!" the man shouted to the crowd.

Julius's arms were trapped in the twisted fabric of his coat and she could see the panic in his bright blue eyes. Using the heavy glass bottle, she struck the attacker over the head with all her strength. He crumpled to the ground, releasing his hold on Julius.

Instead of thanking her, Julius grabbed her hand and tugged her in the direction of the stage. When they reached the edge, he lifted her onto the raised platform and then jumped up after her. They hurried behind the curtains to the backstage area.

Behind the stage was also chaotic. Dancers raced to and fro, shouting at each other while collecting their belongings. Smart ladies. They knew to escape before the riot spilled over in this direction.

"This way," Julius said and clasped her hand once more. He led her to a large steel door in the rear of the building. A giant man stood guard, his tree-trunk arms crossed over his chest. "Hatcher," he greeted, then flicked his gaze to the side.

A woman stood there in the shadows. Miss Desmond. She was bundled now, her recognizable features nearly obscured by the hood of her cloak.

"Julius." She stepped forward and clasped her hands. "May I speak with you?"

"Not now," he snapped, anger punctuating every word. "I'll deal with you tomorrow. Open the god-damn door, Pete."

The guard flung open the door and Julius stormed out of the building, Nora in tow. Before they disappeared into the alley, Nora craned her neck to see Miss Desmond lingering. "You were magnificent!" she called to the other woman.

The actress's lips curved just before Nora lost sight of her.

Chapter Eight

Julius's hands shook as he helped Nora inside his carriage. He couldn't remember the last time he'd been so damned terrified. Noise from inside the Haymarket echoed in the New York City darkness, and he guessed the roundsmen wouldn't be far behind. Fucking Poppy. Why in the hell would she deliberately set out to cause a riot tonight?

He tried to drag in air, kept telling himself he and Nora were safe. Poppy couldn't have known what she was doing. *She doesn't know your history. She doesn't know what you've lived through.*

Most likely, Poppy had thought to make him jealous. After all, everyone knew whoever held the flower at the end of her performance was invited backstage to spend the evening with her.

Once in the carriage, Nora's cheerfulness did not help his mood one bit. She appeared perfectly poised, every bit the English lady. One would never guess she'd just emerged from a brawl.

He, on the other hand, felt rattled to the marrow of his bones. He'd seen violence. He knew how mobs could lose control and human decency, the anonymity giving them license to commit gruesome acts.

He'd been a boy of thirteen during the Panic of '73. He'd never forget the bank runs, the throngs of New Yorkers breaking windows and doors, dragging bank clerks in the streets when the money ran out. Workers lost jobs, their homes. Sometimes their lives. Rallies and protests were organized, but the police often used brutal force to squash any sign of trouble.

In those days he'd worked as an errand boy on the exchange, often running from the broker houses to the exchange floor. One morning the Workingmen's Association held a demonstration on Wall Street to protest the obscene wealth and perceived greed of the traders. When the police arrived on horseback, waving brickbats and ordering the crowd to disperse, the men began to argue and soon fought back.

Julius had been frozen with fear, armed merely with paper and a few pencils, not nearly enough to defend himself against the clubs and fists. The area rapidly descended into an orgy of violence, with horses trampling and blood flying. He only narrowly avoided getting his head bashed in by jumping into a cellar way and hiding until the worst of it blew over.

It was a lesson he never forgot: how quickly savagery and bloodshed could erupt. He blew out a breath and rolled his shoulders. Two more minutes and those jackals in the Haymarket would've torn him and Nora apart.

"Are you all right?" she asked.

"Fine." He fixed his gaze on the street and attempted to calm himself.

"You don't seem all right. Are you upset about your coat?"

"No, I am not upset about my damn coat." Did she truly have no idea? He bit down on the angry words stinging his tongue. Wasn't this disaster what he'd warned her about in the first place?

You let a pretty face and a prettier smile change your mind, idiot.

"Then what are you upset about?"

Jesus. "Were you not there? Did you not see what happened? You could have been killed. Violated. Maimed. I know you were sheltered over there in London, but have you no sense whatsoever?"

Her brows lifted. "Nevertheless, I am unhurt. In fact, you are the injured party." She indicated his forehead.

"Another minute or two in that mob might've produced a very different outcome. These places are not safe for you, Nora."

"Ah. Is this the part when you say, 'I told you so'?"

He leaned in and pointed a finger at her. "It's no less than you deserve. This was a terrible idea."

"Yes, you've made that abundantly clear. However, it was your former paramour who started tonight's riot. I have to wonder over her purpose."

"I cannot begin to guess, but you'd best believe I'll learn of it tomorrow."

"Perhaps your attention is what she wants."

No, impossible. Poppy had more attention in one day than a normal person needed in a lifetime.

Moreover, if she cared to see him there were better ways to go about it. "Doubtful—and don't change the subject."

He wiped his brow with the back of his hand. Blood streaked his skin, surprising him. Then Nora suddenly shifted to his side, sitting close on the velvet bench. She reached into his breast pocket and withdrew the handkerchief resting there. Holding his jaw with her free hand, she dabbed at the cut above his eye. "Let me see if it needs to be stitched," she said.

He inhaled sharply at her gentle touch. She was close, so close that the smell of her—lavender and reckless woman—caused his head to swim. Without her cloak, the cheap, low-cut dress revealed a daring amount of creamy, plump bosom. He wrestled with the urge to cover her while at the same time praying to see more skin.

She pressed hard on the wound and he flinched. Christ, that hurt. He drew back. "What was that for?"

"You're staring at me quite rudely."

As if he could help it. A blind man would stare at her in that dress. "You're incredibly beautiful."

"I thought we established a strict no-flattery rule between us."

"I don't remember such a rule—and I refuse to adhere to it, regardless."

"Rather keen to be flattered, are you?"

Devilment danced in her eyes, captivating him, and he chuckled. "If you feel so inclined, absolutely."

"I hardly think you need flattery, Julius." She folded the handkerchief carefully, avoiding his gaze and leaving him to wonder what she meant by that statement. He let the comment drop as she continued, "Admit it, you had fun this evening."

"*Fun* is not the word I would use." He crossed his arms and reclined in the seat. "*Dangerous*, *hair-raising*, and *foolhardy* seem much more apt."

"Really? I would say *invigorating*, *enlightening*, and *fascinating*—even if our names will not appear in the papers."

How could she not be affected by what just transpired? She was either incredibly sheltered or incredibly reckless. Neither boded well for Julius's purposes. "Can I assume that Robert does not escort you to dance halls over in London?"

"No, he hates those places. He doesn't wish to attract attention when the two of us are together."

He suddenly understood. "He hides you away, doesn't he?"

She scowled, her shoulders stiffening. "Absolutely not. He's careful. We cannot parade through Mayfair, for heaven's sake."

Julius had been to London many times. There were plenty of places to explore where an earl's daughter would not be recognized. "I think not. I think the two of you meet, let's see, in his apartments. And, when you are feeling adventurous, perhaps a tiny tea shop somewhere off the beaten path for a quick cup and a slice of cake?"

Surprise flashed over her features before she hid it, and he knew he was right. Still, she didn't admit it. "There is a large difference between being prudent and being ashamed. Robert is not ashamed of me."

The more he learned of this Robert the less Julius liked him . . . and he hadn't been especially fond of him since the very beginning. No wonder this sheltered English beauty craved the excitement of New York City nightlife.

That craving, however, could lead to Julius's downfall.

He remembered Tripp's advice, to flirt with her and shake some of her regard for the artist. All he needed was for Nora to care about her reputation, to want to stay in society's good graces for a bit longer. Thinking herself in love with an outsider back in London only prompted her to more audaciousness here in New York. "So will it need to be stitched?" he asked, making no effort to shift toward her.

She leaned closer to inspect his wound once more. Her right hand brought the handkerchief to rest above his brow, her body angled across his. A quick tug would bring her on his lap, where her plush bottom would rest atop his groin. A thick, heavy wanting slid over his skin—a reaction that had absolutely nothing to do with distracting her from a fortune-hunting Rembrandt and everything to do with the alluring, intelligent, and maddening woman in front of him.

Her chest rose and fell swiftly, color staining both her cheeks in the low lamplight. The air in the carriage changed, growing thick with anticipation, and breathing became difficult. Their eyes locked, and he saw the recognition, that she understood what was happening between them. Time seemed to stand still as he remembered the kiss from the gardens and wondered what to do next. He could foresee three results:

One, she moved away and pretended this never happened.

Two, he gave in to temptation and kissed her, whereby she pushed him away in anger.

Three, he kissed her and she eagerly kissed him back. Again.

Wasn't hard to calculate the odds. He'd predict a 76 percent chance on option number one. For number two, he'd give it around 23 percent. That didn't leave much chance for number three but, God above, the possibility of tasting her need and passion once more nearly had him jumping out of his skin.

Focusing on the numbers, however, didn't prevent him from noticing the delicate bow of her upper lip. The curve of her jaw. The small freckle on the bridge of her nose, or anything else that added together to create her exquisite face. Why did he find her so tempting?

Her gaze flicked to his mouth and the odds for number three began to climb. Sweat broke out on the back of his neck, the effort to hold perfectly still nearly killing him. He didn't care to scare her so he waited for an indication, a hint of what she wanted.

His hopes were dashed when an unsteady breath escaped her mouth right before she returned to the bench across from him, arranging her skirts carefully. Avoiding his eyes.

He clenched his jaw. Dashed option one. Sometimes he hated being right.

GOOD HEAVENS, SHE'D nearly kissed him.

Panic fluttered behind Nora's ribs, making it impossible to catch her breath. For one brief second, with desire darkening his eyes, his expression hungry and intent, she'd been certain Julius would break their agreement and kiss her. When he hadn't, she'd almost taken matters into her own hands and kissed *him*.

What the devil was wrong with her?

She loved Robert. Sweet, sensitive Robert, who had professed his love for her on countless occasions. She and Julius barely knew one another and were usually at odds. So why on earth had she wanted to taste him just one more time?

The only logical explanation was a momentary fit of madness brought on by the late hour and the excitement of the riot. Any other reason was intolerable. Robert was the love of her life, her future husband, the only man she should be contemplating kissing. The end.

So why, sitting across from Julius, was she now filled with a terrible disappointment?

"Do you regret tonight?"

She lifted her chin and faced him squarely. "No."

"I meant a moment ago, when we almost—"

Had he read her thoughts? "Stop. There is no reason to discuss it." Her words were clipped and precise, and she sounded every inch the English aristocrat. Not that she could help it. First, she *was* an English aristocrat, and second, her brain was still reeling from the almost-kiss.

For God's sake, cease thinking about kissing Julius.

Crossing his arms, he snorted a laugh. "Boy, your British really shows through when you are upset."

She knew this to be true but still asked, "Whatever do you mean by that?"

He waved a hand in her direction, indicating her entire frame. "Your words, the way you speak and sit. You look and sound like the queen on her throne—if the queen were dressed as a Tenderloin trollop."

"You told me I needed to fit in." She glanced down at herself. "Do you not like it?"

"*Like* is not the correct description for a dress such as that. And considering I've thought of nothing but kissing you all night—"

"Julius!" Why would he bring up that topic again? Heat rushed through her belly and down her legs. "We must not discuss such things. Ever."

"Why not?" Slouching on the bench, he extended his legs and crossed his feet at the ankles. His thigh pushed against her knee, yet he made no effort to move away.

She tried to scoot aside, to put distance between his body and hers. "We are friends. That is all we shall ever be. I am attached, as you well know."

"I know nothing of the sort. You might be making this Robert fellow up. And besides, *I* am not attached. So there's nothing to prevent *me* from flirting with *you*." Long lashes fringed his sharp blue gaze. "Worried you cannot resist me, Lady Nora?"

A wave of longing rolled through her at his heated stare, and irritation quickly followed. "You are impossible," she snapped. "Just when I start to believe my first impression of you was incorrect, you remind me of your true nature."

"Yes, but that true nature will get you noticed in New York City. Is that not what you want?" He bounced his leg into her knee. "You cannot bring the tiger indoors and expect him to act as a house cat, my lady."

She pushed his leg away. "I certainly can . . . unless said tiger cares to be tossed back outside with the other jungle animals."

"Which won't get you summoned back to England with any expediency."

Dash it all. The man was right. She needed him—but he also needed her. Otherwise, he never would have agreed to this. In the Haymarket, he'd started to say something about his father. "Tell me why you need to circulate in society."

"I owe you that, I suppose." Now serious, he drew in a long breath and exhaled, the angles of his face sharpening in the low light. "My father was a man of business, a deal-maker. Always after the next investment for a quick buck. We weren't poor but he hated knowing others had more. In '73, he organized a business deal with three society men to purchase the majority stock holdings of a little-known chemical company. The company had just filed for an important patent and my father thought it was a sure bet. He fronted the money through a demand note from the bank, and the men promised to pay equal shares."

He paused as if bracing himself. She sensed this was a topic he did not discuss often. "You don't have to tell me."

"No, I do. It's just . . . It's been a long time since I've spoken of it. See, the timing couldn't have been worse because a bank panic swept over the country immediately after. When the bank called in the note, my father didn't have the money. So he sent them to the three men who had agreed to the deal. Those three denied any knowledge of an investment with my father."

Nora gasped. "That's terrible. Did he not have any proof? A contract?"

"No. My father believed in a handshake, that a man was as good as his word. In the end his naiveté is what destroyed him. He started drinking then, ranting and raving about the Knickerbockers who'd ruined him. He hanged himself a few days later."

Her jaw fell open. Oh, dear Lord. "That's positively awful. Your poor family. How old were you?"

"Thirteen. We lost everything. Moved in with relatives and my mother found work as a seamstress. I went to work as an errand boy." He shrugged. "We survived."

But his father hadn't. The unspoken words dangled there as the wheels clattered along the cobblestone street on their way uptown. Curiosity flooded her, as questions concerning his family, his background, and his father raced through her mind.

"And his investors? What ever happened to them?"

"I couldn't say. He never named them and my family didn't move in those select circles."

"Until now."

He dipped his chin. "So perhaps you understand why I am anxious to stay in society, at least until I can discover these secret investors."

"Yes, but how do you plan to find them? Do you

hope one of them walks up during a dinner party and mentions your father?"

"Yes, though I dare not dream it'll be so easy."

"That's why you've been trying to buy your way into high society over the years."

"Quite unsuccessfully until you came along. I cannot risk being banished, Nora, not until I discover the names of those three investors."

She pulled at a loose black thread on her cheap satin skirts. Staying in society was all fine and good to suit his purposes, but following the rules would not get her summoned home. "So how do we scandalize New York without getting banished from high society?"

"A very good question." The intensity of his regard caused her to squirm. She could read the accusation there, the recrimination over her plan.

"You're attempting to make me feel guilty. It won't work. After all, you see these men around town, at the clubs and restaurants. Why do you need dinner parties and balls to do your sleuthing? For that matter, why not hire a Pinkerton that you Americans seem so fond of?"

"Oh, a Pinkerton!" He smacked his forehead with the heel of his hand. "If only I had thought of that."

The sarcasm behind the words was not lost on her. "I take it he was unsuccessful."

"*They* were unsuccessful. Not one of the four investigators I've hired over the years could discern anything. People, especially Knickerbockers, are absurdly distrustful of any outsider. Which is why spotting them at Sherry's or Delmonico's yielded nothing. They wouldn't talk to me."

"What about the clubs?"

He shook his head. "The only club that didn't outright refuse my application was the Players Club. I've been told to reapply to the Gotham, which I did last week. I estimate my odds at 65 percent in favor of acceptance this time."

"Shall I ask Uncle James to have a word with someone on your behalf?"

"Thank you but I've already spoken to him."

He had? What else had Julius been up to?

"Now," he continued. "I've taken you to the Haymarket, as per our agreement. Shall we discuss the week's social engagements?"

She straightened, her spine coming off the seat as her shoulders pressed back. "But tonight's outing was a failure. We went largely unnoticed and drew no attention of any appreciable kind. This hardly counts toward fulfilling your promise."

"Dear woman, I never promised to get you noticed. I promised to escort you on one outing, which I did. The results of said outing were never in my control. If they disappointed you . . ." He lifted one shoulder.

"That is hardly fair."

"No one ever said life would be fair, milady. Most of us lower types learn that lesson early."

Did he honestly believe he could outmaneuver this new Nora, one who would no longer stand idly by while others made decisions for her? "Fine," she said, holding his electric-blue gaze. "I'll have a list of the engagements sent over to you tomorrow."

He studied her face for a long moment as he stroked his jaw. "Thank you for being so reasonable. Now, am I to drop you at the front door or have you devised a plan to sneak back into the house?"

"The mews, please. My maid will have left a small door there unlatched for me."

He smirked, not showing the least bit of surprise at this news. Letting his lids fall closed, he rested his head on the seat. "Beware. I am quickly learning your tricks, Lady Honora."

JULIUS REVIEWED THE list of social engagements from Nora and burst out laughing.

His assistant, Martin, had already procured the week's engagement list from James Cortland's secretary. Unsurprisingly, the two lists didn't match up.

The woman had no idea with whom she toyed. Did she honestly believe he wouldn't verify her list after last night? The lie had been right there on her face when she'd offered to send over the week's social schedule. Clearly upset over the failure of the Haymarket outing, she no longer cared to adhere to the rules of their arrangement.

Fine.

He could also play that game—and he looked forward to besting her.

He grinned, imagining tonight's dinner party. Rather, imagining the expression on Nora's face when he arrived at the correct location for said dinner party. She would not be expecting him, and he anticipated catching her off guard.

"You certainly are happy today," Martin remarked from his nearby desk, catching Julius's attention. "Did one of your stocks triple in price?"

He set aside Nora's list. "No. Just thinking of this evening."

"With your fiancée?"

"We are attending a dinner party. I plan to surprise her."

"I don't know if that's wise, sir. In my limited experience, women do not take well to surprises."

"Perhaps, but this woman deserves one." Julius had to admit, the English rose did keep him on his toes. Their heated exchanges and discussions invigorated him as nothing else ever had. He actually looked forward to seeing her, more than he had with any other woman.

Speaking of other women, he'd best deal with Poppy. He glanced at his pocket watch. By now she'd be lingering over breakfast before going to the theater for afternoon rehearsals. "I have an errand to run downtown, Martin. I should return in an hour or so. Watch Jackson Consolidated for me, will you? If it goes below three and five-eighths, call the floor and buy as many shares as you can. I expect to see a drop either today or tomorrow, and I can turn around a handsome profit when it does."

"Yes, sir."

Confident in his assistant's abilities, he rang for the brougham. "Anything for me to review on the drive?" he asked.

"A few ideas." Martin dug a stack of paper out from the chaos of his desk. "Some trends that might be worth noting."

"Excellent." Julius accepted the stack and placed it into his satchel. "Let's see if your ideas match mine. Perhaps it's time you started dabbling with your own account."

Martin's cheeks reddened. "Oh, I don't have the capital."

"Allow me to worry about the capital. I believe in taking risks and you've developed a good eye for these things. Let's discuss it when I return."

"Thank you, sir."

Julius gathered his satchel and started for the hall, his leather soles snapping on the Italian marble. The main floor was quiet today, the way he preferred during work hours. Brandywine somehow managed to keep the place running smoothly without chaos. The man was a marvel.

The front bell sounded as Julius was pulling on his gloves. Brandywine appeared seemingly from thin air to deal with the caller.

"I am out," Julius told him quietly. "No matter who is calling."

The butler nodded and opened the heavy front door. "Good morning, ma'am. How may we help you?"

"Good morning. I am here to see my son. I believe this is his house."

Julius froze. He'd recognize that cold, disapproving voice anywhere.

What in hell was his mother doing here?

Dear God. She'd never come to visit, not once in twelve years. He moved toward the door, needing to verify this turn of events with his own eyes.

Sure enough, his mother stood on the stoop, a

hansom at the curb. "Mother. What a lovely surprise."

Brandywine snapped his fingers, summoning two footmen to handle the luggage. Julius hardly noticed, his attention squarely on the woman before him. Dressed in her usual severe and simple black attire, she stepped over the threshold and into the entry. Her wide eyes took in the surroundings, the marble and the stained glass. The smooth stone and priceless art. He held his breath, awaiting her reaction, some appreciation of his success. Some small acknowledgment of what he'd accomplished.

His stomach sank as she frowned, actually *frowned* as if he'd done something wrong in amassing a fortune envied by even J. P. Morgan himself.

He should've known.

Any small amount of happiness at seeing her faded. Suddenly, he was thirteen again, unable to make her understand why he wanted to work on the stock exchange instead of in a factory or on a farm. He ground his teeth together and planted his feet as the door closed behind her. "Why are you here?"

His curt tone must've surprised her. She blinked a few times, blue eyes so like his own staring back at him. "I am here to meet your fiancée, of course."

His jaw fell open. "My fiancée?"

"Yes, a Lady Honora, if I am not mistaken."

"But . . ." *How did you find out? She is not truly my fiancée. Why do you care?* He had no idea where to begin. He hadn't seen his mother in months and she rushed to the city for this? "How did you learn of the engagement?"

"I do still have friends in the city, Julius."

"Of course you do," he blurted, instantly chastised. "I merely thought . . ." *You hated everything about me.* Seemed crass to voice it but the words hung there nonetheless.

"I know you and I have had our disagreements, Julius, but I am still your mother. I should like to meet the woman you are about to marry." She stripped off her black cotton gloves—was that a split seam between the fingers?—and held them tight in her palms. "May I stay?"

"Of course, of course," he heard himself say. "Come in. Let's get you settled. Brandywine?"

His butler moved forward. "Mrs. Hatcher, please allow me to show you to your room."

"My daughter, Agatha, is here as well. She is dealing with our driver and will be along shortly."

Julius cursed under his breath. His sister was also here? Good Lord, it would be the family reunion from hell. "Why did you not allow me to send a carriage for you?"

"We know how busy you are. We didn't want to trouble you."

So they'd rather surprise him by showing up on his doorstep?

". . . show you to the rose suite. It is the finest room in the house," Brandywine was saying.

Julius fought a wince. His mother would hate the rose suite. Undoubtedly, she'd be more comfortable in the stripped-down servants' quarters. Brandywine would choke upon hearing she didn't employ a maid—a fact that would pose a conundrum for the staff with regards to the duties required each day. Julius pinched the bridge of his nose between two fingers.

The footmen passed with her trunk and he heard Brandywine ask, "Just the one trunk, ma'am?"

"Yes. I do not require much."

Unlike my son. She didn't say it but the implication was plainly there. Julius clasped his hands behind his back and stared up at the stained-glass windows he'd imported from a German monastery. While he wasn't religious by any means, he liked the colors and the images of the three saints depicted there. Serious and pious, the trio guarded the entry and reminded him how small and insignificant we all were in the end.

Even more reason to live as grandly as you dared while alive. One had no idea when it could all be ripped away.

He strode deeper into the house, toward his office. Screw the rest of the world. There was money to be made.

Chapter Nine

A dozen or so society types crowded the Griffin salon, a blur of beaded silk dresses glittering under the dull yellow glow of the gasolier. Nora accepted a glass of champagne from Mr. Cooke, an older man with prodigious jowls.

"I had hoped to meet your fiancé this evening. A shame he could not join us," Mr. Cooke said, sipping his own champagne. Drops of liquid caught on his bushy mustache.

She avoided staring at Cooke's dripping facial hair and hid a smile. Yes, a shame Julius hadn't been able to attend. While part of her experienced a twinge of guilt over her deception, she recalled how he'd backed out of their agreement. Ten minutes inside the Haymarket did not constitute an entire evening—and he well knew it.

Cooke continued on the topic of Julius. "He's reported to be a sharp one. Heard he gave a stock tip to Pendleton the other night that paid off quite handsomely."

That caught her attention. She remembered Julius once saying he was asked for stock advice nearly everywhere he went and rarely answered. "I hadn't realized Mr. Hatcher was providing business advice."

"Not merely advice, my lady. Been near clairvoyant from what I understand. I am hoping to get a nugget or two of my own to use on the exchange."

"I thought gentlemen here avoided discussing business." In England, the topic was never raised in society. Discussions regarding money or commerce were incredibly gauche amongst the *haute monde*.

"Officially, yes. The wives like to believe money sprinkles down from the heavens, of course, but most of the gentlemen play the exchange or the ponies. Anything to chase away the boredom."

She sipped her champagne, her mind racing. If these stock tips did not produce earnings, would there be social repercussions for Julius? Undoubtedly he aided these men in the hopes of discovering his father's investors, but Nora still wanted to protest on his behalf. She had the ridiculous urge to protect him from the obvious greed and selfishness behind the solicitation.

Which was insane. Julius hardly needed her protection.

"My father uses Parliament to chase the boredom," she said. "I believe he merely likes to yell at the opposition."

Mr. Cooke chuckled. "As I am certain your ladyship has heard by now, politics in America is a nasty business. Anyone with a bit of sense stays as far away from that as possible."

"Stays away from what?" a familiar male voice asked behind her.

No, it could not be. Nora spun and nearly dropped her glass at the sight before her. Julius stood there in a well-crafted black swallowtail coat and matching trousers. His dark blond hair had been tamed, swept away from his arresting face, and the rugged features she so often tried to ignore hit her square in the chest. Good heavens, he was handsome.

Her breathing turned erratic, her corset tightening like a vise around her ribs. "Mr. Hatcher!"

"Good evening, my lady." He bowed over her hand. "I do apologize for my tardiness." Blue eyes danced as he straightened, his expression filled with unholy glee.

Dash it all. How had he learned the true location for tonight's event?

"Hatcher, we heard you were otherwise occupied this evening," Cooke said, shaking hands with Julius. "Glad you made it. I was hoping to bend your ear for a few moments regarding a stock I've been watching."

That was when Nora saw it. The slight twitch of his eye, the barest hint of her fake fiancé's annoyance. Without knowing exactly why, she decided to rescue him. "While I am certain Mr. Hatcher would love to help, Mr. Cooke, I must steal my fiancé away for a few moments. I hope you understand?"

"Of course, my lady. Perfectly understandable for a young couple. We'll speak on it later, Hatcher."

Julius inclined his head. "I look forward to it."

Cooke tottered off and Nora grabbed Julius's arm. "Come with me."

She led him to a far corner, well within sight of the party but a spot that would allow them to talk privately. He leaned a shoulder against the wall and smirked. "I hope you weren't terribly worried when I ran late."

Little point in admitting any wrongdoing now. Clearly, considering the amusement in his expression, they were both aware of what she had tried to do. "No, not worried at all."

"That's certainly a relief. You appeared quite surprised a moment ago and I grew concerned."

"So that was what concern looks like? And here I thought you were enjoying yourself."

He grinned, the unrepentant rogue. "Guilty— and I'm sorry to ruin your fun."

"No, you are not a bit sorry."

"True. Thwarting you is entirely too enjoyable. But enough about that bogus social schedule. I need to speak with you."

"Bogus?"

He waved his hand. "Fake. False. Complete and utter drivel. A—"

"I understand now, thank you." Americans had some of the strangest words. "What did you wish to speak with me about?"

His gaze bounced around the room, not meeting hers, while he drew in a deep breath. "My mother and sister have come to visit."

"Your . . . mother? I thought she lived upstate."

"She does." He leaned in. "She arrived earlier today. Wants to meet my fiancée."

"Meet your *fiancée*?"

He winced. "Perhaps you could say it louder?

Doubtful the kitchen staff heard you, Nora." He rubbed his eyes with his fingers.

"I apologize," she said quietly. "This is all very surprising. You said she never comes to visit you."

"She doesn't. She's never come to the city to visit me, which is why it's so disconcerting. Regardless, do not visit my home, and refuse to see her if she calls on you. I'll hold her off as long as I can and then hopefully she'll tire of waiting and return to Albany."

"Julius, your mother did not travel all this way to be 'held off' in meeting her prospective daughter-in-law. You must host a dinner party." Which would provide Nora with ample opportunities to avoid any intense conversations with Mrs. Hatcher.

"Absolutely not," he said. "She'd hardly enjoy it if I did."

"Why not? Doesn't she like parties?"

"Not only does she not like parties, she disapproves of my money and lifestyle. Trust me, you don't want to meet her."

She disapproved of his money and lifestyle? Good heavens. What sort of mother would not be proud of all Julius had accomplished?

And why was he so adamant Nora not meet her?

"I am capable of charming your mother, Julius. After all, I am English. We learn how to charm dour old matrons before we can walk."

"She's more than a crusty dowager. Not to mention, if you do meet her, you'll need to pretend. I'd rather not hurt her by telling the truth regarding the engagement. No, it's best if you two never cross paths."

She liked when he needed something from her. It gave her leverage, which she fully intended to use to suit her purposes. "Would you consider it a favor? Otherwise, I may need to call on her tomorrow."

"Yes." Then his mouth twisted with regret. "Wait, is it too late to change my answer?"

She couldn't contain her wide smile. "Yes—unless you do not want to gain my cooperation."

The angles of his face shifted as a muscle jumped in his jaw. "Allow me to guess. In return for this favor, I must escort you on another attention-seeking venture into the underbelly of the city?"

"Yes. That is precisely what it means."

"And if I agree, you'll not cause any more mischief?"

She nodded and held her breath, worried this fortuitous turn of events could disappear at any moment.

"Fine," he said, the one word dripping with unhappiness. "I'll escort you this Friday night. My choice of location."

"Perfect. See how easy that was?"

His lips flattened. "Shall we rejoin the others?"

She nodded but one more thing was bothering her. "Yes, but I have another question. If you dislike giving out stock tips, why not refuse when asked?"

He grimaced. "I usually do. Stocks are rarely a yes-or-no question. There's planning and foresight involved, and each trade is a gamble. Some men like the risk and the results hardly matter. For others, the results could be disastrous."

Like losing everything, something Julius was familiar with.

"Except you gave Mr. Pendleton a tip that earned him quite a bit of money, apparently."

"I need these men to like and trust me. If dropping hints on favorable stocks earns me a spot in society, I'll gladly do it."

"What happens when someone loses money? What if you are held accountable?"

"I'm fairly certain these men can afford a loss here or there. And these are not secrets. I would never give away any information that might work against me or my purposes on the exchange."

"Meaning?"

"Meaning anything that might take money out of my own pocket. Speculation rewards outliers. If you're merely following the crowd, you'll never reap any substantial benefits on Wall Street. I only give away information any serious investor should already have."

"So you consider yourself an outlier, never following the crowd?"

He took her arm and moved in close, his breath warm on her ear. "That is one of the things you and I have in common, Lady Nora. We aren't afraid to break the rules."

AFTER THE LONGEST dinner of Julius's life, the eight gentlemen left the dining room and retired to the smoking room down the hall. The conversation during the meal had been fairly banal, except for Nora's aunt, who had entertained Julius's end of the table with outrageous stories. Hell, he hoped Nora never heard those stories. They might give her ideas.

Now settled with cigars, the men turned to talk of business and mistresses. The only one not smoking, Julius took a seat on the leather sofa and stretched his legs. Within seconds, two men approached and lowered themselves into the chairs opposite the sofa. One was Mr. Whitehouse, an older man who served on the board of one of the nation's largest railroads. The other guest, Mr. Cooke, had clearly come to make good on his earlier promise to talk stocks.

"Hatcher, mind if we have a word?"

Julius hid his irritation behind a polite smile. "Not at all. What's on your mind, gentlemen?"

Cooke leaned in as if they were discussing national secrets. "Reynolds Petroleum. What do you think the forecast looks like?"

Reynolds was as healthy as a rotten apple. The company leadership was abysmal and the board refused to invest in new drilling technology. They'd be lucky to survive the year. "I would not buy it, if that's what you are asking."

Whitehouse frowned. "I have a friend on the board. Says they're predicting double-digit gains in the third quarter."

Only with divine intervention, Julius thought. He lifted a shoulder. "Merely my opinion. Ocean Petroleum is a safer bet."

Two more gentlemen wandered over to their group and crowded around. James Cortland lowered himself directly next to Julius. "Pendleton said he made a killing on that tip you gave him at the opera."

It had been two tips, but Julius refrained from

mentioning that. "Stocks are all about the timing. I sometimes get lucky."

"Dashed lucky, I'd say, considering your record," Cortland said. "You should consider opening an investment firm."

"I might consider it, if only I had the time." Which he did not. Besides, he'd rather earn money for himself than tell others how to do it. "As my father often said, investing in your own future will serve you better in the long run."

"Sounds like a smart man," Cooke said. "Was he a trader on the exchange as well?"

"Not exactly. He was a man of business. Warren Hatcher. Perhaps you've heard of him?"

Blank faces stared back at him. If someone in the group was lying about not knowing Julius's father, he was damned convincing. "Not that I remember," Whitehouse finally said. "Related to the Hatchers of Boston?"

"No. These were the Hatchers of Bedford Street."

An uncomfortable silence descended as smoke wafted and swirled toward the ceiling. No one in New York society liked to be reminded of an acquaintance's common roots.

"Ocean Petroleum, you say?" one of the gentlemen asked. "Any other stocks you fancy?"

"I'm watching Transatlantic Communications. And if you still have Irving Silver, I would dump it."

Heads nodded all around, each man soaking in the knowledge. No doubt cables would be sent to traders as soon as the party disbanded.

"May I have a private word, Hatcher?" Mr. Peter Moore asked from the rear of the group. When everyone glanced at him, he held up his hands. "Non–stock related, I promise."

Julius nearly rolled his eyes. Heaven forbid one of these jackals received private insight not made available to all. Perhaps this was about his father? Anticipation surged in his veins as he stood. "Shall we talk outside?"

Moore nodded and Julius trailed him onto the terrace, shutting the door behind them. They drifted into the darkness where the chances of being overheard dramatically decreased. Julius thrust his hands in his pockets and waited.

Around Julius's age, Moore was a wealthy bon vivant whose focus remained limited to women, horse racing, and the clubs. The two had crossed paths over the years but were not friends. Moore ran in the most exclusive circles and had little interest in business; hence, he had little use for an outsider like Julius.

They stood near the edge of the terrace, where Moore leaned against the balustrade. "I'll get right to the purpose. I saw you the other night." He flicked ashes off the tip of his cigar over the side and into the gardens. "At the Haymarket."

Julius stiffened. His only outing to the Haymarket had been with Nora and he wasn't keen on that information being made public, no matter what Nora hoped. Perhaps Moore was mistaken? "When?"

Moore threw him an impatient look. "Miss Desmond performed and threw you a flower. Whole dashed place nearly crashed down around us."

Shit. Still, what was Moore's purpose in mentioning it? And had he seen Nora? "What are you saying?"

"Now, friend to friend"—he motioned between the two of them—"you must be aware that you cannot subject Lady Honora to those places. While society is new to you, there are certain rules. Standards to be upheld. I would hope you would respect proper ladies by not subjecting them to your other . . . stomping grounds."

Stomping grounds with which Moore was well familiar. Anger simmered in Julius's blood, outrage at being lectured like a schoolboy—especially when the whole damn thing had been Nora's idea. He could not tell Moore as much, however.

God knew he did not want her reputation ruined.

There was only one thing to do. He forced a contrite, amicable tone. "I appreciate the advice, Moore. I thought her ladyship, being a fan of theater, might enjoy seeing Miss Desmond perform. Tried to sneak her in, but obviously that was an error in judgment on my part."

"Perfectly understandable," Moore said, when nothing could be further from the truth.

Julius ground his back teeth together. Any imbecile with a lick of common sense would know not to take a woman of Nora's pedigree to a dance hall/ brothel. Moreover, he hated the superiority exuding from Moore's slick smile. And the insouciant body language, as if Moore did not honestly care about the rules but was forced to relay them anyway. Because, after all, tradition must be maintained.

"I shall keep this under my hat, of course," the man continued.

Julius dipped his chin and the pleasure at thwarting Nora briefly overshadowed the irritation of this conversation. "I would appreciate that, as I know would my fiancée. It would not do to have her reputation smeared about."

"Indeed, it would not. As gentlemen, we must protect the upstanding women of New York. I know your fiancée is British but the same principles apply—and you wouldn't want to make an enemy of her father."

Julius had little information to go on with regards to the earl. Perhaps Moore could be useful for something. "What do you know of him?"

"Old family. No scandals. Very proper." He shrugged. "Like all the other aristocracy over there. Smart idea, marrying into nobility. Wish I'd thought of pursuing Lady Nora myself, actually."

Was Moore implying that Nora would marry him . . . if only he'd asked before Julius? More fury flooded Julius's veins. Nora wouldn't have this pompous prick if—

Dear God, was that burn in his chest actual jealousy? *She's not truly your fiancée, Hatcher.* So why did the idea of Moore and Nora together scrape over Julius's nerves like an old bowstring across an out-of-tune violin?

He exhaled carefully and tried not to think too deeply on the dark emotion rioting inside him. He liked Nora. Wanted to see her happy with a man who deserved her. That was all, nothing more. Jealousy would imply serious feelings, which he resolutely avoided. Marriage meant disappointment and responsibility. No more parties on horseback and rum punch fountains. He'd stick to bachelor-hood, thank you.

Moore extinguished his cigar on the stone railing. "Of course, it would be easier to forget this business if I had incentive of some kind."

The edge of Julius's lip curled. "Is this . . . blackmail, Moore? Are you saying you'll ruin Lady Honora if I don't, what, provide you with a stock tip?"

"You make it sound so sordid. All I want is a bit of information, something you withheld from the others in there."

Julius rubbed his forehead. Had this man no shame whatsoever? So much for honor and tradition amongst gentlemen. Turned out greed lay at the bottom of most every conversation. Yet what choice did Julius have? He could not see Nora ruined, not until after he learned the identities of the men who had destroyed his father. He gritted out, "Hopper Chemical."

"Excellent. Thank you, Hatcher." Moore flicked the remnants of his cigar to the ground. "Incidentally, I hear you and Miss Desmond have severed ties."

Looking for permission to screw her?

Not that Julius needed to give permission. They were all adults, with Moore and Poppy capable of making their own decisions. But was this how the New York set discussed women at their clubs, like chattel? A stock one considered trading, with little regard to how the woman felt about the entire business? The more he knew of society, the less Julius cared for it. "We have. A result of the engagement, I'm afraid."

"So why did she throw you the flower the other night?"

One could speculate, but Julius went by facts and numbers . . . not guesswork. The only person who could answer that was Poppy, and he hadn't been to visit her yet. "She has a unique sense of humor," he hedged.

"She must. The place erupted into a Bowery brawl. I nearly didn't escape in time."

Memories of another narrow escape, of blood and fear as violence rained all around, caused sweat to prickle on the back of his neck. He pushed the dark thoughts away. "A close call for many, I'm certain."

"Indeed, it was that. Shall we return inside?"

Julius swept his arm out. "After you."

"Thank you for being so reasonable. And don't worry." Moore slapped Julius's back. "I shall keep quiet regarding Lady Honora's visit to the Haymarket."

Because I acquiesced to your blackmail demands, you bastard.

"I appreciate it," Julius forced out.

Above all else, he hoped to hell Nora never learned of what he'd done to thwart her plans for notoriety.

DELMONICO'S BUSTLED ON late Thursday evening. White-coated waiters rushed to and fro, carrying glasses and plates to the elite patrons packed into the dining room. Julius loved the frenetic energy, the conviviality of New Yorkers gathered together for a pleasurable night out. He'd spent many hours here, downing oysters and champagne, usually in the company of a beautiful lady.

Tonight he was here to dine with Frank Tripp

and a few other friends. No women, but hopefully plenty of oysters and champagne. Frank's invitation had been a welcome distraction from the week. Between his mother's ongoing visit from hell and thoughts of Nora, his concentration had been fleeting at best. He'd missed a sure thing on an oil stock yesterday.

Once inside he was shown up the stairs to one of the private dining suites. Which meant Tripp had a long, raucous evening planned, one that required privacy. Away from prying eyes in the main dining room. Julius rubbed his hands together in anticipation.

He stepped through the red velvet curtains and into the suite. Blinking in the low light, he searched for Tripp.

"Hello, Julius."

His head snapped over at the sound of the feminine voice and he saw a well-endowed brunette sitting at the small table. Oh, Christ.

A beautiful and talented woman, Poppy Desmond drew eyes wherever she went. Julius had been quite fond of her but never intended for anything more between them, as there was no wife or family in his future and she'd never give up her acting career. So while he wasn't furious that she'd lured him here, he wasn't thrilled, either.

Thrusting his hands in his pockets, he wandered closer. "So that telegram from Tripp inviting me tonight was really from you? Or is this just some astounding coincidence?"

She ducked her head and bit her lip in a familiar, practiced move. He found himself annoyed by it. "I apologize for deceiving you. I wasn't certain you'd come otherwise."

"You are correct. I wouldn't have—not after that stunt you pulled at the Haymarket."

"But that's why I had to see you. I needed to apologize."

"Which you did in a note. Twice." He placed his hands on a chair back and leaned forward. "But you didn't explain why you did it in the first place."

"Please, won't you sit? Let's have dinner."

"Dinner? Are you serious?"

"Of course." She gestured to the chair. "Please, Julius. As friends?"

Sighing, he pulled out the chair and sat. There was no good reason to refuse, not if they were here as friends. He didn't hate Poppy, not by a mile. She could be intelligent and witty, and he was hungry. So as long as they were here . . .

"Thank you," she said as he settled himself. "Now, was that so hard?"

Instead of answering, he asked, "What are we drinking?"

"I ordered a bottle of wine. I hope you don't mind." She reached for a bottle and poured the red liquid into his glass. "It's your favorite. A French cabernet."

He lifted the glass for a long swallow as Poppy signaled to the waiter in the corner to start the dinner service. When they were alone, he asked, "How have you been?"

"Well. Busy. And you?"

"The same. I hear the show is a big success."

Her play was rumored to be sold out nearly every performance. Julius had seen it twice early on and Poppy was fantastic in the leading role.

"Audiences do seem to enjoy it."

Silence descended and they both reached desperately for their wine. It had never been this awkward between them before. No idea why, but he felt . . . disloyal to Nora by being here. A strange sensation, as they weren't truly engaged, but the back of his neck itched with the sudden urge to escape.

He wished it were Nora here with him now. He'd like to seclude her in a private suite where he could feed her oysters, enjoy the sight of her licking the brine from her lips. Feel the press of her thigh to his as they shared a bottle of her favorite champagne. Perhaps he could even bribe the staff to leave them alone for a good long while so he could—

Poppy gave a deep, throaty laugh, interrupting his musings. "This is harder than I thought."

"I don't know why. We've done it hundreds of times before."

"You weren't engaged to a duke's daughter then."

"An earl's daughter, and it's not as if that is news to you."

"I know—and I'm happy for you. Truly. From what I saw the other night, she's lovely and quite genuine. The flower was pure jealousy on my part."

"Poppy . . ."

"I regret it now, believe me. Once I saw the violence I realized my mistake. I shouldn't have thrown the flower at you."

"No, you shouldn't have."

"It was a shock, seeing you there with her." She gave a small chuckle. "It caught me off guard and I acted terribly. Forgive me?"

"Forgiven. Let's leave it in the past."

She relaxed, as if a weight had been lifted off her shoulders. "Excellent. As always, you are nothing if not reasonable. Your calm intelligence was what attracted me most at first."

"And here I assumed it was all the bouquets of poppies I used to send backstage."

"Those certainly did not hurt, either." Her eyes twinkled. "You were very determined."

"As others will undoubtedly be to win your favor now. Have you started seeing someone new?"

"No one seriously, if that's what you are asking. Why?"

"Curiosity." He took a sip of wine, the bold currant flavor rolling off his tongue and into his throat. "Peter Moore asked me about you the other night."

A brown brow shot up, her face tightening. "Asked you . . . about me? As if I am a prized steer on the auction block?"

He held up his hands. "I am merely the messenger. He was interested to learn if we had severed ties, so I presumed he planned to throw in his lot with the rest of the eligible men in New York City to win your favor."

"He's already tried—and failed. He's too arrogant. Expects me to bow to his demands and be available whenever he wishes." She sniffed and lifted her glass. "As if I am some society debutante, with no ambition of my own." Her eyes flicked to his. "No disrespect to your fiancée."

"Lady Nora is anything but a biddable society debutante. Some days I think she's been sent from the devil himself to torment me."

"I think I like this girl."

The waiter returned with the first course, oysters for him and *petites marmites* for her. Once the plates were arranged, the waiter withdrew.

Poppy lifted her soup spoon and took a sip of the broth. "While I do enjoy seeing you, I did have a purpose for asking you here tonight."

"Ah. Allow me to guess? You need a favor."

She wiped her mouth with a linen napkin. "Yes, I do."

"It's not stocks, is it?" Poppy never played the exchange.

"No, it's something else entirely. As you know, I abhor traveling. New York has been my home for so long and I do not wish to work anywhere else. But, despite our recent success, the theater where I am currently featured is closing. The owner lost his fortune at the racetrack, I've been told, and must shut the Athena Theater down."

He shook his head. Horses were a sucker's bet. Too much human corruption and animal unpredictability. "A fool and his money . . ."

"Yes, unfortunately. But there may be an alternative."

"Oh?" He slid an oyster in his mouth, the citrus and brine like heaven as he swallowed. "What's that?"

"I'd like you to buy the Athena and let me run it."

He coughed, nearly choking on his tongue. "Me? Buy a *theater*?" he wheezed.

"Yes." She angled toward him, still maintaining a respectable distance. "Why not you? You have the money and are savvy with investments. I know the theater business and would ensure it flourishes."

"I don't care about the money, necessarily. I just hadn't ever considered it." He drummed his fingers on the table, running the possibilities. Theaters were risky and dependent on the strength of the economy. More importantly, they needed dedicated staff present to keep an eye on things. "Poppy, you have no experience in business. Are you prepared for long, grueling hours on your feet? Dealing with high-strung actors and unhappy patrons?"

"I will hire the right people to do the managerial work. I plan to perform."

"How many weeks a year do you plan to be on stage?"

"Are we negotiating?"

"It appears so. I'm not investing in this venture for any reason other than you. If you have no intention of acting but a few weeks a year, the place will close in six months."

"Fine. Eight weeks a year."

"Thirty."

"Julius, that's preposterous. I'll be dead on my feet. Fifteen."

"Twenty, Poppy. Final offer."

They stared at each other for a long moment. He wasn't the least bit concerned. Poppy was well familiar with his stubbornness and he had no intention of backing down.

"Fine." She struck out her hand. "Twenty weeks a year for the first five years. I'll cable you with the amount tomorrow."

He shook her hand. "Done. May we now enjoy our dinner in peace?"

"Of course." She picked up her spoon. "By the way, where are you hosting the masquerade this year?"

Turning his wineglass on the white linen, he said, "There's no masquerade this year."

"You're . . . not hosting one? I cannot believe it. Why not?"

He took a long swallow of wine, not keen on explaining. No one would understand his reluctance to cause a hullabaloo—and why would they when he'd relished creating them in the past?

Poppy chuckled. "Goodness, I never thought I'd see the day."

"And what day is that?" he asked tersely.

"The day Julius Hatcher was brought to heel by a woman."

Chapter Ten

Though there were three occupants inside it, the Cortland sitting room was as quiet as a church while Nora read the newspaper. When she finally put the newsprint aside, her tea had grown tepid. Probably for the best, seeing as how her stomach now churned with a riot of dark emotions. She placed the cup in the saucer and set it on the table.

Her two new friends, Kathleen Appleton and Anne Elliot, had come to call bearing the unfortunate news from today's *Town Talk* column:

> Mr. Julius H— and Miss D— were back on the town last evening for a private dinner in a suite at Delmonico's. While it had been rumored the two had split since Mr. H—'s engagement, guests oversaw the two leave together afterwards.

"You must be upset," Kathleen said, her eyes full of worry. "I am so dreadfully sorry."

Yes, Nora was upset . . . but not for the reason her

new friend assumed. She hated that Julius had met his former mistress for dinner and the papers had gleefully run the story the very next day—without even mentioning Nora's name. This was precisely the sort of attention she needed, the reason she'd chosen Julius as her fiancé. She had begged him to help create a stir, to come up with a plan to get them noticed, and he'd refused. Instead, he dined with Miss Desmond and now the entire city knew. The sour heaviness in her stomach had nothing to do with jealousy and everything to do with the elusive notoriety escaping her grasp at every turn.

Indeed, how could it be jealousy? She and Julius were friends locked in a mutual agreement, that was all. She liked him, of course. Who wouldn't? The man was charming and intelligent. Handsome. And he treated her as an equal, not like an earl's daughter. He disagreed with her and challenged her as no one else ever had. She appreciated that. Thoughts of him emerged more often these days, as she wondered what he would think about some such thing or another. She looked forward to seeing him, as she did all her friends.

And if the idea of Julius and Miss Desmond together, laughing and touching, caused a sudden ache in her belly? Well, that was best ignored.

"Oh, Nora." Anne reached over to squeeze Nora's arm. "I wouldn't worry. You know how these things are. Many men like to have one last affair before marriage."

The engagement is not real. He owes you no fidelity. She drew in a breath and waved her hand. "I'm not worried. Julius and Miss Desmond are longtime friends. He is free to do as he pleases until the wedding."

Anne and Kathleen exchanged a look. "Of course there is no cause to worry. This is probably common in London," Kathleen murmured. "We do tend to exaggerate here in America."

That last part was true. Americans were certainly a brash lot. For example, though still daytime, both her friends were draped in diamonds. New York women had no concept of reserving the sables and good jewels for the evening. They dressed extravagantly no matter the hour.

But as far as the rest . . . A betrothed man engaging in a very public affair was not common in London. Undoubtedly it would be equally gossiped about there—if not more so.

She lifted a shoulder, attempting to appear more casual than she felt. "I trust him. He has assured me his feelings for Miss Desmond are platonic and I believe him."

The young women stared at her as if she were delusional, which was precisely how Nora would stare at any friend of hers who said the same thing. When Nora's placid expression did not waver, however, signs of resignation washed over the faces of her two new friends.

"You are so devoted to each other," Anne sighed. "It gives me hope about my future marriage."

"Has he tried to kiss you yet?" Kathleen asked, her voice laced with avid curiosity. "He does have a bit of a reputation."

Nora jerked in her seat and blinked stupidly.

And here she'd believed nothing these two could say would surprise her.

Anne sipped her tea. "Katie, stop it. You are embarrassing her. Of course Julius Hatcher hasn't kissed her. She's an earl's daughter, for heaven's sake. Kissing before marriage is quite scandalous."

"A shame," Kathleen sighed. "I bet he's excellent at it."

Her skin as hot as a burning ember, Nora resisted the urge to change the subject. Physical matters were never discussed in England, at least not between the few friends she had there. She'd been taught from birth to swallow any unsavory topic that might be misconstrued or land her in trouble. Because, as everyone knew, young girls were terrible gossips—

She froze. Gossip was *precisely* what she needed to draw attention to herself. Her reputation would suffer, but at least the chatter might reach her father's ears. How had she not thought of this before?

Before she could talk herself out of it, she blurted, "Yes, he has—and he's quite excellent at it."

"Wait, he did? Oh, I want every detail," Anne said, slapping her saucer and cup on the table. "Spare nothing."

Kathleen was even more eager, reaching over to grab Nora's arm and shaking it gently. "You must tell us all about it. When? Where? How long? Did he use his *tongue*?"

Nora smoothed her skirts and tried to contain the devious grin attempting to break through. The gossip would spread all over New York City before nightfall. "Let's see. It was at the Billingses' ball. Outside in the gardens. I couldn't say, but it felt like eons. And yes, tongue was involved."

Kathleen gaped. "That devil. I knew I liked Mr. Hatcher! Well done, Nora."

Anne did not appear so impressed as she faced her cousin. "So if he kissed Nora at the ball, why in the world was he dining with Miss Desmond last evening? And then leaving with that woman? I don't care for it. Even if their relationship is strictly platonic, he should not be so cavalier with Nora's feelings."

"Platonic friends may share dinner, Anne," Kathleen said. "And perhaps he merely dropped her home afterward. Do not leap to outrageous conclusions."

"They are hardly outrageous," the other girl countered with.

Nora's gaze bounced between the two young women, who currently conversed as if she weren't even present. "I am certain Mr. Hatcher had his reasons for dining with his former paramour." Reasons she would inquire about the very next time she saw him, which would be tonight. Would this outing finally be the one to land them in the gossip columns?

She thought of poor Robert, patiently awaiting her in London. She must return as quickly as possible. Then Julius could return to his Miss Desmond and everyone would be happy once more.

Nora figured she may as well come clean about the rest of it. After all, the more gossip, the better. "Have either of you visited the Haymarket?"

"Goodness, no," Kathleen said. "Our mothers would never approve of such a scandalous destination."

Anne, who had been stirring sugar into her porcelain cup, watched Nora's face carefully. The silver spoon clattered onto her saucer. "Wait, are you saying *you* have been to the Haymarket, Nora?"

"Yes. Julius took me there."

"The Haymarket?" Kathleen's hand covered her mouth. "Wait, when? The dance hall, right? We are talking about the same place?"

Anne looked as if she were about to fall out of her seat. "He did? That is astonishing. What was it like?"

"Yes! Spare no detail. Come, Nora. I must know exactly what it's like inside."

Nora proceeded to tell them of her quick trip to the dance hall, complete with the risqué dress and the brawl. "We were only there fifteen, perhaps twenty minutes. Then Julius escorted me home."

Their jaws slack, both girls took a minute to let the story sink in. Kathleen recovered first. "Poppy Desmond is jealous of you."

"No," Nora said, flicking her hand to dismiss the mere thought of the great Miss Desmond being jealous of her. "I think she likes the attention, Julius's in particular. But she has no cause to be jealous of anyone, let alone me."

"You are marrying Julius," Anne said. "Of course she's jealous of you."

"And he fought to get you out safely," Kathleen added with a sigh. "It's so romantic. However did you convince him to take you?"

"I asked." No need to tell them of Robert and her plans to get summoned back to London. Those were for her and Julius alone. "He was reluctant but I convinced him. And, for the record, *I* saved *him* during that brawl."

"I cannot wait to become engaged," Anne breathed. "That is when the real fun begins."

Kathleen beamed at Nora. "Dashed genius of you, Nora. I'm impressed. You found the one re-formed cad in New York willing to take you to the spots the society men wouldn't dare expose you to. Brava!"

"You are my new hero, Lady Nora," Anne said. "And don't worry—Kathleen and I shall not breathe a word about this to anyone."

"Oh, I do not—"

"Exactly," Kathleen cut in to say. "We would never betray your trust by telling anyone about this. Society frowns on this sort of female independence. Which is absolutely ridiculous, but there it is. Never fear, we'll keep your secrets safe."

"You're too kind." Literally. Were they telling the truth? Girls in London gossiped over every little detail, no matter how small, even if promises had been made to keep the news secret. She could only hope that Kathleen and Anne would tell someone and the news would soon spread down Fifth Avenue like wildfire.

A wildfire that reached all the way to London.

A MOORISH-STYLE BRICK and terra cotta building, the Casino Theater had been the first establishment in New York City to build an outdoor theater on its roof. The above-ground breeze and charming setting—not to mention the stiff drinks—kept crowds returning, especially in the summer. Thankfully the owner had the foresight to partially enclose the roof with a glass ceiling, so the space was bearable even in February.

Julius led Nora along the short promenade and past the fragrant flower beds to the rows of covered tables. The place was only about half-full, mostly male patrons wearing heavy overcoats. His fake fiancée had been uncharacteristically silent thus far, her shoulders stiff and unwelcoming. No idle chitchat, no orders. No questions about tonight or how they would shock New York society. Only silence.

Strange.

Unnerving how much he'd been looking forward to seeing her. Most thoughts had been centered on seduction, which had less to do with his plan to encourage a romance between them and more to do with repeating that kiss from the gardens. Had he imagined the passion between them? He didn't believe so. The experience was burned into his memory, and he longed for one more taste of her.

Perhaps this evening.

The heavy black cape swirled around her as she walked, her head high and proud. This could be a drawing room in Mayfair for how she held herself. Did nothing rattle her? She was the bravest woman he'd ever met, utterly fearless and determined.

Robert had best appreciate her. Because if Julius ever caught word that the artist mistreated her . . . Well, there'd be no hole small enough where that fortune-hunting worm could hide from Julius.

The attendant showed them a table in clear view of the stage. "Is this satisfactory?"

Julius waited for Nora to answer, to indicate whether this position was scandalous enough, but she stared off into the dark New York night. "Yes, thank you," he said and slipped the young man a few coins. Then he helped Nora lower herself into a seat. "How did you escape your aunt's careful watch tonight?"

"My maid told them I was unwell and had taken a sleeping draught. Then I snuck out through the delivery entrance."

The answer was clipped, her voice tight. He sat down and asked, "Are you upset?"

"No."

Hmm. While he was not the most intuitive man with regard to women, he could almost hear her gritting her teeth. "Would you rather return another night?"

"No. Is your mother still here in the city?"

"Yes, though I cannot fathom why. I had expected her and my sister to return to Albany within days." They hadn't left his home and had asked daily about meeting Nora. He wasn't certain how much longer he could put them off.

Another silence fell and he could not stand it any longer. "When will you—"

A waiter appeared to take their drink order. Julius ordered champagne for Nora and bourbon for himself. He should probably drink champagne as well, but the mood hardly felt celebratory. Politeness be damned. He angled toward her and lowered his voice. "Please, tell me what is bothering you."

"How are you so certain something is bothering me?"

"Because you've normally mapped out the evening the way a general approaches battle, yet tonight you're silent. What happened?"

She sighed and pulled her cape's collar tighter around her slim neck. "You had dinner last evening at Delmonico's."

"Yes, I did. Were you there?"

"No. I read about it in today's *Town Talk* column."

Christ. He hated that gossip nonsense. Then a spark of realization slid through his veins, energizing him as if a stock had split. This was about Poppy. "You're jealous."

Her brows slammed down. "Absolutely not. That is utterly ridiculous."

Their waiter returned and Nora pressed her lips together. Julius nearly laughed. The truth had been in the clear golden flecks of her dark brown eyes. She hadn't expected him to guess jealousy and therefore hadn't been able to erect defenses quickly enough to hide her reaction. So she was jealous of Poppy. Interesting.

Once their drinks had been poured, he lifted his tumbler and sipped. "So you were saying . . . You're not jealous of Poppy."

"Of course not. This is not a true engagement. Why in God's name would I be jealous?"

"I have no idea. Perhaps you are growing to like me the tiniest bit." He held his thumb and forefinger a hair's width apart.

"I am not jealous, you imbecile—I'm *furious!*"

Her voice carried and the other patrons craned

their necks to check on the disturbance. Julius stood, helped Nora out of her chair, and led her to a secluded spot amongst the shrubbery.

"Tell me why you are so angry," he prompted. "Come now, Nora. Spill it."

She took a deep breath. "I hate that you and she can easily garner attention when I fail so handily. The article mentioned your engagement but didn't bother to note the identity of your fiancée. This should have been ridiculously easy! Instead, I'm plotting and scheming to no avail. At this rate, we'll be married before my father finds out."

"And what else?" He wanted her to admit to the jealousy. He needed to hear it, that he wasn't the only one turned inside out by whatever was happening between them.

"There's nothing else, Julius."

He didn't believe her, not when she wouldn't meet his eyes. "So the idea of Poppy and me together, my hands on her, kissing her—"

Nora's hand shot up to cover his mouth. "Stop talking about it!" He didn't bother to hide his smug satisfaction and she exhaled heavily. "Fine. I am a tiny bit jealous."

He couldn't help it. He had to touch her after that heartfelt admission. His fingertips brushed her cheek, then swept along her temple to push a strand of hair behind her ear. She shivered and he lowered his hand but didn't pull away. The air thickened, blanketing out the rest of the city until they were the only two people in New York.

He put his hands on her hips and shifted closer. "The papers love Poppy because printing her name sells more copies. It has nothing to do with me, I promise, and she arranged dinner to ask me a business question. The dinner was not personal, Nora. I would not secretly see another woman while we are pretending to be engaged."

She pulled her bottom lip between her teeth then grimaced. "I want to say those words do not comfort me, but that would be a lie." Her stare remained fixed on his necktie, her chest rising and falling swiftly, the rapid rate of her breathing matching his own. "I find my feelings grow more confusing every day. You are quite dangerous to my peace of mind."

"Good, because you have already destroyed mine."

Her eyes shot up to his. "What?"

"Is it not obvious? I am attracted to you. Worse, I actually *like* you. I think you're intelligent and interesting, not to mention captivating and shockingly devious."

Music from the stage drifted in the background, along with sounds wafting up from the streets. The cold air burned his lungs but he hardly noticed, his attention focused solely on the woman in front of him. A dull yellow glow from the outdoor lamps cast shadows on her face, and he waited, unable to move, unwilling to even blink and miss her reaction.

"I hadn't expected you to be so forthright and honest. Do all American men speak this way?"

He hadn't the faintest clue. He only knew something was happening between them, something he had no control over, and he owed her honesty. "It's how I speak. I told you I wouldn't lie to you and I meant it."

"So what are we to do?"

His hand cupped her jaw. "Whatever you like. In the eyes of the city, we are engaged."

"This was designed to be purely a business arrangement." She sounded so disappointed that it nearly made him smile.

"I excel at seeing trends and predicting the future. But you are the first person I've met who is truly unpredictable." He studied the fine cast of her features, her high aristocratic cheekbones. The chestnut eyes tipped with brown lashes. He hadn't ever wanted to kiss a woman this badly. Memories of their only kiss plagued him at all hours, a fascination he'd tried hard to shake. Much to his dismay, however, the lure of being with her was only building. "I haven't a clue what we are to do beyond this moment right here."

"And what do you think we should do right now?"

"I think you should kiss me."

Her gaze dipped to his mouth and his heart stuttered. Was she considering it? He prayed the answer was yes.

"That is a terrible idea," she whispered, and he blinked, worried he'd horribly misread the situation. But then she said, "Someone might see us."

Not because she didn't want to but because they might get caught. Anticipation raced through him. His hands found her shoulders and he leaned closer. "No one can see us here in the shadows, my lady."

A dull flush spread over her cheeks. "There are other reasons as well."

He did not want to discuss her worthless beau

at the moment. "Those other reasons hardly matter here tonight on this rooftop. You're in New York, not London, and tonight you're mine."

SHE COULDN'T HELP herself.

Whether it was his words, his deference to her wishes, or the lush, romantic setting, Nora found herself pushing up on her toes to kiss him. There had been this pull between them, an invisible thread drawing them together for days. So it seemed the most natural thing in the world to move in and seal her mouth to his once again. And he didn't resist; instead, he kissed her back. Hard.

It. Was. *Glorious.*

His lips slid over hers fervently, urgent and greedy, as if he'd been waiting years for this. There was a messy desperation along with the skill, the inability to control his reaction in the moment, and proof of his abandon emboldened her, had her shifting closer and threading fingers into his soft hair. Strong hands pulled her flush to his body, cradling her, his wide chest heaving against her own, both of them dragging in precious air.

Every inch of her came alive, as if her blood suddenly moved quicker through her veins and her heart beat faster behind her ribs. Her breasts grew heavy and swollen beneath her corset, and she ached to feel his hands on her. She needed *more*. Her tongue darted out and caught a hint of spirits from earlier, along with something uniquely Julius.

He gave a low growl before his tongue, hot and slick, invaded her mouth. He crowded her, surrounded her, and a giddy weightlessness filled her like champagne bubbles. She was falling, drowning in each gust of his breath, each tiny groan from his throat. Every noise, every shudder ratcheted her own desire higher, and the place between her legs began to pulse, a steady drumbeat of need. She whimpered, delirious with the onslaught of sensation. Drunk with it.

This was nothing like kissing Robert, who—

She broke free, gasping as she put her palm on Julius's chest. Oh, no. She had kissed him *again*. They shouldn't have kissed the first time, let alone once more tonight. What was wrong with her?

Stepping to the side, she tried to put as much distance between her and Julius as possible while collecting her reeling thoughts. Shame burned her skin. This could not be blamed on avoiding discovery in a dark garden. No, *she* had kissed *him*, this man she barely knew.

Everything she'd been raised to believe about love and marriage no longer made sense. She'd fallen in love with Robert, had given him her trust and her heart, and he had done the same. Those pledges meant they would happily spend the rest of their lives together, just as every storybook, governess, and society matron had claimed. So how could she experience these feelings, this burning hot desire, for Julius?

More importantly, how could she have forgotten Robert?

A lump sat in her throat, the urge to cry so strong she could nearly taste the tears. It must have shown on her face because Julius reached for her. "Nora—"

She recoiled, holding up a hand to keep him away. "No, please. Don't touch me. This was an unfortunate mistake."

"Is this about Robert?"

"Do not say his name!" She covered her ears with her hands. "We shall take this to our graves, Julius."

The rogue did not even bother to temper his boisterous laugh. "There are many things I'm taking to my grave, sweetheart, but this won't be one of them. I'm not in the least bit embarrassed by what just happened."

"Well, I am. No one must ever learn of this. No one."

He thrust his hands in his pockets and studied her, his bright eyes shining in the gaslight. "Why? You wanted to act scandalously. Been dying to shock society. This would certainly accomplish both those things. Or, are you worried Robert will hear of it?"

"I already told you not to say his name. What is wrong with you?"

"Perhaps I'm tired of hearing about him," he said with a shrug. "Perhaps I'm tired of all of this."

A fissure of panic worked its way under the surface of her shame. "What do you mean, you're tired of all this?"

"Exactly what I said." He dragged a hand through his hair—hair that had been in her grasp moments earlier. "First, we make this ridiculous bargain, then you prevent me from making any real progress on finding my father's investors whenever we are in society. You push and push for a scandal, never stopping to think of the others affected by your selfishness. You are turning my life upside down—all to return to a craven fortune hunter who doesn't deserve you."

How dare he . . . She poked him in the shoulder. "Robert is not craven or a fortune hunter. And how do you possibly know whether he deserves me or not?"

He took a step closer, his legs brushing her skirts, and her heart thumped in her chest as if they were still kissing. "I know," he said, "because he never should have allowed your father to drive the two of you apart. Any decent man would've married you. Found a way to stop you from leaving his side. That you are here and your Robert is there speaks volumes about how he feels about you."

The words lodged under her ribs like a fist, squeezing her insides until she could hardly breathe. Julius didn't know the circumstances, how hard it was to stand up to a man of her father's position. Robert hadn't had a choice.

But a small sliver of suspicion whispered that perhaps she and Robert should've fought harder. She instantly pushed it aside, even angrier that Julius caused her to doubt herself and Robert. "That is a terrible thing to say."

"It is not my intention to hurt your feelings, Nora, but you must face up to the realities of the situation."

"Realities as you see them."

"Yes. I deal in facts, not emotions or blind faith.

People lie. They conceal their motives whenever possible. You cannot take someone's word that they care about you. It's what they do that matters."

"And how was Robert supposed to keep my father from sending me away? He has no power, no money. No influence to speak of. How could he possibly stand up to an earl?"

"I don't claim to have all the answers, but I would never allow the woman I love to be taken away from me. I would find a way to convince her family, whatever it took."

"Easy for you. You're wealthy, which comes with its own set of privileges. Not everyone is as fortunate."

His expression hardened, eyes growing cold. "My wealth had nothing to do with luck and everything to do with hard work. Your artist is a fool, a hopeless dreamer waiting for the big strike of inspiration to hit. He's doomed to failure."

Her father's similar words rang in her ears. *He will drag you into the gutter if you let him. Artists are failures until they die.* She hadn't expected Julius to sound so much like the earl and less like her friend. Hugging her waist, she said, "You know nothing about him—or me, for that matter. And when I want your advice I'll ask for it."

He pressed his lips together and stared out at the New York nighttime for a long moment. "I apologize, and you're correct. I don't have all the information. Furthermore, none of this is my business. If you want to save yourself for Robert then, by all means, please, do so."

He spun and made his way back to their table, his gait stiff and angry. He threw himself into a chair and reached for his drink, downing the spirits in one gulp. She stood frozen, unsure what to do. Her lips stung from Julius's kisses, the imprint of his fingers haunting her rib cage, while her mind remained a muddled mess.

She couldn't imagine sitting next to him for the next hour after that passionate embrace. Her body still thrummed with excitement, tingles under every inch of her skin. Were they to pretend this never happened? *You cannot leave. Remember your purpose. Remember Robert.*

A fresh glass of champagne awaited her when she returned to their table. She sat down, grabbed the crystal, and swallowed the crisp liquid in one mouthful.

The man at her side remained quiet during the performance—a perfectly bad version of *Taming of the Shrew*—steadily drinking his spirits and watching the actors. Nora hated this awkwardness between them. She never should have kissed him. He'd been quite annoyed when she mentioned Robert. Was he jealous as well?

If so, where did that leave them?

Another glass of champagne arrived and Nora downed this one as well. In all her scheming she'd never imagined that she and Julius would develop an attraction to one another. She wasn't his type, based on what she knew of him, and her heart had already been given away to Robert. But tonight everything had changed.

She had changed.

There was no excuse for this kiss. None whatsoever, other than a desperate need to do so. Worse, the attraction between them had exploded. How could they possibly remain engaged after this?

There was no undoing it, however, and she would still need to find a way to England—with or without Julius's help.

You prevent me from any real progress on finding my father's investors whenever we are in society.

Guilt settled between her shoulder blades, the uncomfortable notion that Julius may be right. She hadn't been much help to him, and the sooner they helped one another, the sooner this charade would end. Besides, the answer seemed so simple, she could hardly believe the intelligent man beside her hadn't already come up with it.

She looked over. "Have you considered luring your father's investors out?"

His gaze locked with hers, one blond brow raised. "Luring, how?"

"With some false promise of payment. All you need is for word to get around in society that you've found something related to your father's investment, something that will benefit these mysterious investors. Then they'll come forward to collect."

He rubbed his jaw thoughtfully, and she could tell he was surprised. "Like stock that has matured, or something along those lines?"

"Yes. If we make it exciting enough, the gossips will take care of the rest. What do you think?"

"I think it could work. From what I've seen, most men of New York society are greedy and lazy. This idea appeals to both." He studied her carefully, intently, with those bright blue eyes, and a familiar heat slid along her spine. "Thank you."

Swallowing, she angled herself toward the stage. "You are welcome."

"And I promise I'll help you return to England as quickly as possible."

She didn't respond, uncertain why those words did not give her more comfort.

Chapter Eleven

Julius entered the foyer of the Gotham Club, a large brick and limestone mansion towering at the corner of Fifth Avenue and Twenty-Second Street. Surprising that the club remained downtown, considering most of the millionaires lived above Forty-Second Street nowadays. He could only surmise how the developments in the surrounding neighborhood—the encroachment of the middle class—infuriated the club's conservative members.

He, on the other hand, relished the upheaval. Perhaps one day soon he'd no longer need to pretend to like these vapid, spoiled men who assumed their last name put them above all others.

The attendant showed him through the marble hallways, past the priceless art, to the dining room. At midday, the airy space bustled with a bevy of New York's elite taking their luncheon, men with names like Cooper, Bennett, Astor, and Jerome. He recognized two senators and a retired general amongst the crowd as well.

Cortland rose as Julius approached the table. "Hatcher, hello." The two men shook hands.

Julius sat opposite Nora's uncle. "Thank you for accepting my invitation."

"Of course. The other two will be joining us shortly. Incidentally, I was a bit surprised you wanted to include Cross and Underhill. Didn't think you even knew them."

"Well, as Nora's future husband, I do owe it to her to try to acquaint myself with the men of society." More importantly, Cross and Underhill were two of Manhattan's worst gossips, according to Nora.

"Happy to hear you say that. I do hope you and my niece plan on staying in New York once you're married."

"We haven't discussed it, but I suspect we'll travel frequently between London and New York."

"That would be nice. Her aunt and I have become quite fond of having Nora about. She's been a breath of fresh air, honestly."

Two men began weaving through the linen-covered dining tables. One was Cortland's age, heavy beard and sideburns covering most of his face. The other man was several years younger, a simple mustache gracing his upper lip. The two greeted diners along the way, more concerned with garnering attention than punctuality. Julius was well acquainted with the type: men who never missed a party, abhorred working, and believed money fell from the skies.

"Ah, here they are," Cortland murmured, standing.

Julius rose as well and waited to be introduced. Then handshakes were traded and the men all sat.

Before conversation could start the waitstaff appeared and it was several minutes as orders were placed. When they were relaxing with drinks, Cross said, "Hatcher, I've heard a number of men sing your praises lately. Said you gave them some sound financial advice."

Julius swirled the contents of his glass, a fine twenty-year-old Scotch whisky. "A few correct guesses here and there. It's nothing."

"Don't need the advice myself," Underhill said with a smug smile. "But some gents ain't as lucky. Good of you to help out."

The condescending tone had Julius gritting his teeth. God help these two if another financial panic were to hit. "I'm happy to be of service."

Talk turned to horses and jockeys for a brief bit. Cross was apparently a connoisseur of New York's racetracks and spent ten minutes comparing Saratoga Springs to Sheepshead Bay. Julius had been to both once or twice but had no insight to contribute. As they ate, his mind instead wandered to Nora. He'd not seen or heard from her since he'd delivered her home after their outing to the Casino Theater. In his daydreams, however, he had relived that kiss a fair number of times.

He hadn't believed she'd actually kiss him. He'd goaded her, fully expecting her to laugh at him or push away with a firm rebuke. Yet she hadn't, and that kiss had exceeded every prurient memory of the first one. In that instant, seducing her away from Robert had become less of a game and more of an obsession.

He no longer merely *wanted* her. He *craved* her.

And that was dangerous. She loved another man and Julius had no intention of pledging his troth for a lifetime of responsibility and failure. Even if Nora weren't attached, pursuing her would be a terrible idea. His affairs, while public, were with ambitious women no more looking for a husband than a trip to the moon. He had no desire to change that.

And still . . .

He hadn't been able to stop thinking about her.

She kissed with every bit of passion in her soul, more depth of feeling than he'd experienced from another woman before. Something about the two of them was explosive. Mind-bending. He hadn't lost himself so completely in a kiss, well, ever.

"Hatcher," Cortland said sharply. "Are you still with us?"

Julius shook himself and gave the older man his attention. "I apologize. You were saying?"

"I understand your mother and sister are visiting from Albany. Perhaps we should host a dinner for the two families to become better acquainted."

A dinner. With his mother, Nora, and the Cortlands? Dear God, no. The idea spelled disaster. He hoped his mother would soon tire of waiting and return home.

When Julius remained silent, Cortland said, "I'll have Mrs. Cortland arrange it with your assistant."

That prompted him to say, "Oh, I'm certain you and Mrs. Cortland are extremely busy. I wouldn't care to impose. My family can be overwhelming." More like unforgiving.

"Nonsense. We'd love to have them to our home for dinner."

His mother would never agree to a dinner at the Cortlands', as she loathed New York society types. She much preferred that Julius host, which he'd flat-out refused to do. But how much longer could he refuse? Agatha and his mother showed no signs of giving up and Julius was running out of excuses. "I'll speak with her," he lied.

"Good. Nothing more important than family."

Julius wasn't so sure about that, but now that the topic of family had been raised . . . "She has come down to oversee a number of my late father's interests, actually. Some very interesting business developments have transpired over the last two months."

"Is that so?" Cortland asked politely.

"Well, I wouldn't want to bore you gentlemen with the tawdry details. Something out of a Poe novel, really." Now that the carrot had been dangled in front of the horses, he focused on his food.

"Poe, you say?" Cross leaned in, eyes gleaming. "I do love a good tawdry story."

"Me as well," Underhill concurred.

Julius carefully placed his knife and fork on his plate. "Well, as long as you keep this between us." Underhill and Cross nodded eagerly, while Cortland seemed quite uncomfortable. Probably because he knew Underhill and Cross were incapable of keeping secrets.

Undaunted, Julius continued. "My father was coordinating a number of investments at the time of his death. One investment had a number of partners but the particulars of the deal were never disseminated before he died. However, it appears my father wrote it all down and buried the details under the floorboards in his study. My mother recently found the paperwork and each investor stands to inherit an obscene fortune. Some stock that has split several times. I've been poring through the legalese to ensure it's legit."

"And is it?" Underhill asked.

"Yes, it appears so. The only problem is we don't know the identities of these investors." He lifted a shoulder. "If I cannot find them, I guess I'll keep the money myself."

Cross's eyes were huge. "That's quite a tale. Are you saying you don't have the names of the other investors?"

"No. They're not in any of the papers I could find. I do know there were four altogether, including my father. So you can understand why I want to keep this between us. If word gets out I'll have every Tom, Dick, and Harry at my door."

"I imagine so," Cortland said. "But how will you recognize the true investors from frauds when they appear?"

"The men who know the details of the deal are the true investors—and I'm guarding those closely. Anyway, what are the odds these men will actually surface after all this time?" Pretty high, if his plan came to fruition.

"Are you actively searching for them?"

"Not really. If they don't show up, then it's more for me, right?" He forced a chuckle that sounded cynical and greedy to his own ears.

"Smart thinking," Underhill said with a wink, though Julius could tell the wheels were turning in the other man's brain.

"I never discuss money—it's so vulgar, you know—but this must be quite a large amount if Julius Hatcher himself is hoping to keep it," Cross said.

Julius merely smiled and lifted his cut-crystal tumbler in a toast.

By the time the luncheon ended, Cross and Underhill could hardly sit still. They all said their good-byes and Cortland walked out with Julius. Before Julius left the dining room he glanced over his shoulder and saw Cross and Underhill leaning over, whispering in ears, gesturing in Julius's direction.

Excellent. Perhaps Nora's idea would work after all. Which meant all that remained was to help her return to London, an obligation about as appealing as turning off his stock ticker for a few days.

However, he'd made a promise and he had every intention of standing by his word—no matter how much he hated the prospect of never seeing her again.

"I AM QUITE looking forward to meeting Mr. Hatcher's mother," Aunt Bea said, breaking the silence as the large Cortland carriage arrived at the Hatcher mansion. "Do you know much about her, Nora?"

"No, not really. She and Julius are not close, from what I understand. I was surprised to get the invitation, really." Stunned, more like it. Julius had been adamant against this happening and she had no idea what had changed his mind. All she knew was that her aunt had arranged the entire thing with Julius's secretary at Mrs. Hatcher's request.

Icy wind and sharp rain pelted the sides of the Cortland carriage. Shivering, Nora drew the sides of her heavy cape more tightly about her and longed for the vehicle to turn around and take her back to her uncle's. How on earth could she play the loving, cheerful fiancée when her mind was such a scattered mess?

You are turning my life upside down—all to return to a craven fortune hunter who doesn't deserve you.

The past few days had been spent trying to sort through her feelings for both Robert and Julius, while examining herself in the process. Nora didn't care for what she had discovered: a woman who could feel such intense attraction—and yes, interest—for Julius when she had promised her loyalty and soul to someone else. A month ago she wouldn't have believed it possible. Yet here they were, posing as an engaged couple while stealing very real kisses in secluded spots.

Kisses her brain hadn't been able to erase, no matter how many times she reread Robert's letters.

Briefly, she'd considered confessing all to Robert but couldn't bring herself to put pen to paper. Julius was a scoundrel, a charming rogue who attracted women like flies. Nora could hardly be faulted for succumbing to his easy smile and handsome face, could she? Years from now, when she and Robert were far from New York and secure in their marriage, she would tell him of her brief fling here and how little it had meant.

Only . . . the burst of happiness she experienced each time she thought of Julius did not feel *little*. It felt huge and all-encompassing. Distracting. To dismiss it seemed like the worst kind of lie, even to herself. Whatever was happening between her and Julius, though inconvenient, was genuine. Perhaps more genuine than anything Nora had ever experienced before . . . and that scared her to her toes.

The wisest course of action was to avoid Julius. To admit he was a temptation she couldn't resist and never allow herself to be alone with him. Remain in public and forgo sneaking off with him down secluded paths. Stop daydreaming about the desperate, determined way he'd kissed her, as if he'd been afraid she'd vanish at any moment. Cease imagining what it would be like if their kisses went further and he satisfied this terrible ache inside her.

I would never allow the woman I love to be taken away from me.

His honesty and recklessness made him dangerous, if only because she found those qualities so disarming and dashed appealing.

But Julius was not the man of her future, a man who wanted a wife and children. He'd said as much himself. So what, then? She would become his mistress? Another in a long line of women he enjoyed and then left?

No, absolutely not. Even if she cared little for the conventions of her class, had always done the opposite of what was expected of her, she still had her pride. She'd been raised to settle her heart on one man—and that had already happened. Julius Hatcher had arrived in her life too late.

"Well, I may have pushed it a bit at lunch with Hatcher," Uncle James said.

That got Nora's attention. "Lunch? You had lunch with Julius?"

"Yes." He peered through the window. "Saw him at the Gotham Club yesterday. Are those *ducks*?"

"Oh, isn't that clever," Aunt Bea said, peering out at the moat. "Don't ducks fly away for the winter? I must ask Mr. Hatcher how he manages to keep his here."

Nora would much rather discuss yesterday's lunch than the ducks. Before she could press her uncle, the footman opened the door. Uncle James descended and helped Aunt Bea to the walk, then assisted Nora. As she stepped to the ground, Nora said, "I am so happy you and Julius are getting along. Was this lunch to discuss wedding plans?"

The edges of his mouth turned down slightly. "Goodness, no. We'll leave all that wedding planning to you and your aunt. We had lunch with a few other men. Nothing to be concerned about."

Ah. Could it be that Julius had taken her advice and started a rumor regarding his father's lost investors? That was good news. At least one of them was close to achieving success in this bargain.

"It's like a fairy tale castle," Aunt Bea whispered, now on the walk at Nora's side and craning her neck to take in the mansion. "All we need is a witch and a curse."

Nora sincerely hoped they found neither of those two things inside.

The front door swung in and Brandywine emerged. When Aunt Bea heard his British accent, she beamed as if the butler was a long-lost cousin, and soon the two were chattering like old friends. He took their things and showed them to a small family salon near the formal dining room.

Julius was already there, his back to the room, leaning on the mantel and staring into the fireplace. His shoulders were bunched tight, unhappiness etched in the lines of his profile. Nora had the ridiculous urge to run a comforting hand down his broad back.

Stop it. He is not really your fiancé.

An older woman rose from the sofa. Her black dress was entirely free of embellishments or adornments and she wore no jewelry. Blond hair was pulled into a simple twist at her nape, smoothed off her face with not a strand escaping. Piercing blue eyes swept Nora quickly and the lines around her mouth deepened. Was that disapproval?

Next to Mrs. Hatcher stood a younger woman who bore a strong family resemblance to Julius. This must be Agatha, the sister who lived with his mother in Albany.

"Good evening," Aunt Bea said, entirely undeterred by the awkwardness in the room. "How nice to meet you both. I am Mrs. Beatrice Cortland."

All the appropriate introductions were made. Mrs. Hatcher's handshake was limp and uninspired, Nora noticed, while Julius's sister had a strong grip, almost as if she had something to prove. "Very nice to meet you, Lady Nora," Agatha said with a hardy pump of her hand.

"You as well, Miss Hatcher. Julius has told me quite a bit about you."

"And yet you still came tonight," her fake fiancé drawled as he snatched her hand away from his sister and kissed the knuckles. "You look lovely, my lady."

Heat flooded her at the compliment. For some reason, she'd wanted to make a good impression this evening, so she had taken extra time with readying herself. Her ivory silk dress was ornamented with lace, beads, and embroidered flowers, with delicate purple-and-green stitching around the skirt and train. Matching flowers had been woven into the elaborate set of braids close to her head. "Thank you."

He smiled, though it did not reach his eyes. He appeared tired, subdued. "Would anyone care for a drink?" he asked the room in general. Aunt Bea requested sherry and Uncle James strode to the sideboard with Julius.

"Nora?" Julius called. "Wine, champagne, or sherry?"

"Champagne, please."

The Hatcher women were not drinking and Nora wondered if she should rescind her request. Julius was drinking, however, as would Aunt Bea and Uncle James. She decided one glass would not hurt. At least then she'd have some liquid courage to get through the evening.

Aunt Bea lowered herself into a chair opposite the sofa. "We were pleased to hear you had traveled all the way to New York."

"I live in New York," Mrs. Hatcher said, her brow wrinkling. "In Albany."

The correction flustered Aunt Bea for half a second. "My apologies. I meant to say New York City."

Nora came to her aunt's rescue. "I have heard lovely things about Albany."

"Except for the government riffraff, it's a decent, upstanding place," his sister replied. "We live in Julius's home there. He bought it several years ago and generously allows us to stay."

Julius "allowed" them to stay there? An odd way of phrasing it, Nora thought.

"You know that's not true," Julius said from the sideboard. "The house belongs to you and Mother."

Aunt Bea accepted the glass of sherry from Uncle James and smiled at Julius's relatives. "I hope you are taking some time to see the city while you are here. No doubt Mr. Hatcher can show you about."

"If we are able to pull him away from his stock ticker," the sister muttered.

Nora saw a muscle tighten in Julius's jaw and her heart went out to him. "He certainly knows the city well," she said, determined not to let these women ruin the evening. Not when she'd worn one of her best dresses. "And the exchange does shut down in the afternoons."

"I'm not fond of staying up late," his sister said. "The hours you society ladies keep are quite different than how we live in the country."

"Undoubtedly that is true. Very often I've retired early with a good book, have I not, Aunt Bea?"

Her aunt nodded eagerly. "Yes, we all do. Not everyone can keep vampire hours for long. Not even vampires."

Julius snickered and the sound lifted Nora's mood considerably. At least he could still laugh.

"Know a lot of vampires, do you?" her fiancé asked as he joined their small circle, a glass of red wine in his hand.

"A few," Aunt Bea said with a wink. "They're a bloodthirsty bunch."

Groans and chuckles erupted from half the room while the Hatcher women frowned fiercely. Nora cleared her throat and gave her aunt a pointed glare. "We should probably refrain from scaring Julius's family, Aunt Bea. At least until after the wedding."

"Yes, allow me to offer my congratulations," Agatha said. "I am certain you and my brother will be very happy. You seem well matched in your interests." The way Agatha stared at Nora's dress suggested distaste with the garment, though Nora was modestly covered. Had that been a compliment?

"Thank you," Nora said, confused but determined to carry on. "I believe we shall be happy together as well."

"Have you thought about a date for the wedding?" Mrs. Hatcher asked.

"November," she answered.

"September," Julius said at the exact same time.

"Well, which is it?" Agatha asked sharply. "September or November?"

Nora waved her hand. "We are having a slight disagreement about the date. Julius is not excited about London in November, but I prefer the cooler weather."

"London?" His mother's eyes went wide. "You are getting married in London?"

"Of course." Nora glanced at Julius, who was watching his mother and sister carefully. Oh, no.

Clearly she'd said something wrong and there was no hope for it but to soldier forward since her fiancé remained mute. "We decided that would be best, considering my father's schedule."

"I cannot travel to London for a wedding," Agatha said. "And neither can Mother."

"I will work out your travel arrangements, if necessary," Julius said. "I'd like both of you there. However, if you'd rather stay home, I'll marry Nora without you present." He held out his arm to Nora. "Now, shall we start dinner?"

THE DINNER PARTY was a disaster.

Beatrice and James Cortland attempted to keep the conversation flowing, while Nora forced conviviality through her confusion. Julius tried not to drink himself under the table while ignoring his mother's pinched expression and Agatha's smug, self-righteous smile. That they both disapproved of Nora, the Cortlands, and his entire existence was perfectly clear to everyone in the room.

At least his family had remained fairly polite thus far. Any overt signs of disrespect to anyone in his home would not be tolerated, even if they were his blood relatives. Both his mother and sister were listening attentively and responding when asked questions, thankfully.

The dinner had been arranged behind his back. The Cortlands reached out to his mother directly, assuming she handled social functions like any normal society matron. How were the Cortlands to know that Rebecca Hatcher was nowhere close to a society matron?

There'd been no choice but to attend once it had all been settled. He had warned both his mother and sister beforehand to be courteous. Agatha, unfortunately, was unpredictable. Julius had no illusions his older sister would behave and the anticipation kept him on edge. Like when a stock started to plummet and you couldn't take your eyes off the tape, waiting to see how low the number would finally drop.

So he drank—and surreptitiously watched Nora. His fake fiancée really was quite lovely. Not a flashy or obnoxious beauty, she possessed a classic elegance where every regal feature drew one's eye. Brows evenly matched and sculpted. A straight and delicate nose. Her proud chin and fierce, commanding brown gaze. Pale, creamy skin that he would bet was every bit as soft as it appeared. Why hadn't he run his tongue along the column of her throat when he'd had the chance?

Heat wound through his belly, along his spine. He'd come to a decision the other night, one that would benefit them both. They couldn't deny there was an attraction between them, a spark that erupted whenever they were in the same room. Considering he had no intention of ever marrying and she was in love with someone else, where was the harm in acting on these base desires? No one would ever know. Besides, hadn't seduction been in his plans since almost the beginning of this farce?

Are you seriously contemplating seducing the daughter of an earl and expecting no repercussions?

Yes, he was. Recalling that kiss from the Casino rooftop, he could contemplate almost nothing but seduction.

"Julius." His sister's sharp tone broke into his reverie.

He looked up. "Yes?"

"I asked if you plan to travel to Albany for Mother's birthday in a few weeks."

Christ, had it been a year already? "Of course. Don't I always?"

"Are you planning to bring your fiancée? We would need to make arrangements, of course."

"What sort of arrangements?" The large house could easily accommodate guests and there were enough servants on staff. What difference was it if he brought Nora or not?

"The house is ill suited for visitors at the moment. We would require advance notice of any guests."

"Meaning?"

"Some of the rooms have been rented out."

What the hell? He straightened in his chair and slammed the base of his wineglass on the cherry tabletop. "Why on earth are you renting out rooms?"

"Julius," his mother said, reproach in her tone. "Perhaps we should discuss this later."

"Absolutely not. I want to know why you are renting out rooms when the entire place is paid for. Not to mention the monthly expenses. So tell me, why are you operating some sort of boardinghouse?"

His mother and sister exchanged a look, one that had Julius bracing for the worst. "It's not about earning money," his mother said. "We do not charge them much rent. The point is to offer folks a reasonable residence, one they can afford." She gestured to the opulent dining room. "Not everyone has a mansion to live in."

A dull ringing echoed in his ears, his skin igniting with outrage. She had the nerve to criticize him when he'd provided her with that house? Were they running this charity as a way to save Julius's greedy soul? If so, his soul did not require saving. And if his mother did not like it, then she could find her own damn house.

His lip curled and he leaned forward, opening his mouth to tell her exactly how he felt—

"Julius, I wondered if you would give me that tour you promised." Nora motioned to a footman to help with her chair.

The wine must have dulled his brain because he hadn't a clue what the woman was talking about. He blinked. "Tour?"

"Yes, of your home. You promised earlier that you would show me the turrets."

She's offering you a way to escape. Leave it to his bold and clever fake fiancée to come to his rescue. "Yes, the turrets." He blew out a long breath and stood. "If you all will excuse us. I promised this charming lady a tour."

"Of course," Beatrice said, waving them toward the door. "We'll relax and talk amongst ourselves. No need to hurry back."

Julius paused, certain he was hearing things. If he didn't know better, he would swear Beatrice was encouraging him toward inappropriate behavior with her niece.

Nora tugged him in the direction of the door. A footman opened the heavy wooden panel and they strolled into the hallway.

He took her hand and led her to the main stairs.

Their shoes ticked on the marble floors and he noted she smelled of lavender. The tension between his shoulders eased up considerably. "Thank you."

"You are welcome. I assumed you would prefer those conversations remain private, which you undoubtedly would have realized had the heat of the moment not carried you away."

"Correct. Also probably shouldn't have had so much wine at dinner."

"Are you drunk?"

He shot a grin down at her. "I might be. Would you mind?"

Her lips twisted into a smirk, eyes dancing with mirth. "As long as you're not on horseback."

"You'll never let me forget that, will you?"

They started up the steps and she chuckled. "It was a memorable first impression, that's for certain. Wherever did you get the idea for a dinner party on horseback?"

"A bet. Friend of mine said it couldn't be done, that the floor couldn't hold the weight. Decided to prove him wrong."

"Allow me to guess, you did the calculations and knew exactly how many horses you could use."

He liked that she knew this about him. "Of course I did. Louis Sherry wouldn't take too kindly to the second floor collapsing onto his dining room."

Once on the landing, she looked up at him, frowning. "Wait, where are we going?"

"To the turret."

She dug in her heels and dragged them to a stop. "That was a fib. I merely wanted to get you out of the dining room."

He eased in close so they were nearly touching. He liked touching her, had daydreamed about stroking her soft skin far too often. Daydreams that had nothing to do with their fake betrothal or flirting with her in an attempt to shake her affections for Robert, and everything to do with how a man drives a woman out of her mind with pleasure.

Recollections of their intense kisses had only sown the seeds of an obsession within him. An unhealthy heap of prurient fantasies and dangerous imaginings that had grown stronger each day. How had she managed to turn this all around and make *him* suffer?

He deepened his voice to ask, "Have you ever been inside a castle turret, my lady?"

"No," she whispered, a becoming blush spreading over her neck and cheeks.

"Then, please, allow me to show you what you've been missing."

He tried to pull her along but she held fast. "Julius, we shouldn't be alone."

"Says the woman brave enough to face down a Haymarket mob. Do not give up on me, Lady Nora."

"It has nothing to do with giving up. You're . . . I think it best if we remain in the company of others."

"You think we need to be chaperoned?"

"Yes, I do. It would make things easier between us."

Easier for her to resist him, in other words. Interesting. So his little English rose was worried. A heady jolt of satisfaction sped through him. "What if I promise to keep an arm's length away at all times? Will that do it?"

The edges of her mouth turned down into a pretty frown. "You're laughing at me."

"A little, but I have no wish to cause you any discomfort. I merely wanted to show you the clever little nook I designed in the east turret while we escape the banal after-dinner conversation. Would you rather return to my mother and sister?"

That did the trick. She shook her head and swept her arm out. "Lead the way, good sir."

Chapter Twelve

Before his fake fiancée could change her mind, Julius spun, took her hand, and hurried toward the end of the family wing. The turret was his own private retreat within the house and for some silly reason he was excited to show it to her. He sensed Nora would appreciate what he'd done with the space.

He pressed on the wall to the right of the last sconce and the mechanism released. The edge of the door popped open, behind it a staircase no one used but him. He held open the secret panel, threw the switch for electric, and gestured for Nora to enter. She swept through the opening and began climbing the stairs, her long train trailing her. Julius followed and tried not to stare at her tiny waist or the sway of her backside. Dashed impossible to do when she was right in front of his face, however, so he stopped fighting it and enjoyed the view.

The stairs curved near the top and ended at the edge of the turret. He heard her gasp when she reached the end and smiled to himself. "Julius, I cannot believe it. It's a tiny . . ."

"Library. I know."

He stepped up into the round reading room and stood beside her. Exposed wood beams in the domed roof met in the center, where a large black metal gasolier illuminated the space. Floor-to-ceiling curved walnut shelves packed with books covered three sides, complete with a wooden ladder to reach the volumes on top. An upholstered bench seat had been built beneath the two large windows, a perfect reading spot that was every bit as cozy as it appeared.

"I love it." She spun around to take it all in. "It's incredible."

"Wait," he told her and hurried to the bench seat. Lifting up the last cushion, he flipped up the top of the bench to reveal the compartment underneath. He gestured to the contents. "See?"

She peered around him into the bench where he kept his favorite bottles and glasses. "A hidden sideboard. How clever."

Reaching in, he withdrew a bottle of brandy—his preferred French Cognac—and two snifters. Then he replaced the seat and the cushion. "Shall we have an after-dinner brandy?"

Nora's attention had already turned to the books. "Sure, fine. Have you read all these books? *The Theories of the Production of Wealth* and *Lectures on the Principles of Capitalism.*"

"Indeed, I have." He handed her a half-full snifter of brandy, which she accepted absently. "These are my personal favorites, as opposed to the library in the main part of the house that contains a little of everything."

"Oh, I loved *Gulliver's Travels*. Heavens, that appears to be a first edition."

"It is. All of the books in this room are original printings." He warmed the snifter with his palms, swirling the contents in the crystal bowl. He took a sip of brandy, then licked the rich flavor from his lips as the liquor burned all the way down to his stomach.

Carrying her glass, Nora trailed a finger over the spines and walked along the shelves. "*Madame Bovary*?" She threw him a glance over her shoulder. "I should have expected you to possess the scandalous books as well, you rogue."

Smiling, he lowered himself onto a cushion at the window seat. "The tale of a restless woman searching to escape her circumstances through assignations and affairs? My dear, it is poetry on every page."

She returned her attention to the shelves. "I suppose you'll tell me that is how you see me."

That hadn't been his meaning, not at all. "No, Emma is almost a child, looking for love and acceptance in high society. When she doesn't find it she kills herself. You are far too brave, too self-assured to be Emma." He lifted a shoulder. "The title character is probably more like my father, actually, though not the affairs. He suffered from the craving for money and the acceptance of one's betters. Perhaps that is why I am drawn to the story."

"To better understand him?"

"Yes, perhaps."

She came to sit by him, her skirts spilling over the bench. "That is the second time tonight you have referred to me as 'brave.'"

"Does that description honestly surprise you?" Had precious Robert never commented on that fact? Her father? "You are fearless, Nora."

"Oh, how I wish that were true," she said with an odd laugh that came out more pained than humorous.

"What do you mean? What has you so afraid?"

She shook her head, her lips pressed tightly together.

"Come on, tell me," he coaxed. "Can it be so terrible?"

"I am terrified of *this*." She gestured between the two of them. "Of whatever seems to be happening when we are in the same room. I am terrified of discovering I am as fickle as I suspect. I am terrified of becoming a—" She pressed her lips together but the rest of the sentence was as clear as if she'd spoken aloud.

Whore. Tart. Loose woman.

His chest tightened with an uncomfortable sensation he suspected was guilt. He had set out to seduce her, to shake her regard for the mythical Robert, without contemplating how that would make her feel. The doubt, the self-recrimination she would experience . . . Hell, he'd never wanted to hurt her.

The realization hit him with the force of a brickbat to the stomach. *Oh, Christ.* He was falling for this woman. Throwing back a mouthful of brandy, he willed the uncomfortable thought away for now.

There would be time enough to wallow in regrets after all this had ended. For God's sake, he deserved a broken heart, the universe's way of keeping life's tally sheet in perfect balance.

At the moment, however, he needed to vanquish the heart-wrenching vulnerability he saw in her eyes. He hadn't told the story in a long time, hadn't even let himself think on it in eons, but he'd willingly crack open an old wound if it helped her. "When I was seventeen I worked as a clerk on the exchange. My boss, an older man with the disposition of a cockroach, had a young, pretty wife named Charlotte. He liked for her to come to the office—to show her off, no doubt—and I began to notice Charlotte staring at me. Coy, flirtatious glances." He grimaced at the memory of his youthful naiveté and took another sip of his brandy. "One day she waited for me outside in her carriage and offered me a ride home."

"I can see where this is headed."

"Possibly anyone could but at the time I had no idea. It started innocently at first, I swear. Her marriage was an unhappy one and I was eager to oblige. I never wanted to marry and here was this attached, safe, beautiful woman who would never ask for more."

Nora shifted toward him so their knees were almost touching. "And what happened?"

"I fell in love with her. God above, I was like a puppy trailing after that woman. Eager. Delirious with both the secrecy and the newness of it. She was older and experienced, and I worshipped her. But her husband soon found out."

"He did? What did he do?"

"Fired me straightaway. All things considered, I escaped relatively unscathed. It could have been much worse."

"Losing your source of income must have been difficult."

"Not in the least. What he didn't know was that I'd already saved up enough to buy my own seat on the exchange. Just hadn't worked up the nerve to do it. I was still young and inexperienced. But losing my position pushed me forward to buy the seat and begin trading on my own." Success had come quickly after that; he'd made his first fortune not even two years later.

"And Charlotte? Did you ever see her again?"

"I did not. He sent her to Paris, I heard. While I was heartbroken I knew this had all happened for a reason. I required a push and life offered me one."

She sipped her brandy and watched him over the crystal rim. When she lowered the glass, she said, "You are saying life is offering me a push. What, through *you*? Through this engagement?"

The way she said it, as if the idea were ludicrous, stung more than he would have thought. His tone sharpened. "Possibly. I couldn't say. But I can tell you that if I had been the one entrusted with your heart, you would not be sitting alone with another man in a turret."

"Even if that other man was merely a friend?"

There was that word, the one he'd hoped to never hear from her lips again. *Friend.*

Setting down his snifter, he reached for her free hand where it rested on the cushion between them.

She hadn't yet put her gloves back on after dinner, her skin soft and delicate in his rough, brutish grasp, and he lifted her hand to his mouth, turning it over. He bent his head and placed his lips on the inside of her smooth wrist. She smelled of lavender and soap, the most delectable treat he'd ever encountered, and his cock began to thicken inside his trousers. Unable to resist, he touched the tip of his tongue to her warm flesh, the merest hint of what he'd like to do all over her naked body. A harbinger of all the pleasure he longed to shower on her. He heard her gasp as her hand trembled.

"Make no mistake, my lady," he whispered, looking up through his lashes to lock eyes with her. "We are not friends. I plan on seducing you, but when I do you'll come to me willingly and eagerly. And when it's over, I promise you'll not regret a single second."

Her eyes glazed over with desire, and Julius nearly lunged forward to kiss her mouth. But they had been gone long enough from the others and once he started kissing her, he wasn't certain he could stop.

Furthermore, returning a ravished Nora to her aunt and uncle would only precipitate a very real wedding date.

Releasing her, he stood. "We should return downstairs before they send a search party after us."

I PLAN ON seducing you, but when I do you'll come to me willingly and eagerly.

Now in the drawing room, Nora fanned her face vigorously as Julius's words rang in her head.

Based on the promise she'd seen in his gaze, she did not doubt his intent. It was his arrogance that bothered her. To assume she would ever go to him with the intention of seduction . . . It was laughable. Wasn't it?

A small part of her suspected he might be right. When he'd kissed, then licked, the inside of her wrist earlier tonight in the turret, she had nearly melted into a pool of desire right there in front of him. The buzzing in her blood had yet to cool, even several minutes later.

She sat next to her aunt on the sofa, while Julius and her uncle conversed over a glass of port on the other side of the room. Rebecca and Agatha were cloistered near the window, whispering. Most likely about Nora's reckless disregard for propriety in stealing Julius away after dinner.

Out of the corner of her eye she could see her fiancé, tall and powerful next to her average-sized uncle. Every now and again Julius sent her a glance, one laden with secret knowledge and mysterious promise.

"You seem distracted," Aunt Bea noted, tipping her chin in Julius's direction. "Though I can hardly blame you. Your uncle is quite a handsome man."

Nora laughed and tried not to blush at being discovered. She sipped her coffee and considered her aunt. Nora's mother had died when Nora was young, much too soon to provide advice and motherly guidance, and Nora had come to love and respect her aunt these past few weeks. Perhaps Aunt Bea could offer insight to Nora's current situation without growing suspicious of the reason. "You and Uncle James appear so happy with one another. Really quite different than the couples I've witnessed back in London. When you first met him, how were you so certain he was the only man for you?"

"Oh, goodness. I wasn't, not at all. I had a handful of suitors that season, even one that I seriously considered. In the end, however, James was irresistible."

"Who was the one serious suitor?"

"The catch during my debut was Lord Hartford, heir to an earldom. Looked like Byron, sounded like honey on warm toast." She leaned back and stared at nothing, an amused twist to her lips. "Smart and witty, and not a terrible dancer, either. Do not tell your uncle but"—she put a hand in front of her mouth and whispered—"Hartford was my first kiss."

"No," Nora breathed, enthralled. "I know Lord Hartford. He has three sons and a daughter who is close in age to me."

"He married a lovely girl from Surrey, a viscount's daughter. They're happy, from what I hear."

"So why did you not marry Hartford instead?"

She lifted a shoulder and reached to drop one more sugar cube in her cup. "Hartford was the infatuation of a girl who hardly knew herself. I realized it as soon as I met Cortland. The two men were vastly different and, more importantly, the way I felt about each of them was incomparable."

Nora understood perfectly, though her situation was not exactly the same. Robert was warm and cozy, like her favorite velvet cape. Julius was a fever, one that invaded your bloodstream to make you delirious. Neither were terrible, merely at odds.

You are fearless, Nora.

Was that only how Julius saw her, or had she grown more determined and independent since living in America? Her life here was drastically different than her life in London, which had been filled with duty and obeying the rules. New York was adventure and exploration. Excitement. And a large reason for those feelings was lounging against the mantel on the other side of the room.

Was Robert a mere girlish infatuation? She could admit now that he had bolstered her, made her feel attractive and desirable at a time when she'd felt overlooked. He'd spoken to her as an equal, not as if she were silly or thickheaded, and had been genuinely interested in hearing her thoughts. Sweet and sensitive, he'd not pressured her for physical intimacies but let her set the pace for their relationship. When she finally decided to take him to bed, it had not been decided lightly. In fact, she'd agonized over it for months. She resolved to after they discussed marriage and decided to remain together forever.

So how could she consider doing the same with Julius, a man who would not marry her? A man who did not love her. A man she barely knew. What was *wrong* with her?

Her fiancé raised the port glass to his lips, the thick column of his throat working as he swallowed. Tingles raced along the insides of her thighs and she shivered.

"I'm so pleased you have settled on Julius," her

aunt said, regaining Nora's attention. "It's clear you'll never need worry about the temptation of another man or second-guessing your choice."

That is precisely what I am doing. "I won't?"

"Based on the way the two of you stare at one another when you believe no one is watching, I'd say not. Hatcher is a man who knows his mind and has strength of character. Takes care of his mother and sister even though they treat him abominably. That tells me he tries to do the right thing, no matter how unpleasant. He'll do whatever is necessary to keep you happy."

If I had been the one entrusted with your heart, you would not be sitting alone with another man in a turret.

Only, Julius had no interest in her heart. He'd made that perfectly clear.

But how do you feel about him?

Like the world shone brighter each time he walked into a room.

Like she might expire if he never kissed her again.

Like her entire life had been turned upside down.

She closed her eyes and drew in a shaky breath. This was no passing fancy. Even though she may never act on them, the feelings she had for Julius were entirely real. Keeping the truth from Robert, allowing him to believe she still pined away for him, was intolerably cruel. The time had come to be honest.

Tears stung her lids and she dug her nails into her palms, hoping to stem the rise of emotion until she could be alone. No good ever came from crying at a dinner party.

Julius's mother and sister suddenly sat, forming a small circle around Nora and her aunt. They helped themselves to coffee. Mrs. Hatcher's gaze locked with Nora's. "Lady Nora, I fear I must speak plainly as I am uncertain when I'll have another chance. Has Julius told you of his father's death?"

"Yes, he has. You have my sincerest condolences on the loss of your husband." A loss that must still pain her, considering the woman remained in mourning dress all these years later.

Mrs. Hatcher dipped her chin in acknowledgment. "I'm afraid that Julius has inherited my late husband's obsession with money and material things. That obsession was . . . a difficult part of my marriage. I never asked for a better lifestyle or more wealth. However, my husband assumed these were things I wanted. He drove himself, often recklessly, to improve our circumstances, though improvement was hardly required. Do you understand what I am saying?"

"If you are worried Julius will act as reckless as his father, I can assure you he's quite levelheaded when it comes to business matters."

"As was my husband, once. But greed is a powerful emotion, one that most men cannot resist. I have watched Julius surpass every hardship, every dream. But still he works. Strives for more. When will it be enough?"

Nora grew annoyed on Julius's behalf. "I hardly see it as greed. He excels at finance, at reading the market. Why should he not put such expertise to good use?"

Agatha made a noise in her throat. "Good use? Look around you. Do you call this house *good use*?

There are portions that remain locked, completely closed off. It is wasteful in the extreme."

"Is that not the American way?" Aunt Bea said with a chuckle, a clear attempt at a joke.

"What happens," Mrs. Hatcher continued, "when the markets plummet? Or when his skills dull and he loses all his money? When you are out purchasing new gowns and expensive jewels each week?"

The tips of Nora's ears burned and she heard Aunt Bea's quiet intake of breath. Was his mother intimating Nora was marrying Julius for his money? Her family was not nearly as wealthy as Julius, but they were not paupers, either. Many British families had fallen on hard times in the last fifteen or twenty years, but the Parkers were not one of them. She would know, as she'd overseen their three homes for eight years.

Remember, you are not truly marrying him.

The reminder should've calmed her, yet she still bristled. She suspected her feelings for Julius could no longer be categorized as friendly or businesslike. Which was terrifying, but did not prevent her from leaping to his defense. "I have no intention of frivolously spending Julius's fortune. And if you are concerned he's about to make a mistake in his choice of bride, perhaps you should take the matter up with him."

"I have. He assures me my concerns are unfounded."

Her tone indicated she still didn't believe it to be true. All this anxiety over an estranged son struck Nora as odd. Was his mother concerned about Julius's happiness or her own financial security? It did not take a genius to deduce that, if he lost his money, then the property in Albany might need to be sold.

She opened her mouth—and Julius suddenly appeared at her elbow, his hand extended. "Lady Nora, a word, if you please." His tone brooked no argument, a stern gaze fixed on his mother.

Smothering a frustrated sigh, she allowed Julius to lead her out into the hall.

TAMPING DOWN HIS anger, Julius held tightly to Nora's arm and directed them toward the dining room a short distance away.

A few footmen were there, cleaning up dinner. "Give us a moment," Julius told them. "I need the room."

The footmen disappeared, the door closing with a soft click. "I suppose it was your turn to rescue me," she said in an attempt at levity. He did not laugh, not feeling particularly amused at the moment. He'd taken one look at her face in the drawing room and known something had been said, something that had upset her. Hadn't taken a genius to assume his mother or sister had been involved. "Tell me what happened in there."

Nora rubbed her forehead, her shoulders slumping. He had the sudden urge to comfort her, to wrap her in his embrace and hold her tight to his chest. He fought the impulse and forced himself to stand still.

"I really tried, Julius. I was prepared to like her, to win her over. Yet I failed. Miserably, I'm afraid."

"Hardly your fault. She is impossible. Still, I would like to know what she said to upset you."

"I do not wish to add to the rift between the two of you. Please, let it alone."

"Absolutely not. You cannot make the rift worse, Nora. She has disapproved of me ever since I pursued a career in finance years ago. And regardless, I'll not allow her to distress you."

"What career path did she hope for you instead?"

"A factory job or something on a farm. A career with less risk, as she called it."

Nora nodded as if this made sense, her dark hair nearly bronze in the torchlight streaming through the terrace doors. She was lovely, this English rebel. That sniveling coward back in London hardly deserved her. If she were truly Julius's woman, he would never hide her or sneak around. He'd marry her and keep her in his bed as long as possible.

The idea of Nora in his bed caused a slow heat to wind its way through his blood. Unable to help himself, he shifted closer and reached for her hand again. He laced her delicate fingers with his and held on. "Now, tell me what was said."

Her mouth flattened, eyes losing some of their shimmer, and it hit him. His mother hadn't insulted *him*. She'd insulted *Nora*.

Every muscle clenched, anger filling his every pore, every crevice, up to the roots of his hair. His free hand cupped her jaw and gently forced her to face him. "Tell me," he said carefully. "Please."

She bit her lip, drawing his attention to her mouth for a brief second. The strong urge to kiss her resurfaced, threatening to distract him, until he found her eyes. He didn't like the distress reflected there. "It's not so unbelievable, all things considered. She is worried I'm marrying you for your money. That I'll spend you into the poorhouse."

He couldn't help it—he threw his head back and laughed. She tried to squirm away and his grip tightened. "Nora, you couldn't possibly spend me into the poorhouse. Not if I married six of you."

"You're not even marrying one of me," she snapped, pulling free and taking a few steps to the side. "In case you've forgotten, this is not a real engagement."

The amusement instantly died and a twinge of disappointment erupted under his sternum. He hardly recognized the feeling and, even worse, didn't care for it. Not when he should've known better. "Indeed. How could that have slipped my mind?"

Rubbing her arms as if she were cold, Nora drew in a deep breath. "I have no idea."

Her frosty tone stung. Even if they were not friends, they were *friendly*. He liked Nora. Enjoyed spending time with her. She challenged him like no other woman he'd met. He never had to impress her or pretend to be someone else. If not for finding his father's investors in society, he'd be showing Nora every saloon, dance hall, and beer garden in New York City. God knew she wouldn't shy away from it.

He studied the tips of his black leather shoes. He needed to keep his head on straight, not become tangled up in his increasingly complicated thoughts and feelings over this woman. She was having no trouble remembering where things stood, obviously, so why was he?

Clearing his throat, he tried to understand her reaction. "Why do you care if my mother believes you an opportunist out for my money?"

"I wish I knew." She lifted her arm and let it fall against her side. "It shouldn't bother me, of course. We are not truly marrying and therefore her fears are unfounded on multiple levels. Yet I cannot stomach it. Does she assume any woman marrying you to be a money-grubbing opportunist, or merely me?"

He liked witnessing her outrage on his behalf. No one had ever spoken up for him before, not since his older sister, Clarissa, left for Chicago. He grinned. "Feeling the need to defend me, fair maiden?"

Instead of laughing, she nodded gravely, her expression serious. "Yes, I rather do, actually. You're intelligent and kind, thoughtful and respectful. You earn an extraordinary living using gifts you've honed over the years, and you are certainly no hunchback ringing a tower bell. Why is she not bursting with pride?"

Julius rocked back on his heels. He'd never had anyone describe him in such a way before, and that it was this woman, the fake fiancée he'd met just weeks ago, stunned him. A desperate longing welled up in his chest, one he resolutely beat back. He could not entertain such foolish tenderness for Nora.

He swallowed hard. "Do not take it personally. She fears I'm too much like my father, obsessed with money and status to the detriment of all else. I have tried to tell her she's mistaken, that I am different from him, but she refuses to believe me. And thank you."

She lifted a shoulder and gripped the smooth

wooden edge of the table with her hands. "You are welcome. I would gladly defend any of my friends."

Friends. There was that word again. He was coming to hate it. "And I know better than to subject friends to my mother alone, so I apologize. I should have joined you the second she sat down. Come, we'll return."

"Fine, but you need not intervene. I'll manage."

He offered her his arm and began to lead her toward the front of the house. "Is that so? How will you manage, exactly?"

"I'll let her say whatever she wants about you and smile serenely."

"I am doubtful there is a serene bone in your body, Lady Nora."

She laughed, her shoulders shaking and bumping into his. "You would be right. But I am able to fake it on occasion."

"Well, I still plan on sitting in whether you need me or not."

A very harried Brandywine appeared, clearly rattled. Julius stopped in his tracks. "Sir, a word," the butler said.

"Out with it," Julius said, his body tense. What the hell had happened?

"Sir, the stables are on fire."

Chapter Thirteen

Covered in soot and ash, Julius stood with his hands on his hips and surveyed the damage to the two-story, twelve-horse stable. It had taken three city fire brigades, four hours, and over forty men to battle the blaze, but the fire had finally been put out mere moments ago. All things considered, it could have been much worse.

Fire had been the fear of every city dweller since the creation of cities. One spark could bring down an entire neighborhood. In fact, damn near the whole city of Chicago had burned a few decades before. So Julius considered himself lucky the fire had been contained to the stables, thanks to the quick response of his grooms and footmen when the flames erupted.

It was now the middle of the night, the dinner party long having broken up. Nora and her aunt had returned home, his family sent to bed, while Cortland had stayed to assist with battling the blaze. Nora's uncle had carried buckets, held hoses, moved horses, and done anything and everything to lend a hand. Julius walked over to where he stood with the horses and clapped him on the shoulder. "Thank you, Cortland. Appreciate your help tonight."

"Of course. You were fortunate. The worst of the damage is there in the back and you can rebuild it."

The battalion chief approached and pushed his cap farther up on his head. "Mr. Hatcher, I think we've discovered the source of the fire, if you'd like to see."

Julius and Cortland trailed the chief into the damp and dirty interior. They picked through the rubble until they reached the rear stall. The remnants of a blackened metal bucket sat on the ground, the area around it not as burned as the ceiling above. "I'd say someone packed that bucket with rags and kerosene, something flammable, and lit it on fire. The grooms sleeping directly above here said they first saw smoke coming up through the floor."

Someone had set fire to his stables?

"You are saying this was deliberate?" he asked the battalion chief.

"Yes, sir. Without question. Based on the burn pattern around the bucket and the smoke, someone tried to burn your stables down."

"God almighty," Cortland exclaimed. "Arson?"

"Yes, sir," the battalion chief repeated.

Julius rubbed his jaw. He would need to interview the grooms. Had anyone seen anything suspicious? Doubtful one of his current staff had set fire to the surroundings, but could it have been a disgruntled former staff member? He wasn't aware of anyone being fired recently, so he'd need to speak to Brandywine.

"If that's all, Mr. Hatcher, I'd like to let my men go on home."

"Of course," he told the battalion chief, and the three of them returned outside. "Please, pass on my heartfelt thanks to all of them."

The battalion chief dipped his chin and touched the brim of his cap. "I will, sir. Good night."

Julius and Cortland stood staring at the burned-out shell that remained of the stables. No horses had been lost, thank goodness, but plenty of damage had been caused all the same.

"Any idea who may be responsible?" Cortland asked.

"None. Hard to believe anyone would want to cause this much damage." He glanced over his shoulder to locate Brandywine and instead saw his valet directing the footmen back inside the house. "Weaver!"

The valet's head snapped up and he nodded at Julius. After one last instruction to a footman, he made his way over to where Julius stood with Cortland. "How may I be of assistance, sir?"

"Weaver, you always know the gossip in the house."

The edges of Weaver's mouth curled up. "Thank you, sir."

"Any disgruntled members of the staff? Anyone fired recently? Is there any obvious person who would want to harm me or someone on the estate?"

"No, indeed not. Brandywine would know more, of course, but the only staff let go in recent memory was a footman found to be romancing too many of the housemaids. From all accounts, he left for Pittsburgh shortly after. I have heard of no grumblings or fiendish plots to set fire to the buildings here."

"Thank you, Weaver. Please keep this to yourself. I would prefer the staff not learn that the fire was set deliberately."

"Of course, sir." Weaver bowed and started to turn, then caught himself. "Perhaps I should mention a small detail from earlier today, if you wish, sir."

"I wish, I wish," Julius drawled and motioned with his hand for Weaver to continue.

"A lamp was found missing from your sister's bedchamber. She rang for a replacement and the original could not be located anywhere."

"A lamp?" A lamp would be flammable enough to start a fire, especially if placed in a bucket with oily rags. Had his sister started the blaze in the stables? The idea was ludicrous. Agatha had never been fond of Julius but she'd never wanted to harm him or his property before.

"Yes, sir. Was there anything else?"

"No, thank you, Weaver." He waved the valet away absently, his mind turning over the significance of a missing lamp, if any.

"Would your sister be capable of something so terrible?" Cortland asked.

"I cannot imagine Agatha responsible for this. She and I are not close, but she hasn't been destructive in the past."

"I sense that she does not approve of the way you live your life, the money and material things. Perhaps this is an attempt at forcing you to mend your ways?"

"Ha. She knows there's absolutely no chance that will happen."

Cortland slipped his hands in his trousers. "Hatcher, this makes me quite nervous. My niece will soon be living here and I would hate to think of her being hurt on your property. Whomever is responsible for this needs to be found and turned over to the authorities—quickly."

Julius could not agree more regarding the culprit, but the comment rankled. "I have no intention of allowing any harm to befall your niece. The person who set tonight's fire will be caught and dealt with as soon as possible."

"Even if that person is related to you?"

"Yes," he snapped, though he knew Agatha could not have done this. Whoever started this fire had done so with foresight and planning. The Agatha he remembered had been too hot-tempered, too reactionary to mastermind something of this nature. And his sister loved horses.

"Good," Cortland said. "I know you care deeply for my niece but she is my responsibility, after all. At least until the two of you recite your vows."

Which will be approximately never. And if Cortland only knew of the salacious plans Julius had for his niece . . . he'd likely punch Julius square in the face.

Not that it would deter Julius in the least. He had resolved himself tonight in the turret. Lady Nora would be his.

"And as long as my ring is on her finger, she is my responsibility as well," he heard himself say. "A responsibility I take quite seriously."

"I am pleased to hear it." They stood in silence for a few minutes, the smoke from the stables disappearing into the cold night air.

"Sir."

Julius spun to find Brandywine a few feet away standing stiffer than usual. Oh, Christ. What now? "Yes, Brandywine?"

"Your office, sir. You should come straightaway."

Hearing this, Julius broke into a run, not waiting for his butler or anyone else, cold panic working its way down his spine. What else could go wrong this evening? His shoes slapped on the marble floor inside and soon he skidded to a stop at the entrance to his office.

The room was chaos.

Overturned furniture. Paintings ripped from the walls. Rugs tossed aside. All his equipment broken and shoved out of the way. Papers everywhere.

Fucking hell.

"I do apologize, sir," Brandywine said behind him. "The staff were all outside and no one noticed what was happening here."

Julius put his hands on his hips. He blew out an angry breath and tried to bring himself under control. Hard when all he wanted to do right now was find the person responsible and pummel him. It was more than the inconvenience of the destruction; someone pawing through his private things felt like a violation.

What had they been looking for?

"This is not your fault, Brandywine," he said through clenched teeth as he righted the broken ticker tape machine. He'd need to have a new one delivered first thing tomorrow. "Nor the staff. The fire was, rightfully so, your first priority."

"Even still, I do not care for thieves and miscreants running about the house. I will speak to the staff in the morning to learn if anyone saw anything out of the ordinary."

Out of the ordinary? Everything during the fire had been out of the ordinary. Julius paused in the midst of collecting ledgers. "Of course," he murmured. The fire had been a way to distract from the real purpose: searching Julius's office for the valuable stock. With everyone outside battling the flames, the intruder would have had ample time to look for the fictional shares.

The realization actually lifted his spirits quite a bit. This meant at least one of his father's investment partners could still be alive—and still greedy.

"In the meantime," Brandywine was saying, "I shall rouse a few maids to come down and—"

"No, that's not necessary. Martin and I can put this all to rights in the morning. There's no need to drag anyone from their bed."

"Are you certain, sir? I would feel better knowing you were not terribly inconvenienced by this."

Suddenly the inconvenience of the mess did not bother Julius. He held up his hand. "I appreciate the concern. But let's all get to bed and handle this in the morning."

THE NEXT MORNING Julius knocked on his mother's door. He straightened his vest while he waited for her to answer. The maid assigned to look after his mother—much to his mother's chagrin—had just informed him that she was awake and dressed. He'd hurried here, eager to set her straight regarding the way she'd treated Nora last night.

Fury still boiled his blood when he remembered the look on Nora's face when his mother had accused her of marrying Julius for his money. Even from across the room, Nora's horror, hurt, and indignation had been quite clear. His mother had no right to disrespect Julius's fiancée, especially in his home.

The door quickly opened and his mother appeared. She couldn't hide her surprise. "Julius. What do you want?"

"To speak with you about your behavior last night." He slipped past her and into the room. A black traveling case rested on the floor, the room neat as a pin. "What's this?"

"I'm leaving for Albany this morning." She folded her hands at her waist.

"Because of the fire?"

"No, because there is no reason to stay."

Yes, now that you've once again decided my choices are unacceptable. Business, home, wife . . . you never fail to find me lacking.

She smoothed the severe black skirts she wore. "We are no strangers to fire, Julius. I should think you would be more concerned with my reaction to your fiancée."

He crossed his arms over his chest. "That is what I came to speak with you about. I'm very unhappy with how you treated Nora last night. You were insufferably rude, Mother."

"I didn't deliberately set out to upset her, but someone had to say something. English aristocracy . . . The notion of it is laughable. Especially considering our family's humble background."

"Nevertheless, I have chosen to marry her."

"And I hope you'll reconsider. A woman like that will cause you nothing but grief."

"How are you so certain?"

Before she could answer, the hall door opened. "Mother, we must—" His sister stopped suddenly, her gaze landing on Julius. "Oh. Hello, Julius."

"I hear you're leaving," he said without preamble.

"Indeed."

"Agatha, Julius was just asking me what we thought of his fiancée." The two women exchanged a look.

"Well, honestly, Julius," his sister said, now giving him her attention. "She's clearly not respectful or demure. That one's got a sharp tongue, and if you think she'll be biddable once you wed her, you are fooling yourself. Is that what you want, dancing to her tune all your life?"

"I would not mind it one bit," he shot back—and realized he meant it. "I happen to like her sharp tongue and a biddable woman would bore me to tears. She's witty and clever, and the bravest woman I've ever met. A shame you two didn't spend more time with her to see this for yourself, but I consider it your loss."

If he ever changed his mind and decided to marry, a woman exactly like Nora would suit him perfectly. She would constantly challenge and surprise him, not to mention she was intelligent enough to be a true partner. And based on the kisses they'd exchanged, he knew the two of them would be more than compatible in the bedroom.

His mother made a sound in the back of her throat, one Julius recognized from his childhood and that never failed to set his teeth on edge. "Though she denied any interest in your money," she said, "I saw what she wore last night. A gown like that probably cost thousands of dollars. Mark my words, she'll expect you to keep her in the lifestyle to which she's become accustomed."

"I can afford a hundred of those gowns and more, Mother. You had no right to ask her whether she's interested in my money."

"I do have a right to know," she said primly. "I am your mother, after all. I must look out for your best interest, even if I must save you from yourself."

"I require no saving, madam. Those matters are private between my fiancée and me. Furthermore, you haven't looked out for my interests since I was fourteen. Where is all this familial concern coming from?"

"Because we care about you," his sister said.

He shot both of them a disbelieving look. "You cannot chide me for the wealth I've acquired and then worry it'll be stripped away in the same breath. None of this makes sense."

His mother crossed her arms. "When she spends you into the poorhouse, you'll see. She shall turn you into a man you hardly recognize, trying to set it right."

"I'm not my father—and do not speak of Nora in such a disparaging manner again. If you disapprove of the match, then do not attend the wedding. God knows, I'll not shed a tear."

His mother gasped, her lips tightening. "That is a terrible thing to say to your mother and sister. I did not raise you to be so impertinent."

"No, you raised me to believe I'll never gain your approval no matter what I do. The difference is I no longer care about it."

He strode to the door and put a hand on the latch. "Oh, and if either of you disrespects Nora to her face ever again, you'll never see another nickel from me. I wish you a safe journey home."

After a slight bow, he walked out and never looked back.

IT WAS DONE.

Nora had agonized over the words for three full days. Through a torrent of tears and a haze of guilt she'd finally finished a letter to Robert, one that expressed her heartfelt sorrow over experiencing feelings for another man. She apologized for not telling him sooner and begged his forgiveness over the shabby treatment. Even though she and Julius would never marry, she didn't see the need to inform Robert of that fact. To have offered him hope would be beyond cruel.

Instead, she told him not to wait on her. To live his life and find a woman who truly loved him back, without reservation. That was what he deserved.

She cried all afternoon after posting the letter. Heartbreak came in many different forms, and despite this being her fault she still felt the keen sting of the loss. Robert had been her first love, her first lover, the first keeper of her heart. She'd never planned to leave him but circumstances had intervened.

Life is offering you a push.

Of course Julius would see it that way. He had no loyalties to anyone save himself. At least what her aunt had said—that she'd learned the difference between infatuation and love when she met Uncle James—made some sense to Nora. What she felt for Julius was more confusing, more intense than anything she'd ever experienced before.

Not that Julius returned the sentiment.

He wanted to seduce her, not marry her. Nora hadn't yet sorted through her thoughts on that, which was why she'd remained a hermit for several days. Better to hide until she'd arrived at some conclusion regarding her future, her fake fiancé, and this new version of herself. No doubt her aunt and uncle thought something terribly wrong, but venturing into society with a smile on her face, when she was actually terribly confused, was beyond her at the moment.

She'd received no word from Julius in that time, which had been fine with her. However, that silence had just ended today. His note had been brief:

> *Take a hack to 10–12 Broad Street. I'll meet you at there at 2:00 sharp. Wear black.*

> Yours,
> *Julius*

She had no idea what he planned and admittedly her curiosity was piqued. Such a mystery was likely the only thing that could've coaxed her out of the house, almost as if her fiancé had planned it.

She wasted no time readying herself and slipping out of her uncle's house under the pretense of a shopping trip. Now, as the hack pulled up to the requested corner, she saw she was across from the New York Stock Exchange. The Italian Renaissance-style building loomed large on the block. Why on earth was Julius bringing her here? Everyone knew women were not allowed inside the exchange.

"Here you are, miss." The driver opened her door and tipped his cap.

She descended and then handed him the fare. "Thank you."

"Sure this is where you're supposed to be?" he asked, indicating the all-male crowds hurrying about.

"Yes, I think so. I'll be fine."

Fascinated, she stepped closer to the men yelling and arguing on the walk. Some were even trading near the front of the building, shouting and waving slips of paper in the air. How could anyone follow this chaos?

Out of the corner of her eye, she saw the profile of a dark-haired figure through the crowd gathered by the stairs. The way he was standing, the worn brown bowler on his head, suddenly reminded her of Robert. She inhaled sharply and craned her neck, trying to see around the streaming bodies for a better look at his face, but there were too many people.

"Hello, my lady," a deep, familiar voice said in her ear.

She spun to find Julius. Before she could say anything, he clasped her hand and began tugging her toward the building. "Wait, where are we going?"

"Patience, my dear woman," was all he said as they approached a door near the end of the façade.

She rose up, walking on her toes to check the spot near the stairs where the man had been standing. No one was there. *It couldn't have been Robert. England is an expensive three week sail away. Robert certainly can't afford the passage.* Her brain must've been playing tricks on her.

After descending a short set of stairs, Julius knocked twice on the door and it swung open. Glancing up and down the street, he held the heavy metal door for her. "Quickly, now."

She slipped inside. An older man stood there, a worried look on his weathered face. "Ma'am."

"Appreciate this favor, Joe." Julius slipped a few coins into the man's hands. "Forget you ever saw us."

"No problem, Mr. Hatcher. No one'd believe me, no how." Shaking his head, the man jerked a thumb at the corridor. "You'd best hurry. Won't be able to keep those stairs closed forever."

"We will. Thanks again."

As they moved quickly down the hall, Nora could hear the old man muttering about "fool kid" and "pretty fiancée." Just what was this about? Was this some sort of sordid adventure in the middle of the day? "Where—"

He turned and put his finger to his lips. "No talking until I tell you."

She nodded and then allowed him to tug her up two flights of stairs. Were they inside the exchange? That would explain the secrecy. The possibility of seeing this male bastion in person had her heart racing.

When they reached the top, he cracked another door and peered around it. He nodded once and then hustled her along another corridor, through a third door and into a large room. Empty chairs faced a curtained window, with a desk and telephone on the rear wall. She lifted up her hands as if to say, *Now what?*

He turned the lock and then drew the shade down over the door, completely shielding them from prying eyes. "It's safe to talk."

She wasted no time. "Where are we and what are we doing here?"

A sly smile broke free on his handsome face. "To explain that I'll need to switch off the lights."

"What?"

He closed the distance between them and took her face in his hands. His palms were rough yet gentle, and the touch vibrated through her entire body. "Do you trust me?"

Her mouth went dry at the tenderness in his eyes, so much sincerity reflected there that her stomach fluttered. Lying never occurred to her. "Yes," she breathed.

"Good girl." Taking her arm, he helped her to sit in one of the chairs. "Are you comfortable?"

"As comfortable as one can be in a situation such as this. Get on with it, Julius."

Smirking, he strode to the switch on the wall and turned it. Blackness engulfed the room. She couldn't see anything at all. A few seconds passed and then she heard his shoes on the carpet. "Here we go."

The curtains parted and bright light stung her eyes, causing her to squint. Blinking, she opened them again and discovered the interior of the exchange before her. *The trading floor* . . . Hordes of men pushed and shoved, screamed and cajoled, bits of paper flying everywhere. Her jaw fell open. It was like a circus, with so much to see every way she looked. The sight was nothing short of amazing.

Julius lowered himself into the chair next to her. "What do you think?"

"I . . . I cannot believe it. How is this possible? Won't they see us?"

He stretched out his legs and crossed them at the ankles. "This is my permanent room in the exchange. No one will come in unless I allow it. And as long as we keep the lights off, the outside light prevents anyone from being able to see inside here."

"This is incredible." She fixed her gaze on the small figures darting to and fro, caught up in the frenetic energy and pace of the trading day. What must it be like down there? "I know absolutely nothing about what is happening on the floor, but it's fascinating."

"The exchange is basically a continuous auction, with those looking to buy and those looking to sell. Those men jostling around the posts down there are trading for investors not inside the building."

"You make it sound so easy."

He chuckled. "It is, if you know what you're doing."

"My goodness. It's absolute Bedlam. Have you ever been on the floor?"

"Yes." The one-word answer caught her attention, a strange tension resonating in his voice. He shifted in his chair and did not meet her gaze.

"You hated it." It was perfectly obvious from the tense lines on his face. "Why?"

"I don't care for crowds." He gestured to the melee below them. "Can you imagine having to fight in that every day?"

She recalled the Haymarket, how rattled he had been when they escaped the brawl. His distaste for crowds must have played a part in the extreme reaction. "Why don't you care for crowds?"

A muscle jumped in his jaw, his strong profile rigid and unforgiving. She did not think he'd answer, he kept quiet so long, but he finally spoke. "I was thirteen during the Panic of '73. I saw buildings destroyed, men stabbed in the street. Mobs taking it upon themselves to steal what they wanted with no regard for common decency or the laws. Police would arrive with brickbats and horses, trampling and whipping through the crowds. Even peaceful demonstrations turned bloody."

"That's when your father lost his money."

"Yes, but the riots went on for years. No one could find jobs, and food was scarce."

"It must have been terrible." Especially for a young boy who'd just lost his father. "Were you or your family ever in danger from the mobs?" He flinched and she knew she'd guessed it. "What happened?"

He cleared his throat. "There was a demonstration one morning at the exchange. I was fourteen, working as a pad shover, running between the offices and the traders on the floor. My closest friend was Andrew, another messenger like me. At sixteen, he'd been somewhat of a mentor, showing me how things worked when I was first hired. We were inseparable. I even spent holidays with his family, since my own was a nightmare of grief and unhappiness at the time." He rubbed his jaw, eyes unfocused as he stared down at the trading floor. "Anyway, this demonstration was just a bunch of workers who couldn't find jobs, protesting the fat cats of Wall Street. It would've remained peaceful if the police hadn't shown up."

Foreboding settled in Nora's chest. She touched his arm. "Julius, you don't have to—"

"No, you asked so I'll tell you. They came on horseback, the police. Swinging clubs and ordering the men to disperse. Andrew and I tried to push through but the crowds were too deep and we were swept along with the demonstrators. He kept telling me to head toward the exchange but . . . I was scared of the horses. It sounds so ridiculous now, but then . . ."

"You were a boy," she said softly. "It's not ridiculous at all."

He folded his arms across his chest and lifted a shoulder. "I suppose, but if I hadn't been so scared we both could've escaped. Instead, I froze, standing in the street, unable to move, and Andrew had to come after me. I saw him trampled to death not even three feet from my face. Crushed under a stampede of hooves and boot heels."

"Oh, Julius. I'm so sorry."

"Somehow I started moving, probably terrified I'd suffer the same fate if I didn't do something. So I darted and ran to a small cellarway and hid. Like a coward."

"Surviving by any means necessary is not cowardly." She touched his arm. "You were caught in an impossible situation as a small child. What else could you possibly have done?"

The darkness in his expression didn't change and she knew this tragedy had shaped much of the man he was today. He carried the guilt and shame, as well as the fear, deep in his soul. "That's why you built that huge house away from the more crowded portion of Fifth Avenue, as a way to protect yourself."

"Don't be ridiculous," he snapped. "I saw a castle just like it during a visit to France and had the money to build one here."

Maybe not, but there was some truth to his choice in a home. An impenetrable stronghold to keep him apart from the chaos of the city. A refuge. A strange ache settled behind her heart, and she steeled herself against the rush of emotion. The glimpse of vulnerability in his expression could have her falling in love with him . . . and that would never do.

Would never do at all.

Chapter Fourteen

To Julius, the inside of the exchange resembled a church, with its gothic arches, smooth
stone, and high windows. Fitting, as this was as
close to a place of worship as he ever got. He didn't
believe in a god—but he did believe in a fair and
free market.

Trading posts capped with signs were erected
at various points on the floor for the high-demand
stocks, allowing them to be located and traded easily. The most popular spot this afternoon seemed to
be oil, probably due to yesterday's rumors of an anti-
trust act coming this summer. Julius had heard this
news six weeks ago, which was when he sold his oil
stock for an unbelievable profit.

Focusing on the floor meant he didn't need to
ruminate on Nora's perceptiveness. He didn't care
for the way she seemed to look right through him,
stripped him to see past the layers he'd created over
the years to protect himself. He'd much rather solve
the puzzle that comprised the fascinating woman

sitting beside him than be picked apart and solved by *her*.

He couldn't believe he'd confessed that story about Andrew. That was a lockbox he hadn't opened in a long time, a painful memory he preferred to keep buried. Yet Nora had asked and he'd promised to never lie to her. She'd been quiet for the last ten minutes and he hoped his revelation hadn't ruined their day.

"Do you have a man down there completing your trades?" She leaned toward the window slightly, not enough to be seen but in a subtle attempt to peer closer at the faces.

He latched on to the topic gratefully. "I have a few, actually. One is over there by the tall post marked 'silver.' Another is over by coal." There were others from his chosen investment firm as well. His trades were executed with marked efficiency, a perk of being the top client.

"How can you possibly see them in that crush of bodies?"

"I knew where to start, based on what I wanted them to watch today. We've been keeping a close eye on both silver and coal this week."

She continued to study the proceedings, her brow wrinkled in concentration. She appeared to be enjoying herself on this adventure, thank God. "I'm trying to imagine how much money is being earned and lost out there today."

He checked the board. Fairly moderate day thus far. "No big drops or gains today. Everything seems to be holding steady."

"Even still, the buying and selling . . . There's so much at risk."

"Not really." He shrugged. "Stocks are meant to be an investment. If you think only in the short term you're bound to lose money."

"I suppose. It's all fairly confusing to me."

Angling closer to her side, he gestured to the trading floor. "So if you had to buy one stock right now, one business or commodity you thought would rise in price, which one would it be?"

"I don't know. It's hard to say what I might do if I were participating."

"So let's take away the hypothetical. I'll give you the money to buy one hundred shares of any one stock right now."

"Julius, that's foolish. I'm not well informed enough to do that."

"Nonsense. You are intelligent. Make your choice."

She narrowed her eyes on him. "Why?"

Because I like to see you happy. Because I am grateful you came this afternoon. Because you're so beautiful my teeth ache with wanting you.

He lifted a shoulder. "Why not? It'll keep the day interesting. Besides, what's the fun in coming to the exchange and not seeing your trade completed on the floor?"

He could tell by the way she stared at the chaos below them, her bottom lip disappearing between her teeth, that she was considering it. "Come now, Nora. What do you have to lose?"

"Your money."

"I can well afford it. Go on. Give us a stock."

She took her time, watching and thinking. He appreciated that. Habitually impetuous, she was the type to rush into decisions, such as seeking him out at Sherry's that first night. But she considered this one for several long minutes. "Consolidated Gas Company."

Without asking for an explanation, he stood and went to the phone on the desk. He put in a call directly to the firm's contact on the trading floor. A voice answered and Julius gave the order, then placed the receiver back in the cradle. "See him there"—he pointed the man out to Nora as he retook his seat—"the tall one hurrying with that piece of paper?"

They watched as the messenger delivered the paper to one of Julius's men on the floor. The man read the note and then ran through the fluttering paper and bodies toward the area where gas and electric were traded. Pushing into the circle, he fought to get the auctioneer's attention. It didn't take long, probably because everyone knew this was one of Julius's traders and they wished to hear what he was buying. The auctioneer nodded and wrote down the order.

"There you go. One hundred shares of Consolidated Gas are yours."

"That is it? We're done?"

"Yes, with the purchase." He pointed at the big board on the wall. "Now you only need watch the numbers to see if the value goes up or down."

Activity around the Consolidated post picked up as other traders came over. The investors were obviously wondering why Julius had purchased the flat utility stock and ordering their traders to do the same. He nearly smiled. The more purchases made, the less supply in the market and Nora's one hundred shares would quickly become more valuable.

She glanced over at him. "Are you not curious why I picked that stock?"

"I've learned not to ask questions where you are involved," he teased, lifting his arms and linking his hands behind his head.

She elbowed his side playfully. "There's no need to be rude." She was genuinely grinning, happier than he'd seen her in a long time. She seemed relaxed, less . . . conflicted. What had changed? Dared he hope that she had resigned herself to his seduction?

"I'll tell you anyway. Lent is approaching," she said. "If New Yorkers are anything like the British, then people will remain indoors more often. Less gadding about the city and visiting."

That was a damned fine observation. He frowned and wondered if he'd ever noted as much in any of his projections for the spring.

She let out a mock gasp, her hand on her heart. "Have I impressed the great Julius Hatcher, king of Wall Street?"

"Actually, you have." He searched her face, so lovely even in the near dark. "And I'm hardly the king. More like a highwayman, out to steal what I can from under their uninformed noses."

"Why did you bring me here this afternoon?"

The sudden question caught him off guard. Their eyes caught and held, and Julius found himself unable to look away. The room was quiet, protected from the roar of the trading floor below them, and a rush of desire swept through him. A fierce longing that was never far each time he saw her. "Because you crave excitement and scandal, and I realized this would solve both requirements while keeping you safe."

He hadn't planned to seduce her today but couldn't keep from touching her. It had been days since he'd seen her and he felt greedy for her. Inching forward, he invaded her space until the scent of lavender filled his head, and he reached to drag his knuckles along the soft skin of her jaw. "Because you, my lady, deserve to be the only woman who's ever been inside the exchange."

A tremor went through her body at his gentle touch but she did not pull away. "The way you say those two words, *my lady*. It's quite seductive." Her voice was thin, her breath coming noticeably faster.

"Good. Then you've not misinterpreted my intent."

Her lips parted on a gasp. With the pad of his thumb, he traced the plump, smooth flesh surrounding her mouth. The need to kiss her tore through him, a powerful urge to taste her, to drink in every moan and whimper. There were a great many things he yearned for at the moment, but mostly he longed to drive her wild.

"You mean to seduce me," she said, her lips brushing his thumb.

"Yes, I do—and you should know by now that I'm a man of action, not flowery words. I'd rather show you what I intend."

"Here?" Her brows shot up. "You must be joking."

"I am entirely serious. There are many ways to bring you pleasure, as you are undoubtedly aware."

Her face showed no signs of recognition and he nearly frowned. Had she no idea of what brought about her pleasure? He'd been certain she was no longer innocent. Perhaps Robert hadn't satisfied her, a prospect that both enraged him on her behalf and thrilled him down to his selfish bones.

The realization urged him on, past whatever scant reservations his common sense clung to. Seducing her was reckless and risky, a foolhardy plan that ended terribly any way he considered it. Yet, his palms moved to cradle her jaw. "Shall I kiss you?"

"I thought you were a man of action, not words," she shot back, her eyes glittering, and he found himself smiling just before he rocked forward to seal his mouth to hers.

His fingers slid into her hair as he kissed her, hard. She met him eagerly, desperately, soon opening her mouth and finding his tongue with her own. At that first slick touch of her tongue to his, a growl erupted in his throat. His cock appreciated her boldness, his shaft filling, lengthening in his trousers.

The kiss grew frantic as it wore on, air in shorter and shorter supply. Her nails dug into his shoulders, hands nearly clawing at his coat to get closer. God, this woman. She unraveled him, took his noble intentions and shredded them. He could not wait to strip her bare and lay her down on a bed. Sink inside her slowly until he was buried to the hilt.

Panting, he broke off from her mouth and trailed

his tongue down the column of her throat, nipping and kissing along the way. Her day dress covered her up to her collarbone and he'd never cursed an article of clothing more. Her breasts were some-where underneath all those damn layers and he dreamed of dragging his tongue over her hard nipples, drawing the taut buds in his mouth . . .

His erection now impossibly uncomfortable, he slid out of his seat and dropped to his knees in front of her, wedging between her thighs. With one hand, he cupped the back of her neck and brought her toward him for another kiss. His other hand dove under the hem of her skirts until he found her stocking-covered calf. He learned the shape of her, mapped the sturdiness of her knee, and explored the firm, smooth planes of her inner thighs. Heat met his fingers as he parted her drawers, the back of his hand brushing the soft curls covering her mound.

She inhaled sharply as he stroked the outer lips of her sex with his thumb, teasing. "Julius," she breathed against his mouth.

"Yes, my lady?" He dipped inside her entrance and slickness coated his thumb. She was so deliciously wet that his mouth actually watered.

Her chest heaved, gusts of air falling from her mouth. "Do not stop."

Had sweeter words ever been spoken?

"I do not plan on it."

He pressed his thumb against her clitoris and she jumped. "Shh," he said, kissing her lips. "You'll enjoy this, I promise."

She crushed her mouth to his and he returned the kiss, using all the skill at his disposal to intensify her lust. Swept tiny circles over that swollen nub at the apex of her core. Deep, hungry licks in her mouth. His free hand cupped her breast through her clothing and undergarments. Soon, she was writhing, her hips canting, chasing the pleasure as he maintained a steady, maddening pace.

She threw her head back, eyes closed in surrender. "God, Julius . . ."

He could not wait any longer to taste her. Flicking her skirts to her waist, he sat back on his heels and pulled her hips forward in the chair. She was pink and glistening, so ripe, and lust raced through his blood, his cock throbbing for relief. Leaning in, he touched his tongue to her center, the sharp taste of her filling his mouth. His eyes nearly rolled back. *Yes, dear God. This, right here.*

"What are you doing?" Brows pinched, she stared at him in disbelief.

Oh, Robert. You fucking fool.

"Do you trust me?"

"Yes," she rasped without hesitation.

"Then close your eyes and allow me to continue." Without waiting, he dragged the flat of his tongue through her folds until he reached her clitoris. He circled, sucked, swirled the bud with his mouth and tongue, listening to the sounds she made to discover what she liked best. When he found the precise pressure and speed that caused her thighs to tremble, he kept at it, relishing the way her fingers threaded his hair to hold him in place. He slid a finger inside her, the walls so tight and hot. Then he added a second finger, pumping a few times with his hand, and her muscles clenched.

She cried out, the pleasure cresting, and her limbs shook. He could feel the pulses inside her body, the tissues clamping down on his fingers. His cock screamed for friction, for release, yet he resisted. He did not want to push her too far and his own orgasm could wait.

When she shivered, the flesh too sensitive, he pulled away, withdrawing his fingers and planting one last kiss on the inside of her thigh. He sat on his heels, hardly able to focus through the haze of lust clouding his brain, and tried to collect himself. His chest heaved as if he'd swum the length of the East River.

"That was astounding," she said, her voice filled with awe. "You are either quite clever or very, very wicked."

She was adorably rumpled, a flush tinting her creamy skin. He loved seeing her like this, his debauched English rose. "Can I not be both?"

"I suppose, though it hardly seems fair to all the other men in New York."

"Good thing, then, that I never play fair."

A KNOCK SOUNDED at the door, quickly obliterating any awkwardness following Julius's ministrations. Nora shoved her skirts down over her legs as Julius rose off the floor and smoothed his trousers. "Don't worry," he said. "No one will see you, I promise. I'll tell whoever is there to go away."

She had no idea how he could appear so put together after doing . . . that, yet he did. The only outward clues to what had happened were the large and obvious erection in his clothing and his slightly tousled hair. Nora, on the other hand, felt unmoored. Unhinged. As if he had untethered her from everything she knew to be true.

For certain, she would never look at his mouth in the same manner again. Or his tongue. Who could have guessed such a thing possible?

Shame washed over her, a bone-deep embarrassment that scorched her skin. It had taken less than two days. A mere thirty-eight hours after casting Robert aside for her to lift her skirts for Julius. Heavens, she'd *begged* him not to stop. What in God's name was wrong with her?

She bit her lip and tried to collect her rioting thoughts. Dwelling on her failings would not serve any purpose whatsoever. *Why do you care what society thinks anyway?* As Julius said, no one need learn what happened between them and the world considered them engaged. Soon enough she'd return to London and reassume her role as the doting, obedient daughter of an earl. Didn't she deserve a slice of happiness here in New York while she could manage it?

After one last check to ensure she was properly concealed, Julius spoke to the closed door. "Who is it?"

"Mr. Hatcher, it is Mr. Hutchinson. A word, if you please."

"What is this about?" Julius asked, impatient.

"If you don't mind, I'd prefer to converse face-to-face."

"One minute."

Returning to Nora's side, he helped her to her feet. "Stand against the back wall," he whispered in her ear. "I'll speak with him in the corridor. He won't be able to see you in here, so just stay quiet."

She nodded and crept as carefully as her skirts would allow to the rear of the room. He paused until she was ready, then he cracked the door and slipped into the hallway. "Well, what is it?" she heard him say.

"I find myself in an awkward situation, Hatcher. We've received an anonymous note claiming you snuck a woman into your office here at the exchange."

Nora froze, every cell on high alert. How had someone learned of her presence here? Would Hutchinson demand to search the office? *Here's that scandal you desired, Nora.*

Only, she wasn't certain she desired one any longer. If she revealed herself, there would undoubtedly be repercussions for Julius, perhaps even losing his seat on the exchange. The man lived and breathed for this place. How could she contribute to the loss of the one thing he loved?

Since when has Julius's happiness come to mean more to you than returning to England?

It hadn't, per se, but was there a reason to return to England? She had mucked up her relationship with Robert, who would certainly loathe her once he received her letter, and her father wasn't missing her. He'd sent her away to find an American husband knowing full well that meant residing permanently in America. Not once had he written or cabled, either.

Then there was the little matter of her scandal, which was still quite the topic of discussion in London. Her friend said the latest rumor was that she'd gotten herself with child and her father had sent her away.

Well, half that story is true.

Hutchinson gave a dry, mirthless laugh, regaining her attention. "Now, I realize it seems silly but we do have to investigate these matters. You know the strict rules."

"Are you seriously suggesting I brought a woman here to the exchange? Good God, man, for what purpose? No woman is interested in stock trading."

"True, but as the president of the exchange I must be certain everyone is following the rules. You wouldn't mind letting me see your office, would you?"

Nora held her breath as Julius snapped, "Damn right I mind. I pay over one hundred thousand dollars a year for that office and I'll not be accused on some coward's word. Let him come accuse me to my face. Tell me why he suspects I have a woman in here."

"Be reasonable, Hatcher. It is well within our right to—"

"The hell it is." Julius's voice turned brittle and unforgiving. "I've already given you your answer. If you step one foot into my office, I'll buy this entire building and have it razed to the ground."

"You—you cannot threaten me," Hutchinson stammered. "Or this institution."

"Can't I?" Menace filled those two words followed by an ominous silence. "Tell me, who holds the most influence on Wall Street?"

It took Hutchinson a moment to grind out, "You do, Mr. Hatcher."

"That's right, and one word from me can send panic through investors all across the city—hell, the nation—and you'll see a crisis worse than the depression of '73. Are you ready to lose everything? Because I swear that is what will come to pass unless you walk away and pretend you never doubted my word."

"I apologize," Hutchinson said, his tone much more conciliatory than confrontational. "We'll consider the matter resolved, then."

"Excellent."

"Good afternoon."

Julius bade him good-bye and then a few long seconds passed. Nora dared not move while she waited, blood rushing in her ears, her heart pounding wildly. Finally, he reentered the room, locked the door, and crossed to where she stood. "Did you hear any of that?"

"Yes," she whispered. "What are we to do?"

"Trading closes in"—he glanced over his shoulder to the big clock on the wall—"fifteen minutes. We merely need to wait until the building clears out and we'll leave."

"How long will that be, exactly?"

"An hour. Maybe a bit more." His piercing blue gaze searched her face. "Why did you not announce your presence somehow? Finally get the scandal you've been chasing?"

She shook her head, mute with thoughts too jumbled to explain. Guilt for being intimate with another man so soon after writing to Robert and confusion over these new feelings for a man she barely knew.

Stop, Nora. You know Julius. You know him better than almost anyone in New York.

It was true. She had no idea when it had happened, but there was something about him that had burrowed under her skin and into her heart. And she had changed as well. She was no longer a girl content to live in the shadows in London while following the rules. Now she was a woman who craved independence and excitement, who no longer needed her father's approval or society's permission to be happy.

"Did I shock you before?" he asked, his hand cupping her head behind her ear. "In the chair?"

"I think I shocked myself by allowing it."

Creases lined his brow. "I don't understand."

"How can I be so inconstant, so fickle with my affections? How could I enjoy that as much as I did?"

"Ah. We're back to Robert." Julius sighed, his jaw tight and angry, and she instantly regretted bringing up the reminder of her former beau. "You're not a tart, if that's what you're worried about. Believe me, I've met quite a few in the course of my life and none—not one—had a tenth of your grace or dignity. Your bravery or your heart. You allowed two men who care deeply for you to bring you pleasure. The end."

He made it sound so simple. But one sentence tripped her up. Hope welled inside her chest like a balloon. "You care deeply for me?"

"Of course." His grip tightened on her as he pulled her closer. "Would I risk my seat on the exchange for a woman I didn't care about?"

"I thought this was an attempt to seduce me."

"It is," he said, flashing a grin. "But I'm beginning to think it is more as well. I know you have your Robert, but I cannot stop thinking about you."

The words surprised her, quickly followed by a rush of elation that reached her toes. *He cannot stop thinking about me. He cares about me.* On a day filled with sadness, the revelation buoyed her. It was on the tip of her tongue to admit that she'd broken off with Robert . . . but she withheld it. The wound was too raw, too fresh, and Julius would want to pick apart the decision like one of his stock predictions. Nora was not ready to have to explain herself.

And it wasn't as if Julius wanted *more*. He'd said many times over that he didn't wish for a commitment—and she would eventually return to England. Whatever this was between them would remain temporary.

He was watching her expectantly, waiting for her to answer. He'd been honest, after all, and she owed him some semblance of the same. "Yes, whatever this is, I feel it, too."

Chapter Fifteen

Julius felt his mouth hitch. "Is that so?" His fingers slid along her jaw and then lower, over her throat, her breastbone, and then between her lovely and promising breasts. She drew in a sharp breath.

"You are the devil, Julius Hatcher."

"I prefer persistent." Sounded much better than *desperate*, although that was a more apt description at the moment.

"Try as you like, then, but I'm not certain this is wise."

"If it helps, what happens is between only you and me. No one need learn how our engagement includes other benefits."

"Benefits?"

"What would you call them, then? Because I consider bedding you a definite benefit."

Even in the near darkness he could see her lips twitch with amusement. "I've agreed to nothing as of yet."

"You will. I'd say there is an 85 percent chance of you coming home with me tonight."

"You're insane. We are scheduled to attend a dinner party at the McPhees' tonight."

He coughed into his hand a few times, then reached for her, smashing her chest flat with his. "I fear a nasty cold has overcome me. There's every chance you are infected as well."

She rolled her eyes as a wide grin tugged at her mouth. "And I suppose I'm to sneak over to your home after my aunt and uncle depart for said dinner party?"

"You cannot pretend this is your first—or tenth—assignation under a guardian's nose. I would assume you already knew how best to proceed."

"The point is not whether I am able to come to you, but whether I *should*." She took a few steps away, putting distance between them. He folded his arms over his chest and tried not to reach for her again.

"And here I thought you were a woman who did as she pleased, not what was expected of her."

"That is true, within reason. I am not exactly reckless—" He made a face, and she grimaced. "Fair enough. I have been reckless recently, but I was a bit more circumspect in London when breaking the rules."

"I am offended, my lady. Circumspect happens to be my middle name."

"Please. You don't know the meaning of the word. You live life grandly on every level—your home, your work, your parties, your affairs . . ."

He wasn't even certain what they were arguing

about any longer. Was she not attracted to him? He thought he'd read the cues correctly, like when she'd ordered him not to stop while he'd been pleasuring her. Perhaps today had been an aberration, a brief hedonistic moment where they'd both been caught up in the pleasure and not thinking clearly.

"Nora, I am perfectly capable of keeping quiet about my private life."

"Whatever happens, I would not wish to disgrace my aunt and uncle. They have been most kind to me."

Disgrace her aunt and uncle? This was certainly a change of heart. "Are you not the same woman who dragged me outside at the Billingses' ball to start rumors?"

"That was a long time ago—and there was nothing happening between us at the time."

He tried to put the puzzle pieces together but they wouldn't fit, no matter how he positioned them in his mind. "So when we were merely platonic business partners, the rumor of impropriety was acceptable. Now that impropriety is regularly occurring, we cannot allow anyone to find out? Do you realize how little sense that makes?"

"Nevertheless, it is how I feel. Perhaps we need some rules."

This was more along the lines of what he expected of her. Plans. Battles. Negotiations. He waved his hand. "Fine, let me hear what you think."

"The first rule we've already touched on. Whatever occurs stays just between us."

He didn't even need to contemplate that one. "Agreed. The second rule is complete honesty on both sides. You tell me what you want, what you like, stop me if I do anything you dislike or are uncomfortable with."

"That is acceptable." She paced a few steps. "The next is that we stick to our original agreement. This ends in five weeks."

"And we still help each other in the meantime?"

"Yes, of course," she said in a strange tone of voice. "Why would that change?"

He clenched his jaw. Indeed, why would that change? Precious Robert awaited her in London, the sweet artist who hadn't a damned clue what to do with the female anatomy, apparently. At least Julius would give Nora all the pleasure she could stand for the next five weeks. Let the foolish painter try to live up to *that* when she returned.

Rubbing his eyes, he blew out a long breath. The idea of her cozying up to another man in mere weeks annoyed him. Yet it shouldn't. Had he truly expected her to change her mind after one teeth-rattling orgasm? He had to be grateful that he had her now and that she wasn't pushing for a scandal any longer.

If she were willing to carry around the guilt of an affair behind Robert's back . . . who was Julius to stop her? Yes, he was precisely that selfish. He wanted her and didn't care a fig if her London beau suffered because of it. "All right, what else?"

"I cannot think of anything more. Even still, I haven't made up my mind."

He closed the distance between them and lowered his voice. "What must I do to convince you? I find myself quite determined, my lady."

He watched the slim column of her throat work as she swallowed. "This is madness."

"Life is madness. The world is madness. Yet there is much to savor . . . like the shell of your ear, for example." He skimmed the tender skin with his finger. "And your perfectly shaped earlobe. I think you might enjoy the bite of my teeth right here." Leaning in, he demonstrated by taking the lobe between his lips and biting gently. She gasped and clutched at his arm to steady herself.

The closing gong sounded to signal the end of the trading day, startling them. Nora jerked and pulled away, smoothing the fabric over her stomach. Through the windows, Julius could see as traders began tossing bits of paper to the floor, turning it into a checkered carpet of missed opportunities and failures. Tallies would now be calculated. Monies collected and fortunes won or lost. He checked the Consolidated final call price.

"Dear God." He squinted. Could that be correct?

"What is it?" She came closer and examined the scene below. "What happened?"

"You've made a considerable investment on that Consolidated stock. Your one hundred shares have almost doubled in value."

"No, really? Where?"

"See, on that board? The G refers to Consolidated Gas. That's nearly double what we bought it for."

"How exciting! This stock-buying business is quite simple."

Julius nearly choked. "Feeling confident, are you? Perhaps we should make a wager—"

"Absolutely not." She put a hand to his chest, her

palm crushing his necktie. "I know better than to wager on stocks with you. And I don't want the shares. You should keep them. You paid for them, after all."

"Then how about we use the earnings for a dinner at Sherry's one of these evenings?"

"Deal."

He held her a moment and she seemed in no hurry to part, either. He pushed a loose strand of brown hair behind her ear. "Will you come to me tonight?"

"If I say no, will you stop asking me?"

"No. If you refuse, I'll merely try all the harder to succeed in seducing you." Angling his head, he took her lips in an easy kiss, one that proved his sincerity as well as his intentions. She met him eagerly, her fingers clutching his vest. There was no hurry this time, just a desire to be in the same space, to breathe the same air as one another. An affirmation of the strong charge that pulled them together at every turn.

When they broke free, they were both breathing hard. Her lips were swollen and red, and a bolt of lust raced down his spine. Christ, she was a vision. "I cannot stop thinking about you and wondering what it would be like between us." Combustible, if he were forced to guess.

"Me as well," she said, albeit rather shyly, and the admission threw kerosene on the ache already raging inside him.

"Then I believe we should satisfy our curiosity. Tonight. At my home."

"Fine," she said on an exaggerated sigh, her eyes

bright with mischief and desire. "I will meet you tonight, if only to shut you up."

A laugh tore free of his throat. "Thank God— because talking is the least interesting thing I am able to do with my mouth."

IN THE END, Julius insisted on sending a carriage for her. He hadn't liked the idea of her hailing a hack at eleven o'clock in the evening by herself. So when Nora snuck out of her aunt and uncle's house, a grand black carriage with matching gray horses sat across the street, waiting.

The ride wasn't long and she tried to remain calm. He'd been right: this was not her first—or tenth—secret outing but this had a different feel to it altogether. She had held Robert at arm's length for months. When their relationship finally turned physical, it hadn't been due to pressure from Robert. In fact, it had been she who'd finally decided to lose her innocence.

And their intimacies had been nice. Not earth shattering . . . but nice. She hadn't regretted anticipating their vows since they would eventually marry.

The circumstances with Julius couldn't be more different. There would be no marriage. They would separate at the end of the engagement—or whenever Julius located his father's investors and no longer needed her. Either way, this would be over and she would be left knowing that two men she hadn't married had seen her naked. Touched her body.

Could she live with that?

On the other hand, could she give up whatever was happening between her and Julius? The air turned positively electric in his presence, a hum that settled under her skin and in her blood. She hadn't ever experienced this strong of a reaction with Robert, who'd felt safe and comfortable. By comparison, Julius was dangerous and wild . . . and irresistible.

No one needs to know. You'll be back in dreary London soon, missing the excitement here. May as well hoard as many memories as you can.

Seize the moment. This was her new plan. Her father and society could go to the devil for all she cared.

The carriage arrived at the side of Julius's mansion. After pulling up her hood, Nora descended and made her way to the secondary entrance he'd told her about. As expected, the rounded wooden door with black hinges was unlocked. A set of stairs waited ahead.

"No one uses the east stairs except for me," he'd said. *"Take them and come find me at the top."*

The stone steps curved higher and higher up into the house. Other than her boots scraping on the rough surface, the tight space was quiet. Soft electric bulbs glowed every few feet to keep her from tripping, and she noted several closed doors in alcoves along the way. Her heart thumped furiously behind her ribs, a wild staccato of recklessness and longing, the perfect sound to accompany a clandestine outing such as this.

Her leg muscles burned by the time she arrived at the top. Leaning over, she put her hand on her corseted stomach and dragged in a few deep breaths.

"Worn out from the climb, my lady?"

Julius put down the book he'd been reading and stood from the turret's window seat. He wore no coat, just a navy blue waistcoat and necktie along with a white shirt, which had been rolled up to expose strong forearms. The look was oddly intimate and incredibly appealing.

"I'll be fine in a moment." She threw back the hood on her cloak and watched his gaze roam over her hair and face. She couldn't be certain but thought he let out a shaky breath of his own.

"I realize it's a long climb, but I thought this best considering your rule for absolute privacy. No one will discover us here."

"I cannot fault your logic; I merely wish you'd had the foresight to install an elevator."

He snorted as he came forward. "I'll take it under advisement for the next French chateau I build." Grasping her fingers, he brought her hand up to his mouth and pressed his lips to her knuckles.

The sweet gesture and playful words relaxed her, alleviating some of the tension residing between her shoulders. "Please, do. I would hate for your knees to give out on you in your old age."

He shot her a glance through his lashes, his irises a deep blue. "Funny. My knees are not at all what I'm worried will give out in my old age."

A very unladylike bark of laughter burst from her mouth. "You have a filthy mind, Julius Hatcher."

His large hands encircled her waist and dragged her flush against his front. So much heat and strength there, the ridges and angles deliciously different from her own frame. "And you'll soon be quite glad of it," he murmured as he began nibbling the side of her neck and removing her cloak. "I am ecstatic that you're here."

The dull yellow light from the gasolier bounced off the books and wooden rafters, a romantic effect in the intimate space. One thing she didn't see was a bed, however. Where did he plan to do . . . that? Her stomach dropped as her cloak hit the floor. "And I am quite nervous."

He ceased kissing her throat, then leaned back to find her eyes. "You have nothing to be afraid of with me. I merely want to bring you pleasure, Nora. That's all."

Seize the moment, Nora. "I'll not change my mind, if you are worried."

Linking their fingers together, he led her to the window seat. "I'm not worried. You are the boldest woman I've ever met. But if you do change your mind, just know I'll not be angry with you."

How did he know precisely the right thing to say at all times? She nodded and he kissed her forehead, then helped her sit. With a flick of his wrist, he uncovered the hidden sideboard. "I have a bottle of chilled champagne ready or we could enjoy brandy. Entirely up to you."

"Champagne, please."

Within seconds he had handed her a glass and joined her on the window seat. "What shall we toast to?"

She raised her glass. "Savoring."

One blond brow shot up. "Indeed. Savoring."

Their glasses clinked and then she took a long swallow of the sweet bubbly.

Once again, he surprised her. She hadn't known what to expect once she arrived, but she hadn't anticipated relaxing with a drink. Quite thoughtful of him, really. "I never asked—have your mother and sister returned to Albany?"

"Yes, the morning after the fire."

She sensed there was more to the story from the way his expression shuttered. "Were they scared by the blaze? My uncle said there was no clear indication on what started it."

"He likely didn't want to worry you, but it was set deliberately."

"Deliberately? Are you certain?"

She watched, mesmerized, as he finished the rest of the champagne in his glass, the muscles in his forearms shifting with the movement. He had quite sturdy hands. A man's hands, well used, with long, rough fingers. The surface of her skin tingled just imagining those hands on her bare skin.

"The battalion chief seemed to think so," he was saying, though she hardly paid any attention. "And my office was ransacked while the staff was out battling the flames. I cannot fathom a reason for any of it, honestly." He rose and retrieved the champagne bottle.

"Your office was ransacked? It must have something to do with the rumor you started, the one about the lucrative stock from your father's investment."

"That certainly seems plausible," he said, refilling her glass and then his. "Especially if the goal was to get me and my staff out of the house to search it."

"I never dreamed that rumor could be dangerous for you."

He lifted a shoulder. "We already knew these men were not honorable. Don't worry. I'll find them eventually."

She sipped her own champagne and tried to contain her nervous anticipation. Part of her could not believe she'd actually come tonight; the other part wondered what was taking him so long to get started. She felt ready to crawl out of her skin.

When he lowered himself to the seat again he landed directly next to her. His leg touched the outside of her thigh as he angled toward her and the proximity of his large body caused her heart to stutter. He raised a hand and swept his knuckles over the side of her face, near her jawbone, and every nerve ending jumped to attention. He twirled a tendril of her hair around the end of one finger. "I love your hair. It's the color of the strongest coffee."

She could drown in the bright blue pools of his eyes. "I find my hair rather boring, though that sounds as if I'm attempting to worm a compliment out of you."

"No worming necessary. I am more than prepared with compliments. My mind has done little else but think on you while keeping me awake at night. You've been quite the distraction." Releasing her hair, he slipped the same finger lower, along her jaw, the side of her throat, until he reached the scalloped edge of her pale pink silk evening gown. The digit slipped inside her clothing to gently scrape the skin over her chest, down to the swell of her breast above her corset. She inhaled sharply as he traced the flesh lazily, carefully, as if he had all the time in the world. Her breasts grew heavy, heat winding its way through her insides, and her lids fluttered closed as she swayed toward him.

Both of their glasses somehow disappeared and then he was pulling her closer. More fingers slid to join the first, his palm cupping her breast over her undergarments, and he pressed his forehead to her temple, his breath steady in her ear.

"I can still taste you," he whispered, sounding almost agonized. "Can still feel you coming on my tongue. It's been enough to drive me mad."

The room lost all its air and she could not breathe. "Julius . . ."

"Kiss me, my lady."

Nora wasted no time in turning her face and joining her mouth to his. In mere seconds she'd turned boneless, a mass of hunger and yearning, with a desperate need to touch him. To get closer. His tongue swept past her lips, demanding, and she opened to welcome him.

These were no soft, comforting kisses; these stirred her soul, roused her lust, and turned her inside out. She clung to Julius's shoulders to keep steady while her senses reeled. Even the kisses they'd shared before tonight hadn't felt this *deep*, this honest. There was no pretending this wasn't happening or that she did not want this with every fiber of her being. She most definitely did.

Palms and fingers tested and explored the shape of her through her clothing. Arms, ribs, stomach, shoulders, neck . . . his hands touched her every-where, it seemed. One hand threaded her hair, di-sheveling the pins holding it up, and long strands tumbled about her shoulders. He pulled back. "My God, you are glorious," he said and sifted a hand through her hair. "I want to strip you bare and see all this dark silk spread on my pillow."

The comment rolled through her like a wave of fire. She cupped his jaw, the hint of evening whis-kers quite roguish, like a Norse pirate, and she brought his mouth back to hers. He captured her lips and drove his tongue inside, melding, caress-ing. Without breaking free, he suddenly lifted her and placed her sideways on his lap, her legs hang-ing over him. She could feel the hard length of him underneath her, undeniable proof of how much he wanted her, and the flesh between her legs pulsed with a distracting ache. Heedless of how wanton she appeared, she rolled her hips, her backside shifting over his erection . . . and they both groaned.

"Nora," he panted, his forehead pressed to hers. "Tell me what you want."

She didn't even need to think on it. "I want ev-erything."

I want all your kisses. All your lingering glances. All your attention. Only me.

He smiled against her lips. "Greedy, are we?"

"Indeed, the greediest. Please," she said, kissing him once more, her nails digging into his shoulders.

Air washed over her stocking-covered legs as he pushed her skirts aside. Clever fingers skimmed her shin and thigh, then pried her legs apart. He found the part in her drawers and stroked her folds. Teased her entrance and tested the slickness there. "You are so wet. I cannot wait to taste you again." Withdrawing his hand, he brought his fingers to his lips. Slipped the one coated in her arousal into his mouth. Blond-tipped lashes swept down over those piercing eyes and he groaned with male satisfaction.

Wicked. So very, very wicked.

He reached between her legs once more, this time with renewed purpose. "Oh," she said when he brushed the nub at the apex of her sex, the place where all her nerve endings were currently screaming for attention. She bucked when he did it again.

He took her lips, harder this time. Flames licked her insides as he circled and rolled that tiny bud, his tongue in her mouth. He was all around her, the two of them, alone, in a tiny hidden sanctuary. The city felt far, far away, forgotten, along with any inhibitions. She wanted this. She wanted *him*.

The pleasure rose and built, a wave that carried her higher, tightening all the muscles in her body until she could hardly bear it. She threw her head back and dragged air into her lungs.

"I need to watch your face this time," he said, his own breathing none too steady.

The idea of him studying while he tortured her with those magic fingers tipped her over. The orgasm rushed upon her, sweeping and lifting, an explosion of white light that obliterated everything else around her. From a distance, she heard herself shout as she trembled from head to toe.

When she floated back to herself, she first saw glittering blue eyes, half-lidded and intense. He held himself very still, tense, as if struggling to maintain control. She would much rather he lost control. Turn his brilliant brain off for a few moments and just *feel*. "Am I permitted to touch you at some point?"

The side of his mouth hitched. "I wouldn't dream of stopping you. But perhaps we should retreat to the bedroom first."

"I thought we were staying here."

"If you are game for a bit of creativity, I'm certain we can manage here. I'd rather you were more comfortable, however." He helped her stand, arranged her skirts, and then rose. "I worried that asking you to meet me in my bedroom would scare you off."

It very well might have. Probably wise on his part. "Now where to?"

"My bedroom connects off the turret stairs. No one will discover us—that is, if you can keep quieter than a few moments ago."

"You have only yourself to blame," she said, though she knew he was teasing her. "And we shall see who is the loudest before the night is through, I suppose."

He kissed her nose. "I look forward to the competition. Follow me."

Hands linked, they traveled down the spiral stairs silently, quickly, until they reached one of the doors built into an alcove. He pulled the knob and the heavy wood popped out from the wall. A mysterious dark nook was revealed, but Nora couldn't see much of it as she stepped over the threshold.

Julius flicked a lever and then pushed on the side of the nook. A large panel shifted, swung outward.

"How very clever," she said, eyes wide as she continued into what was clearly a man's dressing room. "This house is full of surprises."

"It should be. I designed it." He shut the door to the turret stairs and then closed the hidden panel, sealing them into the dressing room.

He took her arm, led her through another door. His bedroom. She drank in the sight of the dark walnut paneling, heavy furniture, thick carpet, and cream papered walls. A blaze had been set in the huge marble fireplace. The space was opulent but functional, exactly what she would have expected of him. "I like it."

"Good. I'd hoped you would."

After locking both doors, he crossed to where she stood in front of the fire. He stared into her eyes, serious for a moment. "Any regrets?" She shook her head, and he asked, "Any hesitations?"

She considered this. The trip to New York had been forced on her, punishment for daring to love someone not of her class. She had thought to punish her father right back with the most outlandish, inappropriate man she could find. That man turned out to be intelligent and kind, forthright and funny, a perfect match for her in every way. And while there was no future for her and Julius—at least not the way she'd been taught, with marriage and children—she meant to enjoy every bit of this while it lasted. Build memories to keep a lifetime.

Life was much too short to play by anyone's rules but her own.

She placed her palm on his chest. His heart

pounded beneath her hand, his body radiating heat. "None."

A sturdy arm encircled her waist, bringing her hips flush to his, not bothering to hide his erection. "Any requests?"

She had the sense of standing at a crossroads, deciding between what was expected of her and the excitement of the unknown. She was ready to take a new path.

"Just one." Rising on her toes, she looped her arms over his shoulders. "*Hurry.*"

Chapter Sixteen

Julius found himself grinning as he bent his head to kiss her once more. Had he ever smiled this much with any other woman? Nora was such an interesting, complicated mix of proper and unconventional, capable and inexperienced. She fascinated him, and he loved that he never knew what she might say or do next.

They kissed until she clung to him, both of them panting, and he broke free to begin working on the fastenings of her dress. She'd worn a silk evening gown, a strange choice for an illicit rendezvous where only he would see her, but he wasn't complaining. She was stunning, the pale pink showing off her flawless, creamy skin. The dress would look even better on the carpet, however, with her naked body spread beneath him.

He loved undressing a woman, anticipation building while layer after layer fell away. Men were so simple, so basic; a cock pulled out of trousers was all one needed in just about every situation. Not much else mattered. With this particular woman, however, he longed to see every inch of her, to find every freckle, kiss every sensitive spot that drove her wild. Lifting skirts for a quick fuck had its uses, he supposed, but he much preferred to take his time with Nora. Reveal her bit by bit, each glimpse of skin tempting him.

The bodice of the dress parted and he pushed it off her shoulders, down her arms. He devoured the sight of her bare limbs and collarbones before unhooking her overskirt and letting it fall to her feet. She wore a pale pink corset cover, which he removed handily to reveal a matching corset beneath. The flesh of her breasts nearly spilled out over the top. He started to reach for the fastenings and she knocked his fingers out of the way to untie his necktie.

"Hardly the right place to start," he murmured, smirking at her.

"I'll work my way there, do not worry." The necktie came free and she asked, "Since you have a particular order in mind, shall I move on to your waistcoat?"

"In America they're called vests. And yes, that is a logical next step."

He toed off his shoes while she undid the buttons, her fingers occasionally brushing his stomach through his clothing, causing ripples of sensation to roll through him. The vest landed on the floor. She pushed his suspenders over his shoulders and then concentrated on his collar and shirt. Finally, he dragged the fabric over his head and tossed it aside. She was already intently working on the tiny buttons of his combination, her brow furrowed, her skin flushed, breathing every bit as unsteady as his own.

The undergarment separated as she moved lower, revealing his chest and the light blond hair covering his sternum. Without warning, she lifted a hand and stroked his bare skin with her fingertips. He shuddered, lust sharp and swift through his gut. His cock thickened further, the tenuous hold on his control beginning to unravel.

"My turn." He started on her corset. One by one, the fastenings parted until the entire piece came off in his hand. He could see the shape of her breasts, full and luscious with dusky tips, through the thin cotton of her chemise. Sliding his hand over her hip and ribs, he cupped a soft mound, the delectable weight filling his palm, before dipping his head and kissing the exposed flesh above the fabric. She smelled like spring. Like lavender and wide meadows. Like heaven. His heart gave an unexpected lurch in his chest, unfamiliar and unbidden.

Stop. She doesn't belong to you. She will never belong to you.

He straightened, returning to the purpose of the evening. "Lie down."

She bent to remove her shoes and then crossed to the wide bed along the wall, her hips shifting with each step. He followed, slower, contemplating all the things he longed to do tonight. Undoubtedly there wouldn't be enough time for the entire list . . . but he would certainly try.

Once on the mattress, she shifted to the middle. Met his gaze, one brow boldly raised. As if she were daring him.

And then she removed her chemise.

Julius's jaw fell as Nora reached for the hem and

then wiggled out of the undergarment. Flames roared through him, like a shovel of coal tossed into a blast furnace, as her naked torso came into view. Slightly rounded stomach, round breasts tipped with taut nipples, milky white skin over long limbs. All that remained were her drawers and stockings.

Fuck. She was a vision. Like every prurient dream he'd dared to allow himself. He could not wait to peel those drawers and stockings off, get her completely naked for the first time. The first of many, he hoped.

His hands shook as he unbuttoned his trousers. He stepped out of them and tossed the garment aside. Her eyes immediately dipped to his erection, which was pushing against the thin fabric of his combination, and widened. She seemed . . . surprised. Was she an innocent after all?

So as to not frighten her, he left the undergarment on and crawled onto the bed, stretching out alongside her. She turned toward him and he placed a palm on her face. "All right? We do not need to—"

"I hadn't realized you were all different." Her brown eyes flicked to his groin, her throat swallowing. "There. I assumed they were all the same."

Oh. "Size, you mean?" She nodded, her cheeks flushing crimson. More pieces about the illustrious Robert fell into place. "I couldn't really say, as I don't often see naked men these days, but there is variation. Like with breasts. All sizes are a possibility. I realize I may be on the larger side but we'll fit. You'll see."

"Easy for you to say, considering your role in all this."

He couldn't help it; a laugh escaped. "True." Leaning in, he kissed the tip of her nose. "But I've never lied to you—and I won't hurt you."

Placing his palm under her jaw, he angled her head and captured her mouth with his own. He lifted her leg and draped it over his hip, opening her to accommodate him. With one roll of his hips, the hard ridge of his cock rubbed her slit and the friction caused them both to groan. His balls tightened, the pleasure nearly painful.

He thrust again.

Her nails dug into his skin. "Oh my God. *Julius.*"

Vaguely, he wondered if he could make her come like this. If he weren't so desperate for her, he might very well try. Rolling her onto her back, he sat up to untie her drawers, lowering them off her hips and down her legs. Stockings next, and then she was bare. In seconds, he shrugged out of his combination and flipped their positions, her knees straddling his hips as she poised above him.

Her forehead crumpled. "What are we doing?"

Using his fingers between her legs, he stroked her until she shuddered. "It will be easier for you this way." He slipped a finger into her heat, the warm slippery walls grasping him, while his thumb circled her clitoris. His free hand toyed with one of her nipples, pinching and rolling, and soon she was rocking her hips, seeking, moaning, so he added a second finger. Then a third. He wanted inside her so desperately. A fine sheen of sweat broke out all over his body from the effort to restrain himself.

When her cries turned to pleas, he withdrew his fingers from her core and positioned the tip of his penis at her entrance. He guided her lower, gently, until the crown plunged inside. *Goddamn.* So hot, so tight. He clenched his jaw and beat back the urge to thrust upward. To bury himself in that nirvana. She held herself still and he could see the confusion in her glazed dark gaze. "Slide down," he gritted out. "Go at your own pace. Take as much as you can."

Nodding, she bit her lip and applied herself to the task, shifting and adjusting. Julius's hands dropped to the mattress, clutching the coverlet in a death grip as he struggled to remain still. "God, yes," he said. "Keep going."

Each wriggle, each twist of her hips was the sweetest torture. He feared he'd never last, that he'd come long before she had seated herself, but he somehow managed it. Her groin finally met his, the two of them breathing as if they'd just run a race.

"Oh my," she whispered, her lids slammed shut.

"You feel so damn good." He gave her another second to adjust, then rolled his pelvis, his erection pleading for movement. She threw her head back, her mouth parted on a silent groan.

"More," she said. Julius gripped her hips and moved her, showing her how to proceed. She caught on quickly, picking up the rhythm and taking over, allowing him to cup her swaying breasts and squeeze her nipples between his fingers.

"That's it," he crooned. "Keep riding me. I'm so deep inside you right now." Pleasure built in the base of his spine, down his legs. He could hardly believe this was Nora, his wild English beauty, riding him with abandon. She was a female conqueror, he her willing captive. She'd never appeared more gorgeous than right now, naked and uninhibited, astride him. Sliding his thumb to where they were joined, he stroked her, desperate to push her over the edge.

Her thighs tightened, nails carving into his stomach. "God, yes. Oh, God. *Julius.*"

"Come for me, my lady." He said it low in his throat, the way she liked, and she seemed to stop breathing, her walls clamping down on him, shudders racking her body. A moan tore from her throat. He drove up then, riding her through her orgasm, waiting until she came down before flipping them over so she was on her back, where he began thrusting hard, his own release unavoidable. In hardly any time at all, his erection thickened, balls tingling, and he jerked out of her just before he started spurting. Long white ropes shot from his tip and onto her stomach, his fist flying over his shaft to milk every drop.

When he stopped shaking, he sat back on his heels and tried to catch his breath. Nora appeared equally undone, sprawled on his bed, legs spread, her eyes hooded. His spend coated her skin and he felt not one ounce of regret. A surge of territorial male pride filled his chest instead. With the tip of a finger, he smoothed the proof of his orgasm into her body, marking her. "I like seeing you like this, covered in me."

She didn't appear shocked or scandalized. No, she merely trembled, her gaze following the movement of his hand. "You are a wicked, wicked man."

"Oh, I've only just begun."

NORA WASN'T CERTAIN her limbs would ever work again. She and Julius were now in his bathing suite, relaxing in the largest porcelain tub she'd ever seen. Warm water lapped over her bare skin, an even warmer male at her back as she reclined on his chest.

They'd both fallen silent in the aftermath of their intimacy. Ever since catching her breath, she'd been lost in a sea of her own thoughts, trying to make sense of it all, not protesting as he tugged her to the bathing suite to clean her up.

Tonight had been unexpected. There had been pleasure, yes. A lot, in fact. However, there'd also been a connection beyond the physical. In those times when he had stared into her eyes, the lust and longing so clear in his gaze, she sensed something deep and powerful between them. As if there could never be anyone else. Her heart had swelled so full it threatened to burst.

Intimacies with Robert hadn't been anything like this.

She wanted to feel guilty. She *should* feel guilty. What woman flitted from one man to another so quickly without being labeled a harlot? Perhaps she deserved the title. After all, it had only been days since she wrote to Robert and ended their association. How could she have forgotten him so quickly? She hadn't thought about Robert hardly at all since posting that letter. Instead, another man had consumed her thoughts.

It's because Robert was an act of desperation. Trying to gain Papa's attention. Julius is for you, no one else. A selfish, temporary slice of happiness.

Perhaps.

And perhaps she was trying to rationalize her reckless behavior, one that could have very real consequences. Her governess had warned her for years against "loose" behavior. Women who had children out of wedlock were doomed to a life as an outcast. She could still feel the mortification when her father had demanded to know if she were carrying Robert's child.

"No," she'd answered, shame burning her skin. "Definitely not."

"Good," he'd said. "Then we'll send you to America and forget this ever happened."

At the time, she'd protested, saying she would never forget Robert or their love for one another.

How quickly that had proven to be false.

Worse, something told her Julius wouldn't be as easy to forget, even though that hardly made any sense. She'd only known him a short while. But in the end, he would not marry her, so she'd eventually need to move on. Hope to find a husband who hadn't heard of her past.

"You are unusually quiet." Using the cloth, Julius squeezed water onto her breasts, the droplets sliding over the pale globes. "Are you changing your answer about regrets?"

"No." She meant that, despite the emotional distance between them since they left the bedroom. Thankfully, he'd given her time and hadn't pushed until now. She broached the one topic nagging at her. "Do you regret that I wasn't innocent?"

He made a noise in his throat. "Of course not. Would be a bit hypocritical of me, considering my experience. Besides, it's not as if we are truly getting married."

A slice of pain went through her at the reminder. "If we were," she continued, "would it bother you if your bride had been intimate with another man besides you?" *Am I everything society believes of me? Have I ruined my chance at a future?*

"Hell, no. Growing up as I did, far below the gilded ceilings of New York society, we were more practical about those things. Women were discreet, yes, and whatever happened outside of marriage was kept private."

"So you wouldn't think less of her?"

His arms wrapped around her tightly, his lips at her ear. "Nora, I want you—not your hymen. You are worth more to me than any useless body part. And any man who bases his need for you on what you are lacking isn't seeing everything you are, everything you will be."

Pressure built behind her lids, a tingling of emotion welling to the surface. "Thank you."

Clever fingers slipped to roll and pinch her nipples, causing her to gasp. "You're most welcome."

She arched her back, pleasure streaking like lightning throughout her body, as if those two taut buds were directly connected to the place between her legs. Each pluck and twist echoed below, increasing the ache. Then he pulled away, reaching for the cloth once more. Frustration bloomed and she squirmed in the water. "Attempting to torture me?"

He nipped her earlobe. "Yes. Is it working?"

Considering the large erection increasing behind her, she wasn't the only one being tortured.

"I wrote to Robert," she heard herself say.

Heavy muscles tensed as he stiffened. "Nora, I'd rather not hear—"

"I broke things off with him."

A long beat passed, the room filled only with the sounds of their breathing and the soft lapping of water against the porcelain. "When?" he asked.

"After the night in the turret."

"I . . . Why did you not tell me?"

She lifted a shoulder. "I wasn't certain you'd be interested. After all, he's never been much of a deterrent for your plans."

"True." He dragged the wet cloth over her arm and shoulder, along her neck. "But that couldn't have been an easy decision for you."

"No, but the right ones rarely are. He deserved to know the truth."

"I feel as if I should apologize, but that would be a lie. I'm not sorry."

"I assumed as much."

"He didn't deserve you, Nora."

She couldn't argue. Robert deserved someone who loved him and only him, not a woman so easily led astray by another man. "This arrangement between us . . . I'll not fault you if you want out. After all, I no longer need to return to England and you've already begun ferreting out your father's investors. Undoubtedly you'll succeed without my help."

He said nothing for a long moment, just continued the maddening swipes of the cloth over her skin. "I hadn't considered that, but I do hate to back out of an agreement. Gentleman's word and all that."

"I thought you were no gentleman."

He bent his head and nuzzled her throat, his lips and tongue sliding over the damp flesh while his hand slipped down below. He cupped her mound possessively. "I'm definitely no gentleman. What gentleman would seduce his fake fiancée not once, but twice in one night?"

"Twice?"

His finger pushed inside her, curling up to press a particularly sensitive spot, and her back bowed from the sudden jolt of pleasure. He nipped the side of her throat. "Yes, I am seducing you now, in case you were not aware."

"Then I, for one, am quite glad you are not a gentleman."

"Good, because I'm not letting you out of our agreement early. You owe me five more weeks. Then we will have worked this all out of our systems and may return to our independent purposes."

Five more weeks. Something twisted in her chest. Silly time limit. How naïve she had been at the start of it all. Here she'd thought the deadline would protect her, ensure that things progressed speedily. Now that time limit felt like a sharp blade hanging above her head, just waiting to fall and strike.

Only a few more weeks. The thought instantly depressed her. At best, she'd see him three times a week, perhaps four. That was a rapidly dwindling set of encounters to last a lifetime once this ended. And it *would* end. He'd made his wishes perfectly clear from the beginning—and even hearing Robert had been cast aside hadn't caused Julius to rethink his stance on marriage and children.

No, he believed that five weeks would help

them forget each other. Nora now knew the opposite would occur. That time would only dig her in deeper, and the heartache when he finally said good-bye might very well break her.

Why could she not have picked a different false fiancé? One who might actually love her back?

Wait . . . *love*?

Her lids fell and she let out a shuddering breath. Dear God, she'd fallen in love with the rogue. The one unacceptable, unattainable man in New York City and she had gone and handed her heart right over to him—not that he wanted it. How could she be so stupid?

He shifted to add another finger, filling her, and any thoughts of stupidity and broken hearts flew right out of her mind. All she could concentrate on was the here and now, and Julius's electric touch. "Oh, yes," she sighed, melting into the water.

He chuckled, his chest rising behind her. "Besides, posing as your fiancé puts me at an advantage over all the other men in New York City. I am permitted certain liberties others are not."

Fingers withdrawing, he circled her entrance slowly, teasing her, stealing the breath from her lungs. She struggled to keep her wits. "Is that what you call this? Taking liberties?"

"No. I call this vital to my sanity. You have driven me to distraction for these many weeks. There were days I feared my cock would never deflate."

With a moan, she tried to reach behind her to comfort said organ. Julius stopped her by shifting to cradle her in his arms. He then lifted her out of the bath. Water rained down over the tub and the floor as he stepped out of the massive piece, handling her as if she weighed absolutely nothing.

"You do not want me touching you?" she asked.

"I want it very badly. So badly that I need to be inside you quickly."

She smiled at his handsome profile, leaning in to run her teeth along his jaw. "More liberties again?"

"Indeed—and I plan on taking them."

JULIUS STARED AT the ticker tape, the small numbers blurring before his eyes. He'd been unable to stop thinking about last night, about finally having Nora naked in his bed. She'd been so much more than he'd expected. Bold and giving, funny and tender . . . Twice hadn't been nearly enough. Even five more weeks did not seem a sufficient time to fully enjoy her charms. Why had he agreed on that ridiculous time limit in the first place?

What would she do at the end of that time now that Robert had been cast off? He hadn't been capable of asking if she planned to return to England or stay in America. He wasn't sure he could handle her answer.

Perhaps she intended to find herself a true fiancé. That caused a pounding ache in his brain. He rubbed his forehead, contemplating. She deserved happiness, of course, but that didn't mean he wanted it flaunted in his face. Better she returned to London and found some tea-swilling, jolly old chap to settle down with in a palace somewhere.

"*Never marry, my boy,*" his father had said during those last drunken ramblings. "*Because when you fail, you hurt everyone you love.*"

And they had hurt. The loss of Warren Hatcher had been keenly felt, as if he'd been the glue holding the entire family together. How could one man be expected to shoulder so much?

Even if Julius were considering marriage, Nora was clearly out of his reach. She should marry a man with hundreds of years of history, with privilege and standing. Not one who'd struggled and narrowly escaped the squalor of the streets.

"Sir, right there—did you see RNJ Corp.?"

Julius straightened at Martin's excited voice. His assistant was reading the stock updates on the tape falling uselessly through Julius's fingers. "I must've missed it. Show me."

"Here." He shoved the paper in front of Julius's face. "It jumped eight whole points in the last hour. As you predicted."

"Ha! Get it sold, then—and my thanks for catching that. I'm as dull as a post today."

Martin hurried to the phone to call the broker and Julius reached for the tepid coffee on the corner of his desk. Before he could take a sip, Brandywine appeared in the doorway.

"Sir, you have visitors. Mr. Pendleton and Mr. Cortland."

Nora's uncle? What was he doing here? With Pendleton? "Of course. Show them back."

He asked Martin for a moment or two of privacy, then stood and slipped on his top coat, which he'd taken off at the start of trading this morning. The two men soon walked in and he shook both their hands in greeting.

"Appreciate you seeing us, Hatcher," Pendleton

said, settling himself in a chair opposite the desk. "I know this is a busy time of day for you."

"Not a problem. Would either of you care for coffee?"

Both gentlemen passed and Cortland leaned forward. "We wanted to let you know the status of your membership application."

Oh, the Gotham Club. He'd nearly forgotten all about it, what with Nora naked in his bed and all. "And what has been decided?"

"The board has accepted your application," Pendleton said, a little too smugly. As if he'd been single-handedly responsible. "But then we all knew this was just a formality. We're honored to have you."

"Excellent. That is good news." Did membership acceptance generally warrant a personal visit from the president? Highly doubtful. So why were they here? Julius remained silent and tried to work out this puzzle in his mind.

"Yes, everyone is looking forward to seeing you at the club. Perhaps you'd care to share dinner one of these evenings?" Pendleton lifted a brow, and Julius suspected additional stock tips were at the heart of this request.

"I'll ask my assistant to check my calendar and let you know," he hedged.

"I look forward to it." Pendleton rose and extended his hand. "We gentlemen must look out for one another."

Julius felt himself frowning at the words as he shook Pendleton's hand. Why did that phrase sound familiar? He must have read it stitched on a pillow in one of the Knickerbocker drawing rooms he'd frequented lately. "Indeed. My thanks for bringing the news yourself."

Pendleton waved a hand. "Wouldn't have it any other way. We're friends, after all, aren't we?"

Julius merely smiled to hide his annoyance. He'd met the man exactly once before today. Friends seemed a bit of a stretch. He extended his hand toward Cortland, but Nora's uncle turned to Pendleton instead. "If you don't mind, I need to have a word with Hatcher. I'll take a hack when we're through."

Instantly, Julius worried that Nora's uncle had discovered what had occurred last evening. Perhaps Nora had been caught sneaking back inside the Cortland house. Or maybe she'd confessed to her aunt and uncle this morning. Bracing himself for the worst, Julius rang for Brandywine, who quickly appeared and escorted Pendleton to the front door.

When they were alone, Cortland asked, "Any further trouble on the property?"

"No," he replied carefully. "Though I've hired men to keep watch on the premises, so perhaps they've been a deterrent."

Cortland nodded. "And your office? I know there was a break-in the night of the fire. Was anything missing?"

"Hard to tell in the chaos, but it appeared intact. I don't anticipate any further incidents, if that's your concern."

"Nora is quite dear to us. I would hate for her to come to harm."

"As would I. And I assure you that I'll do everything in my power to protect her." *While giving her bone-rattling orgasms.*

"Good. I knew we could rely on you. I'll leave you to your work." They both stood just as the door swung open. Brandywine had returned, this time with Frank Tripp right behind him. Christ, would Julius get any business done today?

Cortland and Tripp said a quick hello before Nora's uncle departed. Frank strolled in, a packet of papers in his hand. "Ah, still cozying up to the father-in-law, I see. Does this mean all is going smoothly in the land of fake engagements?"

Julius didn't want to admit things were going much better than smoothly. The soreness in his lower back today was proof of just how well things were going between he and Nora.

"Oh, indeed?" Tripp dropped into a chair, tossed the papers to Julius, and propped his feet on Julius's desk. "Progressing that well, is it?"

"Mind your own business, Frank."

Tripp's brow shot up. "First names, are we? My, my. She has gotten under your skin quickly."

Julius narrowed his gaze at the man across from him. "Have you a purpose this morning or are you here merely to pester me?"

Tripp grinned easily, not offended in the least. He pointed at the packet he'd tossed onto the desk. "First, those are the insurance papers from the fire. All you need to do is sign them for the claim. Second, I came to see how the plans for the masquerade are coming. Lent begins—"

"I'm not holding the masquerade."

Tripp's feet fell flat to the floor as he straightened. "You were serious about that? You're not holding it?"

Though certain to be unpopular with his friends, the decision was the right one under the circumstances. Julius did not want to host a drunken orgy while he and Nora were still . . . doing whatever they were doing. "That's correct. No masquerade this year."

"This is because of your fiancée." Tripp's head cocked as he studied Julius. "Christ, you're in love with her."

Julius felt his entire body recoil. "I'm not in love with her, for fuck's sake. I'm merely not interested in cavorting with half-naked dancers while stumbling drunk right now."

"Right now, while you're engaged."

"Yes."

"But I thought this was a fake engagement, that she's got some beau back in London and you've no interest in marrying her. Am I wrong?"

Tripp and his goddamn lawyer's logic. "You're not wrong, except there's no beau any longer."

"Oh, I see." His friend didn't even bother fighting his smug grin. "Yes, this all makes perfect sense."

"I'm not amused," Julius said.

"Only because I'm pointing out the truth. You're in love with your fake fiancée, which also terrifies you. Because what will you do if she decides she wants to keep you?" Tripp then rose and whistled on his way out of Julius's office.

Chapter Seventeen

Nora strolled along Sixth Avenue beside her aunt. This was the posh shopping district in New York City, or Ladies' Mile as it was called. Large ornate department stores with their cast-iron façades lined the blocks, the elevated occasionally rumbling by overhead. The bitter weather prevented casual shoppers today, the crowds thinner than she'd seen on past trips.

"We must see about ordering your trousseau," Aunt Bea said.

Nora blinked, nearly tripping on the walk. She hadn't expected this topic to come up so soon. "Oh, there's plenty of time for that. Perhaps after Easter."

"No, that won't do. We'll let Worth do the dress, of course, but your trousseau takes time as well. I made an appointment at Lord & Taylor for today. We may at least start to narrow down your fabrics and colors."

Today? Good heavens. Her aunt had not mentioned a thing about a trousseau when they'd departed earlier, else Nora would have invented an excuse to stay home. She didn't want to order clothes for a wedding that would never transpire.

"You owe me five more weeks. Then we will have worked this all out of our systems and may return to our independent purposes."

A lump formed in her throat, a knot of misery that nearly choked her. Last night, while glorious, had proven two things. First, she had fallen desperately in love with Julius; and second, their fake engagement would not end with a real wedding.

Of course, she had no one to blame but herself. This whole plan had been flawed from the start. Julius had been irresistible from the moment they'd met, and every second in his presence had slowly weakened her feelings for Robert as well as her resolve to return to England.

Just over one month.

What would she do then? She hadn't ever contemplated a life without Robert. They had planned to travel Europe—more his idea than hers—and she had quickly found herself looking forward to seeing a bit of the world. Perhaps she could still fill this craving for adventure and excitement on her own.

You're the brave one, Nora. You don't need a husband or a fiancé to show you that.

"Aunt Bea," she said as they continued toward Lord & Taylor. "I really think we should—"

A man slammed into her shoulder, jostling her. Gasping, Nora glanced up—and froze. His hat was pulled low and he appeared gaunt, scruffier than usual, but she would recognize those soulful brown eyes anywhere. *Robert.*

"I beg your pardon," Robert said in a low voice

and strode the opposite direction. Mind reeling, Nora watched him dart into an alley.

What in the name of St. Peter was he doing here?

She had to speak with him, to find out why he was in New York. How long had he been here? Goodness, perhaps that had been him standing outside the exchange after all.

Her hands trembled as she reached for her aunt's arm, pulling the older woman to a stop. "Aunt Bea, I need to run into a store a block past. Why don't I meet you inside Lord & Taylor?"

"Of course, dear. Shall I come with you?"

"No, that's not necessary. I'll only be a moment. Then I'll come to the bridal department."

"Excellent. If I'm not there, look for me in hats. I've ordered Easter bonnets for us."

Nora nodded, then started off in the direction Robert had taken. Checking over her shoulder, she ensured her aunt had continued on. Then she hurried to the alley and darted inside, peering into the gloom of trash bins and boxes. "Robert," she whispered, creeping farther into the dim space.

She picked her way through the refuse and garbage on the hard ground. Suddenly, a hand clamped over her mouth and she was jerked into the shadows. Panic rose but she fought the sensation. *It's Robert.*

Sure enough, when they were concealed from view he dropped his hand. He'd removed his hat, and hair hung in his handsome face in his familiar affected style. His brow was lined with unhappiness.

"Robert, what are you—"

"I cannot believe you are marrying him," he said with no preamble. "How could you do this to us?"

She blurted, "What are you doing in New York?"

"I came to find you. I wanted to surprise you."

"But your letters . . . They never stopped."

"I had a friend post them—and you are avoiding the question. Who is this Hatcher fellow and why are you *marrying* him?"

He was agitated, upset, and she had no wish to hurt him. He'd been kind and real in a world where she had experienced little of either. Clearly he hadn't received her letter breaking things off, and she needed to do that gently—not in an alley on Sixth Avenue in the cold while her aunt awaited.

She held up her hands. "I'll explain everything, but not here. Not now. Meet me this afternoon in Central Park. Four o'clock, near the animal menagerie."

"Fine." He frowned but did not challenge her. "I'll be there."

"As will I, I promise." She lifted her skirts and hurried to the mouth of the alley.

"You look beautiful, as always," Robert said behind her.

Guilt sat like a stone in her belly. She did not relish the pending conversation but he deserved to know. "Thank you. Until this afternoon."

He dipped his chin. "Until this afternoon."

AT FOUR O'CLOCK, Nora waited near the leopard's cage. Most of the visitors at the Central Park menagerie crowded around the elephant area, so hopefully Robert would have an easier time locating her here. She'd left her maid near the entrance, needing privacy for this conversation.

Dread had permanently taken up residence in her chest. Robert had come all the way from London to see her and now she would be sending him away without so much as a welcoming kiss. *Thank you for coming to see me. I've fallen in love with another man. Best of luck on your voyage home.*

Good Lord, she was a horrible person.

As hard as this would be for Robert—and for her—she could not regret her time with Julius. She loved him, much more deeply than she'd ever cared for Robert. Though the admission made her feel inconstant and flighty, she wouldn't lie to herself any longer.

Nor would she lie to Robert.

She saw him step out from behind a nearby tree. Hands in his pockets, he approached her, a wary expression on his face. His cheeks were red from the cold. "Hello, Nora."

"Hello. Any trouble finding me?"

"No, not really. I've been here a while."

She gestured to a nearby seating area. "Shall we sit?"

He nodded and the two of them walked to the wooden bench. When they were settled, she asked, "How long have you been in New York?"

"Long enough to hear about your engagement."

Had it been in the papers? She hadn't seen her name linked to Julius anywhere, but how Robert learned of it wasn't important. "I wrote to you about everything but you obviously never received my letter."

"Why don't you tell me now?"

"Robert . . ." How could she even begin? There was so much to say.

"You're in love with him, aren't you?"

She squeezed her eyes closed, absorbing the hurt she heard in his voice. "Yes," she answered quietly.

Robert put his elbows on his knees and dropped his head into his hands. "I cannot believe this. You said your father was sending you away to find a husband but you swore you loved me, that you would return to London. And now you're in love with this . . . this tycoon?"

"I didn't intend for it to happen. My goal was always to return to you. I convinced Mr. Hatcher to pose as my fiancé, knowing my father would never approve of Mr. Hatcher's reputation. However, we began spending time together and affection developed. I neither planned for it nor encouraged it. The feelings just happened."

"Feelings do not just happen," he snapped, his tortured gaze locking with hers. "All that time you were writing to me, telling me how much you missed me? Those were all lies, weren't they?"

"No, I never said anything I did not mean—and once I realized the depth of my feelings for him I wrote to you and broke things off. I never wanted to hurt you."

"You broke things off? Oh, of course. I see now. You wrote it in a letter that would take weeks to reach me, while you gallivant around New York with your beau. How convenient for you." His voice dripped acid, a bitter, hateful tone that she'd never heard from his mouth before.

"Robert, I know you are shocked and hurt, but none of this is convenient for me. This has been agonizing."

"Indeed, I've no doubt." His tone suggested he did not believe her. "Have you kissed him?"

She had no intention of wounding him further by admitting the truth. "It hardly matters—"

"It matters to me. It matters a great deal. We promised each other that we would marry, have children, grow old together. How could you say those things and then kiss another man?"

Hadn't she wondered the very same thing? Unmarried women in her world were supposed to wait for their wedding night before even kissing, let alone engaging in any other intimacies. While she had never expected to wait that long, she hadn't thought there would be two men in her past.

And while her future with Julius was uncertain, she knew she didn't love Robert any longer.

"It just happened," she explained quietly. "I never expected to love anyone other than you but circumstances change. People change."

His brows shot up. "You are saying you have changed?"

"Yes, I believe I have."

He let out a bitter laugh. "I suppose if you're attracted to that audacious house and all his money, then you are definitely not the person I loved. The woman I loved would have laughed at Julius Hatcher and his ridiculous moat instead of following him around to dinners and the stock exchange."

She gasped. How did he know all that? "Have you been following me? God above, it was you at the stock exchange. Did you . . . did you write the note telling them I was inside?"

He shot to his feet and stared down at her, his limbs vibrating with fury. "Can you blame me? I traveled here to be with you. Your father came to see me and offered me money to stay away from you. He tried to buy me off, but I refused to take his blood money—money he's made off the backs of simpler men who had the terrible misfortune of being born without a title."

"He offered you money?" She hadn't thought her father capable of such deviousness, and the knowledge hurt.

"Yes, a lot of money. More money than I'll likely see anytime soon. And I turned it down for *you*, Nora. Because I love you and I want to marry you someday."

Emotion cracked his voice and the sound had tears building behind her lids. Her father and Julius both had accused Robert of being a fortune hunter, but Nora knew better. His feelings were genuine. Which made this conversation all the more difficult.

"Robert, I'm terribly—"

"This is where you tell me you're sorry?" he scoffed, kicking a rock angrily with his boot. "That is little consolation when I've come all this way and poured my heart out. *'Thanks for coming, old Robbie. Now totter home and try to forget me.'*"

"It isn't like that at all. But I cannot change the way I feel—and I do not love you anymore."

"You fucked him, didn't you?"

Nora flinched at both the crude word and the vitriol behind it. "You overstep yourself," she said.

"While I wish things hadn't worked out this way, we're through. I do not want to see you ever again."

JULIUS HADN'T BEEN to the menagerie in ages. All different kinds of animals were kept in this "zoo" in Central Park, like elephants, leopards, birds, camels, and more. Hordes of visitors gathered here to glimpse the exotic beasts each day. Julius skirted the edge of the crowds, searching for one particular person in the masses.

He'd come to pay Nora an afternoon call, only to find her out and about. According to Beatrice Cortland, Nora had wandered to the park today with her maid to see the menagerie. With the exchange already closed for the day, Julius had no excuse not to join her in the excursion. After all, there were plenty of secluded spots in Central Park perfect for an intimate encounter.

Smiling to himself, he craned his head back and forth, eagerly looking for her. He hoped she hadn't wandered into the park itself because he'd never find her then.

He caught sight of a young man near the leopard cage, waving his arms around dramatically and shouting at a woman on a bench—

Julius's feet stopped working. Damn it, that was Nora sitting on the bench. And just who in God's name was shouting at her? Fire ignited in his gut, blood pumping, and he hurried toward the bench. "Ho, now! What seems to be the problem?" he called out.

Nora's troubled gaze met his a second before the young man spun around. Julius didn't recognize him and his plain clothing did not identify him as well off.

"Julius!" Nora exclaimed.

"*You*," the young man snarled at the same time—right before he took a swing at Julius's face.

Julius sidestepped the blow, grabbed the man's arm, and yanked it behind his back. "You do not want to do that," he snarled in the other man's ear. "Now, if I let you go, you'd best not speak one cross word to my fiancée."

With a roar of rage, the young man ripped out of Julius's grip and staggered a few steps. Nora was on her feet, her hand covering her mouth. "Julius, do not hurt him."

"You think *he* could hurt *me*?" the other man snarled. "This overly dressed, pompous—"

"That is enough," Julius cut in, his voice terse. "Who are you?" Then it hit him. The irrational anger, the English accent, the almost pretty features . . . *Holy Christ*. "You're Robert."

"Oh, so she's told you about me, has she?" He laughed, a broken, angry sound. "Allow me to guess. The two of you have read my letters together in bed, had a good laugh over my regard for Nora."

"Absolutely not," Nora insisted, indignant. "I would never do that to you."

"Yes, well you also promised never to love anyone but me. And look where that got us. You now love *him*." He gestured toward Julius.

Love? Julius nearly laughed. He and Nora were undoubtedly attracted to one another. Fond, certainly. But love? No, she didn't love him. She was an earl's daughter, a woman who could have her pick of husbands. Why would she settle on *him*, a man who had no intention of marrying and saddling himself with a wife and family?

Nora deserved better.

Better than him—and certainly better than the inexperienced fool Robert.

But Robert's presence here in New York surprised Julius. How long had the young man been here? More important, why? Nora had broken things off with him, she'd said, but it seemed Robert was not ready to let her go.

Too fucking bad.

"Did I not tell you to speak to my fiancée with respect?" he warned the young man, stepping closer. "You had best be careful."

"Or what?" the artist snarled. "You shall pummel me? If you try, I should warn you—I don't come from a fancy neighborhood with champagne and caviar. I'm no stranger to using my fists."

Julius crossed his arms over his chest. "Unfortunately for you, I also did not always live in a fancy neighborhood. I grew up in much different circumstances, a place where fighting on the streets was a regular occurrence."

"Oh, for heaven's sake. Enough!" Nora stepped between them. "No one shall be pummeling anyone else. Robert, I've told you how I feel and I'm sorry you've traveled all this way for nothing. But my mind is made up."

Robert's anger dissipated, sorrow and devastation sweeping over his face before he masked it. He drew himself up, proudly. "I wish you luck, then.

If you change your mind, I am staying at a rooming house on Thirty-Third Street and Lexington Avenue."

Nora nodded in acknowledgment, not speaking.

Robert started to turn, then stopped. "One more thing. I know it doesn't mean much because you have moved on but I love you, Nora. And the woman I love would never be so cavalier with her affections. She never would have allowed a large fortune to turn her head. So perhaps you really have changed—and from what I see, not for the better." He stomped toward the exit, lost in the sea of tourists out on a cold winter's day.

A shaky breath caught Julius's attention and his gaze swung toward Nora. Eyes glistening, her lower lip trembled. The sight nearly knocked him to his knees. He hadn't seen her so sad before and it tore at his insides. "Nora," he said, leading her behind the animal enclosures to gain some privacy. "Tell me you are not upset by what he said. About you changing."

"No, he's right," she said, two fat tears breaking free and rolling down her cheeks. Julius dug into his coat and withdrew a clean handkerchief. She accepted it and blotted her eyes. "I have changed."

"That's not always a terrible thing. From what I see, you would have been miserable with him."

"Your preternatural ability to see trends and predict the future?"

He stroked her jaw with the backs of his knuckles, eager to touch her. To soothe her. "No. Even a fool could see he's not right for you. You need someone to challenge you, to be your equal in all things. Furthermore, for all his bluster today, Robert still *left*."

"As if he had a choice. You were threatening to fight him."

"And he should have fought me. Instead, he took one swing and missed. If he were the man you deserved, he would still be fighting for you."

"We British are not as hotheaded as you Americans. He fought but in his own way." She pinched the bridge of her nose while inhaling deeply, trying to get herself under control. "He's been following me. He knew about our outing to the stock exchange."

"*What?*"

"Yes. He found me today on Sixth Avenue. I should have known then that it wasn't a coincidence bumping into him."

The idea of Nora being followed, even by Robert, disturbed Julius. How closely had the artist been watching her? Had he observed Nora sneaking into Julius's home last night? If so, that information could be used against them. Her guardians would be furious if rumors circulated. "At least we know who wrote to Hutchinson to tell him I had a woman in my office at the exchange."

"You think Robert responsible?"

"Without doubt. Who else would possibly want to hurt us both?"

"How can this be happening? It's like I don't even know him. The things he said . . ." She sighed, as defeated as he'd ever seen her. He hated witnessing her anguish.

Grasping her hands, he threaded their gloved fingers together. "We all change based on our daily experiences, like stocks that go up and down based on perceived worth. Nothing remains constant—and that's a good thing. For example, I never know what you might say or do next and that is a very intriguing quality."

"Inconsistent, you mean?"

"No, more like paradoxical, endlessly fascinating."

"You and your puzzles."

He couldn't help but smile at that. He liked that she knew him so well. "Robert's wrong about one thing, however."

She pulled her hands out of his grasp and wrapped them around her waist. "About my cavalier feelings?"

"Yes. Your decisions haven't been made lightly. Furthermore, he knows nothing of our new arrangement."

Wariness crept into her expression. "Our new arrangement," she said flatly.

"Yes. We have a few more weeks together. It's not as if either of us has made promises or expects anything more."

"Indeed. Merely something that needs to be worked out of our systems."

He hadn't heard her use that flat tone of voice before but he plodded on, nodding. "Exactly. We both know this cannot go any further. But I'm definitely looking forward to these remaining five weeks. Having you again is all I can think about today."

Color rose on her cheeks that had nothing to do with the cold. She glanced around, even though they were definitely alone, then let out a long breath. "I don't believe I'm the type of woman who is able to carry on a casual affair and then walk away—mostly because this no longer feels casual to me."

The weight of that statement recalled Robert's earlier words. He had to ask, "Did you tell Robert you loved me?"

Her gaze remained steady. "I did, which I realize is inconvenient to everyone involved, but there it is."

"I . . ." He had no idea how to respond. Words failed him, the puzzle pieces scattered all over the ground. Everything was shifting, unraveling, in this very moment, yet he was powerless to stop it. The leopard roared nearby—a wild, fittingly angry sound to fill the silence. Julius felt a bit like howling himself.

Tripp had warned him this would happen but Julius had been too stubborn, convinced Nora couldn't fall for someone like him. He thought they were clear on the arrangement and their expectations. She knew he'd sworn never to bear the responsibility of a wife and family, that he'd never carry the burden of failure for the rest of his life. So how had this come to pass?

Nora stared at him, awaiting a reaction, but he had none. Her honesty humbled him. Fearless and stubborn, beautiful and strong, she was unlike any other woman—and he was utterly unworthy of her. "I don't know what to say," he offered, lamely. Her eyes dimmed significantly and he knew he'd disappointed her.

"I cannot say I'm surprised," she said. "I hadn't intended for you to find out, but perhaps this is for the best. We began honestly and now we may end honestly."

His stomach dropped somewhere to his toes. "What do you mean, end? We agreed on—"

"Yes, I'm aware we agreed upon five more weeks. But like you said, people change. Circumstances change. I cannot pretend I do not want more and your feelings on the matter have been made perfectly clear." She shivered and rubbed her arms, tendrils of her brown hair blowing around her lovely face. "I am releasing you from our arrangement."

He hadn't expected her to say it, and the words hurt more than he'd imagined. Memories of last night mocked him, the knowledge that he'd never touch her again. Never kiss her. Never feel her silky skin whisper over his own. He thrust his hands in his pockets to keep from reaching for her. "What if I do not wish to be released?"

"Then I do apologize for your disappointment. Good-bye, Julius."

Chapter Eighteen

The next few days passed slowly. Through sheer force of will, Nora resumed her morning walks through the city. They helped to clear her head now that the whirlwind of her engagement had ended.

A fake engagement, yes. But at some points, near the end, it had begun to feel quite real.

She drew in a shuddering breath, the cold stinging her lungs. The large buildings dwarfed her, ostentatious limestone exteriors that reminded her of how new everything was here. Not like London, a city that had been the center of the globe for hundreds and hundreds of years, now dirty and grimy. New York was fresh and vibrant, a city of hope and new beginnings. It truly did feel as though anything was possible here.

She would be sad to leave it.

People rushed by her but she hardly noticed, so despondent over the mess she'd made of things. She certainly hadn't expected Robert to come here. The conversation at the menagerie had been painful and heart-wrenching. His anger, while surprising from such a normally gentle soul, had been well justified. He'd traveled to New York expecting a reunion and found her engaged—albeit falsely—to another man. A cruel blow, and one she would have spared him, if at all possible.

As if that hadn't been enough, Julius had arrived. *What had you expected, Nora? A declaration of undying love?* Julius Hatcher preferred solitude, a man perfectly happy in his huge castle, overseeing an empire without interference. He had no intention of ever changing. Ironic, for someone so enamored with the ever-shifting stock market.

"We all change based on our daily experiences . . . Nothing remains constant—and that is a good thing."

A good thing except, it seemed, when change pertained to himself. All she could do was move on.

After wallowing in her own grief for a while, she finally returned to her uncle's home. A large carriage sat just down the block. As she passed, the door swung open and she heard a male voice call, "Lady Nora."

Glancing over, she found a man she'd never met headed straight for her. One of her uncle's footmen had been following at a discreet distance, and Nora now waited for him to catch up before addressing the stranger.

The man was fairly young and handsome, and dressed like a gentleman. He tipped his bowler at her. "Lady Nora, forgive my rudeness but I wish to speak with you."

"And who are you, exactly?"

"I am Frank Tripp, Esquire. Attorney at law and good friend to Julius Hatcher."

The last two words caused her stomach to turn over. She didn't want to hear whatever this man had to say. Lifting her skirts, she made to move around him. "I really must be getting back. If you'll excuse me, Mr. Tripp."

"I know you'd probably rather ignore me but I'm begging for five minutes of your time." He seemed quite earnest but she wasn't certain her heart could take news of Julius right now. While she thought it over, he said, "Please, my lady. Hear me out."

Had something happened? Was Julius all right? Had he learned the identity of his father's investors or who started the fire in the stables? Questions burned on Nora's tongue, yet she didn't voice them.

"Milady?" the footman asked. "Would you care to return home now?"

Curiosity won out. "No, Patrick. I'll just be a moment." She then allowed Mr. Tripp to lead her to his carriage.

They climbed inside and he closed them in, taking the seat opposite her. "Thank you," he said. "I know this seems a strange request, considering we've never met, but I had to speak with you."

Might as well come straight to the point. "Is Julius unwell?"

"To put it mildly. I've never quite seen him like this, actually."

"Like how?" She didn't want to care but couldn't stop herself from asking, apparently.

"He's . . . Well, I thought there had been a death

in the family until I pressed him and he admitted the truth. Your ladyship broke off the engagement."

"Fake engagement," she corrected. "We were never truly betrothed."

Mr. Tripp's handsome features softened as he smiled at her. "I have known Julius a long time. One thing about him, he's incapable of telling a lie. He cannot do it. Me, I lie for a living. It's in my blood. But Julius is different. He never pretends to be something he isn't. Ever. Do you understand what I am saying?"

"No, I'm afraid I don't. Are you saying he wasn't pretending to be my fiancé?"

"I'm saying that whatever happened between the two of you was real. That his acting skills could not begin to convince anyone he felt something for you if he truly didn't."

"It hardly matters what he feels. As he himself once said, words mean little if they are not backed up by actions."

"True, but sometimes it takes a man's brain a few minutes to catch up. To make matters worse, Julius's father did everything he could to ensure his son wouldn't marry." Nora must've shown her confusion because he said, "Has he told you about his father?"

"About the investment going under and taking his own life, yes."

He settled back in the seat. "That's just the tip of it, I'm afraid. You see, Julius's mother turned her back on her husband when everything fell apart, made Julius sit with the old man during his drunken ramblings. He was thirteen, forced to listen to his father rant and rave for days about the perils of having a family and the weight of responsibilities. And the instant he left the old man for a minute, his father killed himself."

"That's awful." She could only imagine the guilt Julius must carry.

"Lost his mother as well, for all intents and purposes. She closed herself off after that, struggling to keep the family afloat. To Julius, family means failure. And his mother reinforces that notion every time he sees her."

Nora disliked Mrs. Hatcher even more now. Her heart ached for his loss, for the poisoning of his future happiness. How could a mother be so cruel to her children? At least Nora had never had her father's approval and affection. You couldn't miss what you'd never had. "I still don't see what this has to do with me. He doesn't return my affections."

"That's where you are wrong, my lady. He is besotted by you. Completely over the moon. In short, he's in love with you."

"You're wrong. He thinks whatever is between us is merely a phase, an ailment to work out of our systems."

Mr. Tripp was already shaking his head. "He braved his mother for you. He allowed himself to be humiliated, blackmailed, and insulted by these society types to keep up your ruse. *He risked his seat on the exchange for you.*"

While some of Mr. Tripp's logic made sense, it didn't erase the fact that Julius had let her walk away. As he'd said many times, if he cared for a woman he would never allow her to walk away.

Not to mention Julius had endured those society types because he'd needed the ruse to continue every bit as much as she had.

"I'm sorry. I appreciate you coming this morning but "

"I'd like for you to come to the theater with me on Friday night."

She frowned at him. Was Mr. Tripp attempting to make Julius jealous? If so, he shouldn't waste his time. "Why?"

"Julius has purchased a failing theater. There's a grand reopening performance Friday night and all of society will be there. I think you should also attend."

Julius had purchased a theater? That was unexpected—but then this was the man who had hosted a dinner party on horseback and built a French castle. The only time he hadn't acted outrageously was when they'd pretended to be engaged, apparently. "Thank you for the invitation but I must decline."

"Hiding away and cowering hardly seems your style, Lady Nora."

She bristled at the insult. "Are you trying to anger me into accepting? If so, I should tell you it will not work."

He brushed imaginary dirt from his trousers. "Of course. It was silly of me to try. It's probably for the best. Miss Desmond will undoubtedly prefer to have him all to herself anyway."

Poppy Desmond? Nora's stomach clenched at the mention of Julius's former mistress. "What do you mean?"

"Oh, I thought you knew. He bought this theater to give Poppy a place to perform."

Nora inhaled sharply, the news like a swift blow. He bought that woman a theater? Why in God's name would he have done something like that? Furthermore, he'd done it without even mentioning it to Nora. *How dare he . . .*

Anger and hurt twisted in her veins, growing, until she knew what she had to do. Sit home while he romanced his mistress in front of all society? Then everyone would assume Nora was a heartbroken fool, sitting at home and crying over him.

Absolutely not—not even if it killed her.

Looking up at Mr. Tripp, she nodded. "I changed my mind. I would very much like to attend the theater on Friday."

ONE OF THE things Julius had always loved about his large home was the quiet after dark. No dogs running about. No babies squalling or nannies scrambling. Just quiet. He could wander the halls and long rooms, never seeing another soul. The servants knew to give him his space and he paid them well for it.

The tranquility was hardly soothing on this particular evening, however. He was restless, sitting in his dark office and drinking his favorite whiskey. Only a sliver of lamplight from the street peeked through a far curtain, the rest of the room cloaked in gloom.

A gloom that perfectly matched his mood.

Hard to pinpoint each of the emotions churning inside him. He was furious at that ridiculous artist for showing up and ruining everything. Then there was the shock over Nora's admission. Disappointment in himself that he hadn't handled it better.

Most of all, he regretted the end of his fake engagement.

He drained the rest of the whiskey in his glass and poured another. He'd grown quite attached to Nora. Had anticipated seeing her, even if just to talk to her.

"I cannot pretend I do not want more and your feelings on the matter have been made perfectly clear."

What exactly were his feelings on the matter?

Damned if he knew. Yes, he had thought the attraction was something to be worked through. He usually tired of a woman after about three or four months. Why should Nora be any different?

Yet she was different. He felt it down to his soul. She was no selfish jezebel or scheming dance hall girl. Nor was she an actress who wanted him for his name and bank account. Nora had fallen in love with him—a man with a terrible family history far from the elite types she normally associated with. Never once had she treated him as being from a lower station, though he was indeed that.

And brave. God, was she brave. She never shied away or backed down, not even when admitting her love for him. She easily could have lied or made up a story to appease Julius's curiosity. Yet she'd done neither; she had admitted the truth without shame.

Though he hadn't been ready to hear it, he respected the hell out of the admission.

The question was, what was he going to do about it all? The idea of giving her up for good made him

want to punch something. The alternative, however, was to really marry her . . . and he couldn't
very well do that. If her father hadn't approved of
the weak and banal Robert, then he certainly would
not approve of a man with Julius's reputation.

*"Never marry, my boy. You shall hurt everyone you
love."*

It was better to be alone. That was how Julius had
always lived his life, free of familial responsibilities.
Yes, he provided for his mother and sister—and
neither could stand him. They snubbed their noses
at his career, his home, his bank account . . . His
mother had never approved of anything Julius had
done. Somehow he'd managed to disappoint the
one woman who should love him unconditionally.

A noise suddenly caught his attention. He paused
and listened for it again. There, a soft thump. The
staff had long gone to bed. No one else was in this
part of the house. Who was here?

He remained still, waiting. A scratching sounded
in the keyhole. He'd locked the door earlier for privacy and never bothered to unlock it. Someone was
now trying to open the tumbler with a pair of lock
picks. He could hear the pins working to find the
right position to disengage the lock.

Anticipation surged through his veins, his heart
beginning to pump furiously. Oh, how he longed
to pummel someone tonight.

Without making a sound, he stood and crept behind a large curtain near the window, completely
concealing himself. It only took a few minutes for
the intruder to find the correct combination for the

pins and the lock tumbled open. The latch turned slowly, quietly, and soft footsteps fell on the carpets.

Shutting the door, the intruder lit a lamp he must have brought with him. Julius could see the dull yellow bouncing off the walls as the person moved toward the desk. He did not move, breathing evenly and silently, curious as to the intruder's intent. Was this the same person who had destroyed his office the night of the fire? It could very well be one of his father's investors, hoping to steal the fictional stock certificates.

The drawer in Julius's desk slid open. Papers crinkled as hands swept over them, searching. Another drawer, more rustling. Blood rushed in Julius's ears, the irritation and frustration at this violation building until he could not tolerate one second more. This had gone on long enough.

Throwing back the curtain, he stepped away from the window . . . and came face-to-face with William Pendleton.

Pendleton's eyes went wide with alarm, his body freezing as he reached into the bottom desk drawer. "*Hatcher*."

Julius put his hands on his hips and glared at the older man. "You had better have a good goddamn reason for what you are doing right now, Pendleton, or I'll be calling the roundsman."

"I . . ." Pendleton glanced around, likely looking for an escape route.

"Don't even try to run. You've got twenty years and fifteen pounds on me at least—and I know every square inch of this property. You'll never make it."

Sweat beaded on Pendleton's forehead. He cleared his throat and straightened, giving a lame attempt at a smile. "I think there's been some misunderstanding here. I left something the other day during our visit and merely came back to retrieve it."

"In the middle of the night? Using lock picks? Uninvited? You don't really expect anyone to buy that tale, do you?"

"It's the story I'll tell, regardless." A sneer twisted the other man's lips. "Now who do you think they'll believe? Me, an upstanding member of New York society and president of the Gotham Club—or the new-monied banker one step up from the gutter?"

"They'll believe me when they find the lock picks in your pocket."

He lifted his hands in the air as if innocent. "Those were planted on me. I've never seen them before in my life."

Fury colored Julius's vision like a mist. He clenched his fists and stalked forward. "Then I suppose I shall merely need to take matters into my own hands. After all, this is my home and you are trespassing."

Pendleton began backing up, real fear flashing in his eyes. "You cannot touch me. I'll see everything you care about stripped away."

"Nice try, Knickerbocker. You don't have even close to that sort of power over me."

Pendleton lunged for the door, as Julius expected he might. Julius pounced and caught Pendleton's shoulder, pushing the older man against the wall. Before Pendleton could escape, Julius wrapped a hand around his throat and squeezed. Pendleton gasped and clawed at Julius's grip, trying to loosen it to no avail.

"I should squeeze the life out of you right here."

"No!" Pendleton wheezed. "Stop."

"Why should I?" He tightened his fist and bumped the other man's head into the plaster. "Tell me what you were looking for."

Airway further restricted, Pendleton's eyes began to bulge. He shook his head.

"Fine. If you are that eager to die . . ." He watched as Pendleton's mouth tried to form words. Julius eased up his grip. "Something to say?"

"I'll tell you. Just let me go."

"You get one chance, Pendleton. Best make it count." He let go of the other man and stepped back, allowing Pendleton to collect himself momentarily.

Pendleton leaned over, dragging air into his lungs, his hand on his throat. As Julius watched him, something nagged at the back of his brain, something familiar.

"We gentlemen must look out for one another."

Pendleton's words from the other day . . . Julius hadn't remembered at the time, but now he knew where he'd heard that expression before. His father had said it before he'd taken his own life. It hadn't made any sense to Julius then but Warren Hatcher must have fixated on that expression he'd overheard from Pendleton.

"It was *you*," Julius snarled. "You're here searching for the stock because you were one of the investors that ruined my father. Goddamn you!"

Julius moved to wrap his hands around Pendleton's throat once more, but the other man put his hands up. "Wait, don't."

"Why in hell should I let you live when you are responsible for my father's death?"

"Your father was an inept fool," Pendleton spat. "He offered up collateral to the bank and signed that demand note without thinking it through. Always eager to make a quick buck."

"And you left him to face the creditors alone, never paying your share—a share that might have saved my family from losing everything."

"That was not my problem. I never signed anything."

"No, you merely shook his hand and promised you were good for the money—except when it counted, apparently."

"There was no point in paying money for a deal that had fallen through!" Pendleton shouted. "Why should we all lose out to help the bank recover their losses?"

"Because you could afford it," Julius gritted out. "And my family could not."

Pendleton laughed, almost a sneer. "Your father was nothing more than a charlatan. He talked a good game but he was greedy."

"Greedy!" Julius's muscles clenched, ready to strangle Pendleton once more. He shoved the other man into the wall and leaned in his face. "You have now broken into my office *twice* looking for stock that does not belong to you and you have the fucking audacity to talk about greed?"

"I was not the one who broke into your office before," Pendleton choked out.

"What?"

Pendleton took advantage of Julius's momentary surprise and pushed him back a step. "That's right. Your fiancée's precious uncle was responsible for that."

Former fiancée, but Julius didn't bother correcting the man. News of the broken engagement had been made public today, even though Julius refused to believe it was truly broken. "Cortland?" Julius could hardly believe it, breath escaping in a rush. Why would Nora's uncle destroy Julius's office?

Pendleton snickered. "You've never even asked who the other investors were. Are you not curious?"

"Of course," Julius forced out. "Are you saying Cortland was one of them?"

"Yes, he and a man named Allenson, who died of cholera a few years back."

"Jesus Christ."

"Puts you in a bit of a spot, doesn't it, Hatcher? Can't have you exacting revenge on your fiancée's uncle. And you can say good-bye to your social standing and membership at Gotham if you try anything with me."

Pulling back his arm, he punched Pendleton square in the jaw, and the other man slumped to the floor. "I don't give a damn about my social standing or Gotham. I'm prepared to make you wish you'd never been born, Pendleton, and to hell with the consequences."

THE POSH UPTOWN crowd packed the downtown Athena Theater. Nora surveyed the ostrich plumes and diamonds and tried not to be hurt that Julius hadn't invited her. Hadn't even told her of buying the theater. So much for honesty, she supposed.

I have never lied to you.

Yes, but secrets had the power to wound as well.

Mr. Tripp, or Frank as he'd insisted, had allowed her to invite Kathleen and Anne, along with their parents, as well as the Cortlands. The atmosphere was gay, their large festive group surrounding Nora with a joy she could no longer feel. She only hoped that Julius bought her charade.

God above, she missed that man.

Missed him with a fierce longing she hadn't experienced before, as if part of her heart had been carved out of her chest. News of the broken engagement had swept along Fifth Avenue, even— ironically—a mention in the *Town Talk* column of the newspaper. She caught the pitying glances, the smirks, as the ladies didn't bother to hide their curiosity or their whispers. *His former mistress . . . bought her a theater . . . poor Lady Nora.*

But Frank had been right: cowering was not in Nora's nature.

The largest box, the one directly in the center, remained empty. It didn't take a genius to guess the box was reserved for the theater owner. Should Julius actually sit there he would be well within Nora's line of sight. The prospect of staring at him all evening almost had her out of her seat and heading for the exit.

Then again, the box remaining empty meant he was likely somewhere else in the building, like Poppy Desmond's dressing room. Her throat closed as she imagined him kissing another woman, whispering those naughty words in another ear. She dragged in a shaky breath and started to rise, determined to get some air.

"Don't you dare," Frank said softly, handing her a fresh glass of champagne. "Don't run away from."

Kathleen sat next to Nora. "You can do it. Perhaps he's not even in the building."

"More than likely he's backstage with *her.*"

"If he is, then he doesn't deserve you," Anne said as she joined their group. "And you are better off."

Little consolation, Nora thought, when her mind couldn't stop conjuring images of the lush actress and her former fiancé in a passionate embrace. At least she would see him tonight, let him know that she'd discovered his secret.

The gaslights in the interior dimmed and Frank took the seat immediately to her right. The curtain parted and Julius, handsome and formidable in a black swallowtail coat and matching trousers, strolled out onto the stage. The crowd broke into polite applause as they took their seats.

Nora drank in the sight of him, his sandy blond hair swept off his clean-shaven face. Sharp blue eyes twinkled in the stage lights, his gaze sweeping the theater. She stopped breathing when he turned her way even though there was little chance he could see her with the bright lights shining in his face.

"Good evening," his voice boomed. "Thank you all for coming to the reopening of the Athena Theater." More applause. When it died down, he continued. "I hadn't ever pictured myself a theater owner. But, as I told someone recently, people change. Circumstances change."

Nora's stomach clenched at the reminder of their conversation and she held perfectly still, willing herself not to care.

"So here I am," he said with a self-deprecating laugh. "In the end, I found I couldn't allow such a beautiful theater to close. So please, enjoy tonight's production, the first of many I hope you attend at the new Athena."

He left the stage, the crowd clapping, anticipation rising in the air. Not a seat remained available from what Nora could see, except for Julius's box. She glanced over and wondered, would he have a companion tonight? She couldn't fathom his attending alone, not since their engagement ended. He could now return to his devil-may-care ways without suffering any consequences.

Heavens, watching him with another woman would be torture. Why in God's name had she decided to come?

The play started and Nora tried to ignore the empty box. She flinched when Poppy Desmond took the stage, the crowd applauding madly at the actress's first appearance. But even she had to admit that Miss Desmond was a true talent. Her voice captivated the entire building, every eye riveted on her each time she opened her mouth.

Nora was so caught up in the song that she almost missed when Julius slipped into his box. He took the front-and-center seat, and she proceeded to study him through her lashes. He leaned back and crossed his legs, eyes fixed on Poppy down on the stage. No one else joined him.

Was he enjoying watching his former lover? Had

the two rekindled their acquaintance? She searched his face for any sign, any hint, to what he was thinking but came up empty. Just as she was about to give up, his head slowly pivoted and they locked eyes. Her battered heart thumped madly as he continued to stare, no light of recognition or warmth in the blue depths. Had he known she was here?

He gave no outward sign of regret or sorrow as they gazed at each other and Nora began to feel foolish. She had put all her feelings on the table and Julius hadn't been interested. What more needed to be said?

Swallowing hard, she forced her attention back to the stage. Her skin prickled, however, with the knowledge that he was still focused on her. Pride refused to let her turn to see, however. If he could not love her back, then she needed to forget about him.

Somehow.

After what seemed a century, the first act ended and the interior lights grew brighter. Kathleen and Anne began to chatter on about the performance while Nora snuck a glance at Julius's box.

It was empty.

Chapter Nineteen

Throughout the first act, Julius had felt as if he might crawl out of his own skin. Nora was here, only a few hundred feet away, and he could not touch her or hear her laugh. Make her shiver or see her smile. It was pure hell.

He'd known the instant she entered the building. As if every cell in his body were attuned to hers, he'd watched from backstage as her party settled into the box. Fucking Tripp. Undoubtedly Julius's friend was to blame for Nora's presence tonight.

Not that he was complaining. She was stunning, with her brown hair swept up and artfully arranged with diamond clips. Poised and strong, she exuded an iron will, a refusal to back down from any challenge. He adored that about her.

He wished for a fraction of her composure. Since she broke off their engagement and he'd discovered Pendleton in his office, Julius felt as if he were cracking apart at the seams. He had no idea what to do about his tangled feelings for her—and now he also had to figure out how to handle the revelation about her uncle.

Hard to believe that James Cortland had backed out on Julius's father all those years ago. Not only that, he'd ransacked Julius's office the night of the fire to search for the fake stock. Destroying Pendleton had been easy. The man's bank accounts had been laughably thin, possibly why he'd been so determined to find the high-valued stock in Julius's home. A few telephone calls and telegrams had wiped out all Pendleton's assets. Last Julius heard, the man was bound for family in Virginia.

Cortland was a greater challenge. Julius couldn't very well ruin Nora's uncle, engagement or not. Hurting Cortland would crush Nora . . . and Julius hadn't a clue on how to proceed. He shouldn't care—after all, Nora was the one who had walked away from their arrangement—but he had no interest in causing her more pain. And yet, he could not allow Cortland to go unpunished. He needed justice.

Near the end of the first act, he slipped out of his box. The corridor behind the boxes was empty, thanks to Poppy's extraordinary performance tonight. No one wanted to miss a second of her on stage, apparently. Lights still dim, he entered the rear of Cortland's box and tapped the older man on the shoulder. "A word."

James Cortland nodded and rose, following Julius into the corridor. There was an unused service staircase at the end of the hall, and Julius steered them there, holding the door open for Cortland to pass through. They took the stairs down to the ground floor and Julius pushed on the large steel door that led to the back alley.

Cool night air washed over them as he shut the door and leaned against it. The smell of rotting lettuce and horse permeated the alley, but Julius didn't want this conversation overheard by a soul. He crossed his arms over his chest. "Give me one reason not to bury you, Cortland."

Thankfully, Nora's uncle did not play dumb. After a long moment, his shoulders slumped. "Pendleton told you."

"Yes, he did. He also told me you were the one to break into my office the night of the fire."

Cortland sighed. "I only did that to make it seem as if someone had broken in. I didn't take anything, I swear."

"That makes even less sense. Why would you wish for me to think there had been an intruder?"

"It wasn't for your benefit. It was for Pendleton's. He was . . . blackmailing me to find the stock certificates. He was determined to get his hands on them."

"What could he possibly have to blackmail you with?"

"Nora." He dragged a hand down his face. "With Nora engaged to you, Pendleton kept threatening to tell you the truth about my involvement. I had hoped you would never find out."

Jesus, what a mess. "So you started the fire to get me out of the house that night."

"No, I never started any fire. But it was an opportunity I couldn't afford to waste."

Complete coincidence? Julius doubted it. "Did Pendleton start the fire, then?"

"Not that he admitted to me. And I can't imagine he'd dirty his hands in such a manner."

Julius squinted disbelievingly. "We are talking about the same man who picked the lock on my office door the other night, are we not?"

"I suppose," Cortland said, lifting a shoulder. "But he never wanted to hurt anyone. He only wanted the money."

Julius rubbed his eyes with the heels of his hands. "Why didn't you tell me? There were ample opportunities to come clean."

"Shame." He heaved a sigh. "I am not proud of what happened all those years ago. Your father, while possessing a poor head for business, had a good heart. He did not deserve to be ruined over something so trivial. I know it's little consolation but I did reconsider about my share . . . only it was too late. He'd already taken his own life." He thrust his hands in his pockets. "So now you know. What do you plan to do?"

Julius clenched his jaw, debating. Part of him longed to strip Cortland of everything he held dear, as Warren Hatcher once had been. But then he thought of Nora, how kind James and Beatrice had been to their British niece. She would never forgive Julius if he harmed the Cortlands. He would never be able to win her back.

Wait, did he want to win her back?

"Damn it," he clipped out. "I hadn't expected this."

"I apologize. I know your life was forever changed by those events and I'm deeply sorry for my part in it. I never guessed that Warren would be destitute as a result, but ignorance is hardly absolution. I'm prepared to provide whatever recompense you demand."

Nothing could change the events of the past. Julius knew that. And he believed Nora's uncle in that he hadn't anticipated the dire circumstances that would result from breaking the deal. Cortland's attitude was worlds away from Pendleton's, who had lied and twisted the facts to make himself appear blameless. Cortland was not trying to shirk the blame at all. Julius respected that.

"I do not need your recompense." He blew out a long breath. "I had held on to this idea of vengeance for so long, but it's time to let go. There are other greater concerns to be dealt with and I need to set this aside."

"Are you certain? It hardly seems fair that Pendleton paid a price while I did not."

"Pendleton broke into my office and insulted me to my face. He exhibited no remorse and threatened me. Considering he was also blackmailing you, I'd say Pendleton got exactly what was coming to him."

"Fair enough," Cortland said. "What now? What will you tell Nora?"

A burning ache settled behind Julius's breastbone. "We are not exactly speaking, in case you haven't noticed. The engagement's over."

"Is that why the two of you were staring at each other the entire first act?"

Julius felt his cheeks warm. Hell, was he blushing? "I miss her."

"She bought a train ticket, you know. Tried to hide it, but Beatrice is far craftier than anyone gives her credit for. Nora plans to leave for San Francisco next week."

San Francisco? Christ, Nora couldn't go that far away. Why would she not return to England? To her father and friends? "You cannot let her leave."

Cortland shook his head. "Have you met Nora? I suspect she'll find a way to leave whether Beatrice and I allow it or not. I'd much rather *you* not let her leave, because I suspect you are the only person she'll listen to."

"Why me?"

"Because she's in love with you, Hatcher." He put a hand on Julius's shoulder. "And if you want her, you'd best figure out how to win her back. Quickly."

"I don't believe she'll have me, no matter what I do. I—" A faint distinctive smell floated through his nostrils. "Is that . . . ? Jesus Christ—that's fire!"

He spun and pulled on the handle of the door leading back inside the theater . . . except it was locked. "Damn!" He pounded on the metal once. "I told them to leave this unlocked. We have to get everyone out!"

Breaking out in a run, he sprinted toward the street and the theater entrance. Before he even reached the mouth of the alley the screams started. No, no, no. They could not panic. He had to help everyone get out in an orderly fashion, use the exit doors and fire escapes. A stampede could kill hundreds, if not thousands, of people.

And Nora. Dear God, Nora was in there.

The idea of losing her nearly sent him to his

knees. No more scandalous outings. No more teasing smiles or looks full of longing. No more standing up to him with her sharp intelligence and even sharper tongue. Her death would kill him, drown him in grief until he could not function. She was his best friend, his confidant, his lover, and the keeper of his undeserving heart.

She was everything.

And he had to tell her at least once.

When he rounded the corner, people were already streaming out of the main exit doors. Patrons were shoving and yelling, while smoke billowed into the night above them. What disturbed him most was that everyone was dry, which meant the brand-new sprinkler system hadn't yet kicked on to douse the flames. Sweat broke out on his forehead. If the fire continued unchecked, the casualties would be high.

"Someone sound the alarm! Rouse the fire brigade!" he shouted as he pushed his way toward the doors. With everyone trying to get out, he could hardly find purchase in the crowd to fight his way in. With every two steps forward, he was shoved one farther away.

"Stay calm and move away from the building as quickly as possible," he told them, using all his strength to withstand getting swept away by the mob of people. "Do not push, and help anyone having trouble."

Chaos swirled all around and the old fears threatened to choke him. But finding Nora urged him on.

He could not let her die.

NORA WAS DROWNING her sorrows during intermission with a few glasses of champagne when the first hint of alarm reached her ears.

"Did you hear that?" Kathleen asked.

"Is someone . . . screaming?" Anne cocked her head. "I thought—"

Another scream, this time closer. Then they heard the word every theatergoer dreaded: *Fire.*

The men had all departed for the smoking lounge, leaving just the ladies behind. Aunt Bea appeared at their elbows. "I do not know what is happening but I believe we should leave just to be on the safe side." She gestured to the orchestra floor, where patrons were pushing toward the rear of the theater. Actors and theater workers were running across the stage—just before the fire curtain came down, blocking them from view.

"Oh, God. Look!" Kathleen pointed to the ceiling. Gray smoke was gathering, rolling, to cover the beautiful painted mural above them. There were sprinkler heads installed but no water shooting out of them.

"Dear heavens. We need to get out of this building before it goes up in flames." Aunt Bea hurried them to the back corridor, where a large number of patrons were running to the main staircase.

"Go, go, go!" Nora told them. Kathleen's and Anne's mothers grabbed their hands and began tugging the girls along to safety. Nora took Aunt Bea's arm and the two women joined the stream of society men and women rushing to leave.

When they reached the mouth of the corridor

they encountered a living nightmare. A sea of patrons stretched in front of them, leaving absolutely nowhere to go. People were shoving and yelling, climbing on top of one another, fear thick in the air as they debouched from the upper levels. Older women stumbled and risked being trampled before they were helped to their feet. The screams grew louder.

Nora blinked, the gathering smoke stinging her eyes. Soon it would be difficult to breathe. "We have to find another way out," she yelled to her aunt.

Aunt Bea nodded, a lace handkerchief held over her mouth. Nora took her aunt's hand and they started to push through the bodies back toward the boxes. "I think I saw fire escapes on the outside of the building," she shouted.

The crowd thinned bit by bit as they moved away from the main stairs. The lights suddenly went out, the corridor engulfed in total blackness. Nora held tight to her aunt and felt her way along the wall. The other end of the corridor led out into an alley. There must be a way out at that end. Briefly, she wondered about Julius and whether he'd escaped the building. Hopefully he knew of a secret exit for the cast and crew.

She prayed he was all right.

As they rounded the corner, she spied a small gathering huddled at the end of the corridor. Because the stairs were clogged with patrons, the group was trying to force open a large metal door, likely one that led to the fire escapes. *Oh no.* If that door would not budge, they were all in serious jeopardy.

The door suddenly cracked open as if pushed on the other side. Everyone rushed forward to help, pulling it wide to allow access. Julius stepped into the smoky gloom, an axe in his hand. "Hurry, all Go quickly and quietly. The fire escape is already in place."

Nora hurried toward him. "Julius!"

His head snapped up and relief filled his eyes when he saw her. With both hands, he reached and pulled her close. "Christ, Nora. I am glad to see you."

She buried her face in his dirty necktie, clasping him tightly about the waist. "You saved us."

His lips touched the top of her head. "Almost, sweetheart. Hurry and take your aunt along the fire escape."

Aunt Bea had already disappeared through the door. Nora grasped Julius's hand and started pulling him. "Let's go."

He broke free and pushed her toward the opening. "Not yet. I need to turn on the sprinkler system."

"No! Julius, no." He was going into the theater? Everything was getting hotter, smokier. Soon, the air would grow toxic. Her fingers dug into his rumpled clothing. "You must come with me."

"Nora, go." He was gentle but firm. "I cannot allow anyone to die. I must go behind the stage and turn on the sprinklers in the basement. Go!"

"I don't want to leave you here," she nearly screamed, panic residing in her throat. "You'll never make it out."

"I will, I promise." He smoothed her hair back. "I love you. Now go and get to safety, please." Forcibly, he lifted her out onto the small platform leading to the fire escape. She grabbed at the rail to steady herself. When she looked over her shoulder, Julius was gone.

Tears sprang to her eyes. *He will make it. He cannot die, not now.* She drew in a deep breath and started forward. Her aunt had just reached the ground, a few gentlemen in the alley helping her off the fire escape. Unfortunately, not many people were on the ground, and she thought of those still struggling inside, the patrons on the main staircase who would never guess to come down the corridor behind the boxes to reach safety.

It was an easy decision, really.

Turning, she went back inside and ran toward the main staircase.

THE AIR WAS hot, stifling, as Julius wound his way toward the side boxes. He needed to get backstage quickly but the staircases were too crowded. Instead he climbed over the railing on the box closest to the stage. Legs dangling, he let go and dropped more than ten feet to the floor. A sharp pain erupted in his ankle when he landed, as if a white-hot poker had been shoved under the bone. Gritting his teeth, he got to his feet, picked up the axe, and limped as fast as he could to the area behind the stage, feeling his way in the dark.

The valve for the sprinkler system was in the basement's maintenance room. Julius knew this because the system had been tested recently when the crew refurbished the theater; he'd seen the sprinklers work himself. He had no idea why it hadn't yet turned on, but he had to do something before the fire brigade arrived.

At least Nora was safe. No matter what else happened, she was outside and away from the danger. The backstage area was quiet, the crew and actors having used their own exits in the rear of the theater. He coughed, the smoke seeping into his lungs. Withdrawing a handkerchief from his inner coat pocket, he covered his mouth and went as quickly as he dared in the pitch-black down the small stone stairs that led into the bowels of the building.

His ankle throbbed with every step. Probably no more than ten minutes had elapsed since he smelled smoke in the alley but a fire could spread rapidly. Add in the hysteria and the risk of smoke inhalation and none of them had much time.

Though he could not see, the basement was blessedly smoke-free, which meant the fire hadn't originated down here. It also meant he wouldn't instantly die of smoke inhalation while trying to find and fix the sprinklers. He turned the corner and pushed open the door that should be the maintenance room—and drew up short.

A lamp had been lit, casting a soft yellow glow about the room. Robert, Nora's former beau, stood in the middle of the floor, his feet braced and his hands clenched, eyes narrowed on Julius.

"What are you doing in here?" Julius barked, striding forward. "This room is off-limits."

"So was Nora, but that did not prevent you from stealing her."

Julius knew better than to argue. He had stolen

her, at least temporarily, and regretted nothing. He hadn't lied when he'd told her he loved her a few moments ago. He merely wished he had told her sooner.

"Whatever you've done, Robert, we can undo it. People do not have to die." He walked in briskly, cradling the axe in both hands. "No one has to die."

"You are supposed to die. *You*," Robert snarled. "And if you kill me, you'll never learn where I hid the handle to the valve. That's what you're here to do, is it not? Save the day by turning on the sprinkler system."

He'd hidden the handle to the valve? Sure enough, the pipe was missing the round wheel handle to manually engage the water. Without the handle, he'd need a pair of pliers to turn the valve. "Tell me where to find the damn handle. *Now*."

A sneer emerged. "You would like to play hero. Save all these people and be able to brag about it. Get Nora back in bed with you—"

Lunging forward, Julius slammed Robert into the side of the ventilation system, his forearm in Robert's throat. "There are hundreds of people fighting for their lives upstairs. You cannot let them die merely because she cast you adrift. *Think*, Robert. This is terribly cruel."

Robert lifted his chin, anger flashing in his eyes. "I grew up with no one and learned to look out for myself. I feel sorry for those people up there, but they are a small price to pay to get what I want."

"She won't love a murderer. Give me the valve and let me turn on the sprinklers."

"She won't ever know. No one will suspect me.

This'll just be noted as a tragedy in which the theater owner lost his life, and Nora will return to me."

Madness shone in his gaze and Julius believed this conversation had gone on long enough. He did not have time to argue. "I am giving you one more chance. Where is the handle?"

"Go to hell."

Julius lifted the axe and brought the handle's end down on the side of Robert's skull. Robert's eyes fluttered closed and he sank to the ground, unconscious. Julius quickly checked the man's coat pockets. Nothing. Craning his neck wildly, he searched the immediate vicinity for the handle or a box containing tools. Anything with which to turn the valve.

Sweat rolled off his brow as he checked the floor. Seemed logical that Robert would remove the handle and then toss it on the ground under the equipment. Nothing. *Damn it.*

Quickly, he leapt to his feet and began investigating the room. One of the workers must have left some tools behind; after all, Robert couldn't have removed the handle without one. Behind the coal furnace he found a set of tools. Located the pliers and raced to the valve. It wasn't an easy fit but he forced the mouth around the bolt and turned hard. The bolt shifted the slightest fraction, so he put all his strength behind it and yanked. It moved a bit more and Julius kept at it until he had the valve completely open and the sound of water rushed and rumbled through the pipe.

Leaning against the wall, he tried to catch his breath. *Thank God.* At least the flames could be contained until the fire brigade arrived, if they weren't already here. The only thing left to do now was leave.

He stared at Robert's prone form. "Damn it. I'm going to have to carry you out of here, aren't I?"

Robert didn't answer, of course, and Julius had no choice but to bend down and hoist the other man up as best he could with an injured ankle. He draped Robert over his back and shuffled out of the equipment room. The scent of smoke grew stronger as he continued along the hall, the heat nearly stifling, overpowering lungs strained from exertion. Each step on his bad leg was excruciating. His progress was slow and torturous.

When he turned the last corner, the stairs waited a few feet away. He could hear the water falling from overhead, smell the damp soot and acrid smoke. His leg muscles ached, his ankle pleading for a rest, but he trudged onward.

Less than two feet away from the stairs, an ear-splitting crack sounded above—and then the roof caved in.

Chapter Twenty

Nora stood at the fire escape, inhaling smoke and wiping sweat off her brow, and continued to help patrons safely out of the theater. She refused to leave. After Julius had disappeared, she raced to the main stairs and started leading a line of patrons to the fire escape off the boxed tier. She kept them calm and organized as they descended the iron ladder attached to the building's exterior.

Every second that went by with the sprinklers dry and closed stole a tiny piece of her soul. Julius was inside somewhere, and the lack of water pouring from the ceiling meant he could be hurt . . . or worse.

She would not allow herself to consider the possibility of worse.

I love you.

Had he meant it? Her heart swelled with hope and fear. He had to live—if only so she could find out if he had been telling the truth.

The first fire brigade arrived a few minutes later, the bell clanging on the truck as it tore down

Broadway, with a second and third truck right behind. The heat and panic inside the building had
been steadily rising, and a cheer went up outside
when help finally arrived. Still, she kept guiding
a never-ending stream of patrons toward the fire
escape. Each was rattled, scared, and, most of all,
thankful to get out alive.

When the sprinklers overhead began to spew
water, Nora nearly collapsed in relief. He had done
it. *Oh, thank heavens.* With the sprinklers working
and the fire brigades on the scene, this nightmare
would soon be behind them.

Firemen appeared in the alley to assist the injured and elderly. One approached Aunt Bea, who
merely shook her head and pointed up at Nora,
presumably refusing to leave until Nora reached
the ground. Nora continued shouting at the patrons waiting in the corridor to remain orderly, no
pushing. Everyone who emerged was soaked, be-
draggled, but not complaining. They would live.

Where is Julius?

She longed to find him, to see his impish grin
once more. Those bright blue eyes that held keen
intelligence and steely determination. Hear the
low, teasing timbre of his voice. Had he already left
the building?

"Miss, I can take over." A fireman, in a long dark
coat with shiny buttons and a tall hat, now stood
next to Nora. "You should take the ladder out of the
building before you are hurt."

"Is the fire out?" she asked.

"They have the hoses pointed at the worst of it on
the roof. The sprinklers appear to have taken care

of the flames inside. Go on now, miss." He nodded toward the door.

Nora didn't want to leave but she knew it was foolish to try to do his job for him. Additionally, she was anxious to reach the ground and search for Julius. She nodded and started for the exit door. Then a huge splintering sound rent the air, as if the building were collapsing. She turned toward the noise and watched as a huge section of the roof collapsed behind the stage.

She gasped. "Oh, my God." An ominous feeling settled in the pit of her stomach. Julius could be there somewhere.

"Go, now!" the fireman urged the patrons. "No pushing but step lively!"

"I cannot go!" Nora told him. "My fiancé, the owner, went backstage to the basement. He turned the sprinklers on."

The fireman wrapped his hand around her arm and forced her onto the landing of the fire escape. "And if he is, you cannot help him. We'll get down there as soon as we can."

"Please, let me help. I cannot leave him!"

"Miss, the whole building is unsound. It could come down at any moment. You won't help him if you're dead."

People behind Nora began pushing, urging her forward, and she had no choice but to start down the iron fire escape. "Please, find him!" she shouted as her feet moved woodenly, her chest feeling as if it were splitting in two.

"We will," he yelled, not looking at her as he continued to hustle the patrons along.

Tears blurred her vision and she clutched the railing to keep from stumbling as she descended. When she reached the ground, Aunt Bea rushed over and enveloped Nora in a hug.

"Are you all right? What was that sound?" her aunt asked.

"The roof collapsed right over the stage." She patted her aunt's back and then pulled away. "I have to go around, see if there's another way out." She started moving farther into the alley, toward the back of the theater.

"Nora, wait!" Her aunt grabbed her arm. "We should go stand across the street, where it's safe."

Nora shook her head, fresh tears pooling on her lashes. "Aunt Bea, Julius could still be in there."

"Oh, goodness. Well, let's go." She gave Nora a gentle shove and the two of them wove through the chaos in the alley. People were crying, yelling, searching for loved ones. The scene was heart-wrenching as more men and women spilled out of the theater via fire escapes and doors.

Behind the theater was equally disordered. Actors and actresses, stage crew, and patrons were sobbing, holding each other for comfort, while firemen soaked the theater roof as well as neighboring buildings with their hoses. Policemen were attempting to get the bystanders out of harm's way. All the black exit doors were open . . . and no one was emerging.

Nora frantically searched faces. She did not see him. *Please, please, please . . .*

"Nora!"

Turning toward the male voice, she found Frank Tripp racing toward her. "Oh, thank God," he said, grabbing her by the shoulders. "He'd never forgive me if something terrible had happened to you."

The woman with whom Frank had just been speaking joined them. Nora immediately recognized Poppy Desmond, though her costume was soiled with dirt and soot. The actress's brows were lowered in concern. "My lady," she said with a curtsey that seemed out of place, considering the circumstances.

"Miss Desmond."

"Have you seen him?" Frank asked. "Did he make it out?"

"I was about to ask you the same question. The last I knew, he went into the basement to turn on the sprinklers."

Frank closed his eyes and pinched the bridge of his nose. "Idiot."

Nora didn't have time to debate this. She turned to Poppy. "Is there another way out of the basement? The roof collapsed and I fear he may be trapped."

The actress spun and studied the length of the building, squinting. "All these doors lead backstage. If he's in the basement, the only other way out is the coal chute."

Poppy grabbed Frank's hand and they ran to a black cast-iron cover on the wall. They worked together to pry it open.

"Ladies, you need to step away—"

"There is a man trapped down there!" Nora shouted to the fireman. Not a lie; she could feel it in her bones. Julius was trapped inside—and she wouldn't rest until she found him.

The fireman came forward, pushing her out of the way to help Frank secure the coal chute cover. "Hello?" Frank shouted into the basement. "Anyone alive down there?"

"Julius!" Nora yelled. "Come to the coal chute!" *Please let him hear me. Please let him be alive.*

The fireman bellowed for a ladder while Nora continued to call down the coal chute. Only silence answered. Nora was not ready to give up. She said to the fireman, "Lower me in there."

"Absolutely not," Frank said. "If anyone's going in there, it'll be me."

"Nora!"

Julius appeared below, his handsome face covered in grime. He was carrying a man over his shoulders.

"Oh, thank God! Julius!" she said, her voice cracking. *He was alive.* Relief flooded her and she dropped to her knees.

His mouth hitched into a tired half smile. "I'm all right. Though I'm going to need some help getting out."

Within seconds, a ladder arrived and the fireman placed it down the chute. He descended into the basement to help Julius and the unconscious man. Frank, along with several other strong hands, assisted in getting the injured man up the ladder. Nora didn't take her eyes off Julius, however. The fireman ordered Julius to ascend and within seconds he reached the top.

She nearly tackled him, never so grateful in her entire life. "You scared the life out of me," she said into his soot-soaked waistcoat.

He kissed her head, his arms winding around her. "I apologize. But I'm here now."

"Were you trapped, then?" Frank asked.

"Yes," Julius answered. "When the ceiling collapsed."

"Your fiancée refused to give up on you." Frank clapped Julius on the back and nodded toward Nora.

"Is that so?" Julius squeezed Nora as he caught her gaze with his own. "Thank you."

A man moaned and Julius stiffened, his head swinging around. Nora looked over as well—and the breath caught in her throat. "Is that . . . Robert?" She searched Julius's face. "You saved Robert? But what . . . ?"

Julius scowled at the man on the ground. "He was the reason the sprinklers never turned on."

"Robert? But why?"

"He had no idea you were here tonight. He'd hoped I would perish and then he could win back your affections."

"*What?* That is utterly insane. Did he start the fire as well?"

"I don't know, but it's probably safe to assume he did. Otherwise, why sabotage the sprinklers? I wouldn't be surprised if he were responsible for my stable fire as well."

She stormed over to Robert, who struggled to gain his feet. "Did you do this?" she demanded. "Are you responsible for this fire?"

The flash of anger and madness in Robert's eyes was like nothing she'd seen before. He sneered. "He is lying to you. I came here to see the show. I was trying to escape the smoke and ended up in the basement."

She didn't doubt Julius's word for one moment. Not only that, she knew Robert. This was a new, unfamiliar side of him, one capable of violence. "I cannot believe you did this. People might be killed, Robert. Innocent people. This building is destroyed. All to win me back?"

"I didn't do this," he snarled and pointed at Julius. "He is trying to cause you to hate me."

A policeman was walking by and Nora grabbed his arm. Pointing at Robert, she said, "Sir, this is the man who started the fire. He is responsible."

Robert spun and sprinted away, only his legs must have still been woozy from his injury because he fell to the cobblestones. The policeman easily snatched him up. "This one, miss?"

"You were not supposed to be here!" Robert snapped. "Only him. He should have died, Nora. Then everything would have gone back to the way it was."

She closed her eyes, the words like daggers in her chest. He'd caused all this destruction, all this terror and death, to kill Julius in the hopes she would reconcile with him? It was too terrible to absorb. What happened to the sweet poet she had been in love with for months? How could he be capable of something like this?

The policeman dragged Robert away while another officer approached Julius. "Mr. Hatcher, we'll need a statement, sir."

"Of course, but not until the fire is out and we've done all we can here. Where are they taking the injured?"

"The hotel on the corner, sir."

"Do we know how many lives have been lost?"

"Not yet, sir. It'll be some time before that's been determined."

Julius sighed and, after shaking the officer's hand and promising to make his way to the hotel, he put his palm on Nora's cheek. "Why don't you go home and get some rest? This figures to be a long night."

"Not a chance. I am not letting you out of my sight again."

A chuckle rumbled in his chest. "That may be hard to explain when I need to go home and rest myself."

"A fiancée is allowed to see her injured future husband home and settled in his bed."

A sandy blond brow rose. "Is that so? Are you still my fiancée, then?"

"Did you mean what you said in the theater, before you left?"

"I never say anything I do not mean. A man's only as good as his word, you know."

"Will you say it again?"

He leaned down close to her ear. "I love you, my lady. I'm only sorry it took me so damn long to spit it out."

A shiver worked its way down Nora's spine, a wildly inappropriate response considering the grim circumstances around them but one she could not control. But still, he had let her walk away before. How could he be sure? "When did you realize it?"

"I think I've known for a while, but I couldn't deny it any longer when I was trying to push through the pandemonium to get inside to you. I was outside when the fire started."

She thought of the mob on the staircase, all headed toward the main entrance. "You fought through that crowd?"

His expression softened, his gaze sweeping over her face. "I would walk through the fires of hell doused in kerosene if it meant saving your life."

Forgetting they were surrounded by people, she raised up on her toes and pressed a kiss to his mouth.

"Now, now—none of that until after the wedding," Aunt Bea suddenly said from beside them.

Startled, Nora spun toward her aunt, who stood with Uncle James a few feet away. Her uncle slapped Julius's back. "Glad to see you made it, Hatcher. I heard from the battalion chief that the sprinklers likely saved many lives tonight. People stopped panicking once they turned on."

"Thank Christ," Julius breathed. "I must speak to him and then go to the hotel to meet with the police."

Nora took his arm, not ready to let go of him just yet. "I'll come with you." He opened his mouth to argue, so she held up her free hand. "Do not bother attempting to talk me out of it."

"Love, honor, and *obey*, Nora. Emphasis on the last one."

"Then it is a good thing we have not exchanged those vows just yet, Mr. Hatcher."

THE RELEASE CAUGHT Julius by surprise, the fierce pleasure of being inside his fiancée—his true fiancée, it seemed—too damn much to take. "God, yes," he bellowed, his stomach heaving. "*Nora.*" His seed spilled inside her as she continued to ride him, her legs astride his on the mattress, breasts bouncing, her own release having occurred seconds before. He gritted his teeth and grunted, the pulses coursing through him.

He stopped shaking and she collapsed on top of his chest. They caught their breath as he stroked her sweat-soaked back, his semi-hard penis still buried inside her warmth. "I will never get tired of that. Not even when we're old and feeble."

"Good, because I am liable to want *that* at least once a day."

"Whatever my lady wants," he said and kissed the top of her head.

He was exhausted. They had stayed late, helping tend to the wounded and cataloging names to reunite families. Nora had surprised him, selfless and tireless in her efforts to lend aid. He had learned of her efforts during the fire, diverting those stuck on the main stairs to the boxed tier fire escape, and loved her all the more for it. His brave English lady.

In the end, the police had taken pity on the two of them and promised to collect Julius's statement the following day. The police and fire departments were still piecing together all that had happened, but it appeared the death toll would remain low. Almost all the patrons had been able to exit using fire escapes and the balcony had only been half-full.

Nora had confirmed Robert's identity to the police and gave a brief description of recent events. Robert had been arrested and led away, yelling the entire time of his innocence.

In the early hours of the morning, Julius and Nora

had returned to his house, with Nora sneaking in because he "needed help with his ankle." He hadn't really, but who was he to complain?

After a bath to wash away the horrors of the night, they'd ended up in his bed, naked, grateful to be alive and to be together. Julius had no doubt that James Cortland would be on his doorstep first thing after sunrise—towing a justice of the peace along with him.

Which was fine by Julius. The sooner he married Nora, the sooner he'd have her by his side every day. "Are you going to marry me?" he heard himself ask.

She sighed dramatically, her fingers skimming his collarbone. "I suppose I'll have to. Otherwise, how will you hold your head up in society?"

Happiness spread in his chest, warming him. "Thank you for your noble sacrifice."

"You are most welcome. And, just so there is no misunderstanding later, I have no intention of obeying you."

He chuckled and yawned. "I would expect nothing less."

She remained silent for a long moment. "Why did I never realize Robert had this . . . darkness inside him?"

"Hard to say. He may not have even known it himself until provoked."

"I cannot fathom it. I almost married him, a man who just set fire to a theater. People *died* tonight because I broke off with him."

"Because of *him*, Nora." He tightened his grip on her. "People died because of his choices, not yours.

You share no blame in what happened. Only Robert is responsible."

"If that is true, then why did you pledge a small fortune to each of the twenty-one families who lost a loved one in the fire?"

Twenty-one families forever changed. The deceased had been patrons too old to keep up with the crowds, trampled or crushed underfoot, then asphyxiated in the smoke because they'd fallen. All because Julius had underestimated Robert. He'd been too busy seducing Nora to concentrate on discovering the party responsible for the fire in the stables. If he'd figured it out sooner, perhaps tonight's tragedy could have been prevented. "Because I can. It's a small token of kindness during a tragedy no family should have to endure. And I plan on seeing that other theaters institute safety measures to prevent anything of the same happening again."

"The police and fire departments said the theater was not at fault," she said softly.

"I realize that, but there are improvements that would help. Like having exit signs that are in easy-to-spot places and well lit in the dark."

"Will you rebuild the Athena?"

He hadn't considered it. "Perhaps, if only to ensure it's done correctly. If my wife approves of the idea, of course."

"She might allow it, if husbandly duties are not sacrificed to the cause."

"Perish the thought," he said and cupped her breast, fingers rolling her nipple, pinching. She gasped and heat flared in his groin. God, this woman. "I promise to take husbandly duties quite seriously."

"Even though you never wanted to be a husband?"

"People change. Circumstances change," he said, recalling his words from days before. "And if I fail, at least I shall have you by my side . . . because I'm not letting you go."

She was all he needed, until he dropped dead. He'd even set aside his notion of revenge for her. While Pendleton had rightfully paid for his actions, James Cortland did not deserve to be ruined. More to the point, he didn't want to hurt Nora by destroying her uncle.

She kissed his jaw, then nipped the skin with her teeth. Sensation shot through him like a jolt of electric current, his hips bucking. She chuckled. "I apologize, then, for ruining your plan to spend your life alone."

"I never wanted to be alone," he said, though they both knew it to be a lie.

Pushing up on her elbows, she smirked up at him. "If that's true, then why did you build yourself a castle?"

He rolled her onto her back and loomed over her. "Perhaps I was waiting for a princess to come along and save me."

Chapter Twenty-One

A knock on the door brought Nora slowly awake. Where was she? A naked man was wrapped around her, his arms holding her close even in sleep. Oh, yes. *Julius.* She shifted to elbow him. "Julius, wake up. Someone is at the door."

"What?" His beautiful blue eyes fluttered open, unfocused from sleep.

"Someone is knocking."

He lifted his head. "Go away!" he shouted.

"Sir, a word, if you please." It was Weaver, Julius's valet.

Nora stretched to see the clock on the mantel. Already half past nine. Panic rose in her chest. She hadn't meant to sleep this long. Last she remembered, she'd planned to shut her eyes for just a few minutes before sneaking home to her uncle's house. "Oh God, Julius. Get up!"

She started to rise and he put a hand on her shoulder. "Do not move. Let me see what he wants."

Turning, he angled his long and lithe body out of bed. Utterly and gloriously naked, he strode to the door. After ensuring Nora was properly covered, he cracked the wooden panel. She could not hear the words exchanged, but she saw Julius's shoulders stiffen.

"Here? Now?"

"Indeed, sir."

"We'll be along in ten minutes."

Julius closed the door and came to stand by Nora's side of the bed. She tried not to stare at his naked flesh, but it was not easy. The man was dashed gorgeous. His face had her sitting up, however, clutching the sheet to her chest. "Who's here? Is it my uncle?"

"No, it's your father."

Nora's ears started ringing and she wobbled. Her . . . father. Here? How?

"Whoa, steady there." Julius grabbed her shoulders. "Breathe, Nora. Take a deep breath for me, please."

She dragged air into her lungs, her mouth working like a fish on a dry riverbed. Julius sat on the end of the bed and cupped her jaw with one large hand. His serious expression did not reflect the terror currently clawing her insides. "It will be all right," he said. "Stay calm."

"Easy for you to say," she wheezed. "He is . . . He will know we . . ." She gestured to the bed.

"Yes, he will." His mouth curved into a smile. "Something tells me your father is not a stupid man."

"Oh, heavens." Her forehead dropped onto his shoulder. "I've disappointed him again."

He smoothed a hand up and down her back. "In

this instance I don't think you are the one he'll be most upset with."

She inhaled sharply as something more depressing occurred. "What if he disapproves?"

"Do you honestly think that would stop me? I don't need his approval to marry you, Nora. He has no power over me and I'm perfectly capable of standing up to him." He shifted to stare into her eyes. "I will not let you go. Do you hear me?"

She nodded and kissed him quickly. "I won't let you go, either."

"That's settled, then. We should dress and face him."

"Together? Perhaps I should go down first—"

"Absolutely not." His lips flattened into an unhappy line. "We go into the lion's den together. Now get up and I'll help you dress."

They were quiet as they donned their clothing. Julius had been kind enough to send someone to fetch a fresh day dress from her maid last night, as the clothes she'd been wearing reeked of soot and smoke. At least she would face her father with a small amount of dignity.

He's caught you in flagrante delicto *once again.*

This would be the last time, thankfully. She didn't think she could survive the mortification again.

Trembling, she held on to Julius as they traveled along the corridors. Julius's hold on her never wavered, however, his countenance calm and resolved. It was as if he told her not to worry with every step.

The earl stood as they entered the intimate family receiving room. He appeared grim, his silver hair swept off his forehead, mouth turned down in a frown. His eyes missed nothing as he took in Nora's appearance: her hastily twisted hair, the freshly pressed day dress. His gaze narrowed on where she clung to Julius's arm.

Julius released her but did not move from her side. He gave a neat bow. "My lord, I am Julius Hatcher."

Her father's eye twitched and Nora swallowed. "Hello, Father."

He said nothing, merely strode forward, long legs eating up the distance until he loomed in front of them. Ignoring Nora, he addressed Julius. "Do you plan to marry my daughter?"

"Indeed, I do."

Her father struck out his hand. "That was the correct answer. I trust expediency in that regard will not be a problem."

Julius quickly shook the earl's hand. "Not a bit, my lord."

Her father was entirely too businesslike. Was he brokering for votes in Lords or his daughter's future? "Are you not upset?" she blurted, confused.

He turned to her for the first time. "I am furious— but I am also relieved."

"I don't understand." She glanced at Julius, but found him equally confused.

"Hatcher, may I have a moment with my daughter?"

"Of course." Julius bent to kiss her cheek. "I'll be in my office, if you need me." The two men shook hands once more and she watched with trepidation as Julius departed. Nerves fluttered in her stomach at facing her father alone.

"Shall we sit?" He gestured to the small sofa. "I fear I haven't yet gained my land legs."

"When did you arrive?" she asked as they settled themselves on the furniture.

"Last evening. Quite a shock, arriving to learn that my only child almost died in a theater fire. I believe that shaved several years off my life."

He'd been worried about her? The man who sent her away to find a husband in another country?

"I see you do not believe me." He sighed. "Honora, I realize you and I have not always been close, a situation I am no doubt to blame for. Your aunt believes your actions in the last year have been about gaining my attention, good or bad." He shrugged. "Perhaps they were, but I regret I ever caused you to doubt my affection for you. I do not say it often but I do . . . love you, you know."

She closed her eyes briefly, absorbing the words. She hadn't realized how desperately she'd needed to hear them. "Then why did you send me away?"

"You know why. You were caught with that boy in front of six prominent men of London society. What was I to do? The only chance we had of saving your reputation was to get you away from the scandal as quickly as possible. New York seemed the most logical place, with your aunt here."

"So you were protecting me, not attempting to get rid of me?"

He stiffened as his brows rose. "Get rid of you? Good God, no. I thought you'd look at New York as a grand adventure. You've always been so fiercely independent."

"A grand adventure that would lead to marriage."

"Yes, I had hoped. In addition to skirting the scandal, I thought you might find a husband here unimpeded, a man who loved you and would make you happy. And I must say that Hatcher is an excellent choice."

"You approve of him? I had thought . . ." *I had thought you would hate him.*

"He had a wild enough reputation to scare your father into bringing you home?" he finished, tilting his chin in that familiar scholarly way of his. "Hatcher's not as wild as everyone thinks. The man's taken some knocks in his life and yet look where he ended up." He indicated the room, the big mansion. "Loyal to a fault, a wizard with stocks, and intelligent as well. Even if I hadn't seen the way he looked at you a few moments ago, I would have known you two were perfect for each other."

"So you . . . knew about Julius? About my plan to get summoned home?"

"I've known from the beginning." He chuckled at her expression. "You don't honestly believe I was unaware of all you were doing here in New York, do you? Your aunt may be exactly like you, but that's what makes her the perfect spy."

A spy! Nora's mouth fell open. "You had Aunt Bea spying on me?"

"Yes, a role she relished, I must tell you. The woman could have had a stellar career working for the crown—now don't be cross with her. She reported on you at my request."

"She told me you hadn't asked after me."

He patted her hand where it rested on the sofa—a

stunning show of emotion from him. "I asked her to keep my involvement a secret. I knew you would chafe at my meddling in your affairs."

All of this was causing her head to spin. So much had been kept from her. "Yet you did meddle by offering Robert money to stay away from me."

"Indeed, I did and I would gladly do it again. After you left, I learned unpleasant things about that boy and grew concerned. He was raised in the foundling hospital, you know, and there had been recurring problems with his behavior over the years. They let him come back as a way to keep an eye on him, keep him on the straight and narrow. Do you understand?"

She nodded, the news not entirely surprising after last evening's events. "He was responsible for the fire at Julius's theater."

"I read that. It's a terrible tragedy and I feel partly to blame. I wasn't having him watched carefully enough and he disappeared. However, your aunt assured me there'd been no sign of Robert here in New York and you were happy with Hatcher, so I boarded a ship without cabling anyone of the possible danger. I never thought something like this would happen."

A knock sounded an instant before Julius poked his head inside. "Everything all right?"

"Yes," Nora told him, touched he'd come to check on her.

Her father took Nora's arm and pulled them both to their feet. "I must get to my hotel and send some cables. I shall see you both later this afternoon."

"This afternoon?" Nora asked with a quick glance in Julius's direction. What was happening this afternoon?

"For the wedding." The earl bent to kiss her cheek. "I still care about your reputation, you know." He strode toward the door, pulling on his gloves as he went. "We'll discuss terms later, Hatcher?"

"Yes, sir."

With a final nod, the earl disappeared, leaving Nora and Julius alone. Julius came over, placed his hands on Nora's shoulders, and dropped a quick kiss on her mouth. "How do you feel?"

She grinned, the wide smile threatening to split her face in two. "Like I cannot wait for this afternoon."

Epilogue

September 1890

In the end, they married twice.

The first time was the afternoon after her father arrived when they officially married in front of just the earl, Frank Tripp, and Nora's aunt and uncle. Julius had been so sure, so steadfast, his voice clear and strong as he pledged to love her until his dying breath. Nora could tear up merely remembering the moment.

And now, in front of all New York society, they were "married" inside St. Bartholomew's Church on Madison Avenue. Crowds had lined the street, eager to see the bon vivant bridegroom and his English bride. Yet no one but those few present at the first ceremony had any idea this was a second wedding.

Nora leaned over to where her husband reclined in his chair, relaxed as he watched over the revelry at their wedding reception. "Tell me again why we needed a second wedding?"

Bright blue eyes met hers, a small smile playing around his sinful mouth. "I'm not allowing you to miss out on a proper wedding merely because I dove under your skirts a minute after we met."

"I am quite grateful you dove under my skirts," she murmured, hooking her foot around his leg under the dining table. "I'm hopeful you'll dive again as soon as I can get you alone."

"That'll be sooner than you think if you keep that up, Mrs. Hatcher."

Her foot slid higher, stroking his calf. "Promise?"

He swallowed hard, his lids falling briefly to shield his gaze. "Behave, Nora. I want you to enjoy being the center of attention today. To celebrate with all of New York, as is your right as the daughter of an earl."

Oh, this again? "I don't need fanfare. In truth, I believe *you* are the one who wanted to hold the outrageous wedding and reception."

"I do love a good party." He threw her a smirk, the rogue. Nora's insides simmered, the need for him a constant hum under her skin. Would this reception never end?

They had lived apart the entire summer, under her aunt's insistence. Aunt Bea said no one knew of the marriage and appearances had to be maintained, even in New York. Since April, all she and Julius had managed were stolen hours in a race to touch and feel, drown themselves in pleasure before returning to the charade of a betrothed couple.

But this last week apart had been torture. Wedding guests and preparation had precluded any contact whatsoever.

"Julius, have pity on your bride. I haven't seen you or touched you in six days. I've missed you."

Shifting, he put his mouth near her ear. "My cock has been hard since you walked down the aisle. I don't think I can stand without embarrassing myself."

"There you two are!"

Nora jerked away from her husband and found Aunt Bea beside them, Uncle James at her side. The couple appeared positively gleeful. "Hello," Nora said. "Are you both having fun?"

"This is unbelievable," her aunt said. "Positively over-the-top. The moat full of English roses . . . the giant ice sculpture castle . . . the entertainments in nearly every room . . . Mr. Louis Sherry here himself to oversee the food! Good heavens, they'll be talking of this wedding for *years*."

Julius's mouth hitched in what Nora recognized as satisfaction. Her husband had wanted to make a point today . . . and he'd clearly made it.

A trio of women approached—Julius's mother and sisters. Two of the women looked quite miserable. "Julius, I believe we'll return to the hotel," his mother said. "This is too—"

Nora cleared her throat meaningfully, catching Mrs. Hatcher's eye, and the older woman blinked as she reconsidered her comment. "This is too late for us."

It was four o'clock in the afternoon.

Still, Nora had to give Mrs. Hatcher credit for attempting to spare her son's feelings. It was a start. Julius rose and took her arm. "Of course. Nora, I'll just see them into a carriage—"

"Julius, why don't I see your family off? You can settle things down here and then meet me in the turret."

His nostrils flared slightly and he nodded. "I'll be there."

Nora excused herself to her aunt and uncle while Julius gave his good-byes to his family. Nora then escorted the Hatcher women through the house and to the front entrance. She nodded and greeted guests as they went, turning down glasses of champagne thrust at her from all directions. A footman ran to fetch Julius's carriage, leaving the four women standing together.

Nora crossed her arms over her chest. "I trust we understand each other?" She stared each of them in the eye.

"No criticisms or complaints in his presence," Agatha said. "We understand."

"Very good. Because if any of you break that promise, I'll be forced to break mine."

Earlier in the summer Nora had done a little discreet digging into the lives of the two Hatcher women in Albany. It turned out they had become friendly with a local reverend who'd taken to exploiting Mrs. Hatcher's zealous religious beliefs and Agatha's loneliness over the last few years. He'd collected their money—really Julius's money—by convincing them it was evil. Persuaded them to take in boarders and donate the money to the church. Had very likely manipulated Agatha into an affair.

Using her status, a large donation, and Frank Tripp's keen legal mind, Nora had managed to get the reverend assigned to a small parish in Indiana.

She then promised to keep what she knew from her husband . . . as long as Mrs. Hatcher and Agatha treated him politely and with respect. If they didn't, Julius would sell the house in Albany and there would be no more money or assistance, ever. The women had readily agreed.

She could not repair a mother's relationship with her son, but she could damn well try to keep them from hurting one another further.

The carriage arrived and Nora bade them goodbye. She breathed a sigh of relief, eager to get to the turret and to her husband. She wouldn't even bother changing out of her elaborate Worth wedding dress.

The east wing had been closed off to the guests, so the corridors were deserted as Nora lifted her skirts and dashed along the carpets. She opened the door and started climbing the stairs that led to the turret. There were . . . petals on the steps. Pink rose petals, exactly like the flowers filling the moat. The higher she climbed, the more petals appeared. Her husband, the surprising romantic. She bit her lip in anticipation, heart thumping in time with her feet.

At the top, the petals continued in a line across the floor, all the way to the window seat, where a very naked, very aroused handsome man awaited her.

He'd trailed the petals up onto his flat stomach.

She came to the window seat and gazed down adoringly at the banquet of male beauty stretched out before her. Long limbs, lean muscles, light crisp hair dusting his skin . . . Her mouth watered at the sight, lust swift and fierce in her belly.

While he might be the prettiest man she knew, that wasn't why she loved him. There were a hundred small details that made him the man he was, utterly unique, and one entirely perfect for her. She reached for a petal and slowly swept it up over his chest. "Subtle."

He shivered, gooseflesh rising in the wake of the petal. "I thought as much."

"I love you, you insane and generous man."

Turning sober, he clasped her hand on his chest, holding it against his warm skin. "I never wanted you to regret marrying me. You deserve to have the wedding every girl dreams about."

She shook her head. "I never dreamed about a wedding. That never mattered to me. I dreamed of a husband, one who would be kind and intelligent. Decent. Someone to make me laugh."

"And handsome."

"And handsome," she agreed through a chuckle. "I have every one of those things. That's all I need— *you* are all I need."

"You humble me, Mrs. Hatcher. I love you, and I'll marry you as many times as you like. As long as you stay mine."

"I'm yours, though I do wish the groom would get on with the wedding night."

In a flash, he sat up and snatched her, bringing her down until her back was on the seat, her legs over his thighs. She frowned. "What are you doing? Help me out of my gown first."

"Not just yet, my love. There was some discussion earlier regarding your skirts." He began flicking layers of silk off her legs, uncovering her one bit at a time. "I believe I have a promise to uphold."

Acknowledgments

I have long been fascinated by the opulence, excess, and wealth of the Gilded Age elite. Nothing was too outrageous or too costly for this select group, and they hosted events I couldn't begin to make up. For example, the party on horseback actually happened at Sherry's Restaurant in 1903. (Search the photo on the Internet. It's hilarious.)

The "Four Hundred" refers to the top four hundred members of New York society, as decided by Ward McAllister, a partner-in-crime to reigning social queen Mrs. Astor. This was supposedly the number of people Mrs. Astor's ballroom could accommodate.

This story could not have happened without the guidance and support of so many. Thanks to Tessa Woodward, without whom this book wouldn't exist. I'm so grateful for her advice, ideas, and love of this time period. Also thanks to the entire Avon Books team for shepherding this book into the world and getting it into the hands of readers.

To Laura Bradford, who never sugarcoats anything, and I love her for it. To Michele, Dora, and Julie—my eternal gratitude for the laughs, long talks, and advice. Also to Janet, Maria, RoseAnn, and Tina for always having my back. Thanks to Lin—I'm so lucky to have you in my life! And thanks to the Gilded Lilies, who share my enthusiasm and excitement about the Gilded Age on a daily basis.

To my husband, daughters, parents, and family, who are all endlessly supportive and make this writing career possible. I love you all.

Lastly, thanks to the readers! Thank you for supporting romance and allowing me the privilege of creating these characters for you. It really is the best job in the world.

Coming soon from Joanna Shupe,
the next scintillating Gilded Age romance
in her Four Hundred series

A Scandalous Deal

Pre-order today!

*G*ive in to your Impulses!

**These unforgettable stories only take a second
to buy and give you hours of reading pleasure!**

Go to ***www.AvonImpulse.com*** and see what we
have to offer.

Available wherever e-books are sold.

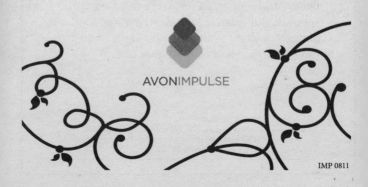

AVONIMPULSE